Divine Heiress

Divine Heiress

The Virgin Mary and the creation
of Christian Constantinople

Vasiliki Limberis

London and New York

First published 1994
by Routledge
11 New Fetter Lane, London EC4P 4EE

Simultaneously published in the USA and Canada
by Routledge
29 West 35th Street, New York, NY 10001

© 1994 Vasiliki Limberis

Typeset in Baskerville by
Florencetype Limited, Kewstoke, Avon
Printed and bound in Great Britain by
TJ Press (Padstow) Ltd, Padstow, Cornwall

British Library Cataloguing in Publication Data
A catalogue record for this book is available from the
British Library.

Library of Congress Cataloging in Publication Data
Limberis, Vasiliki
    Divine Heiress: the Virgin Mary and the creation of
    Christian Constantinople / Vasiliki Limberis.
        p.   cm.
    Includes bibliographical references and index.
    1. Mary, Blessed Virgin, Saint – Cult – Rome. 2. Mary,
    Blessed Virgin, Saint – Cult – Turkey – Istanbul.
    3. Christianity and culture – History – Early church,
    ca. 30–600. 4. Hymns, Greek – History and criticism.
    5. Orthodox Eastern Church – Hymns – History and
    criticism. 6. Istanbul (Turkey) – Church history.
    7. Byzantine Empire – Church history.   I. Orthodox
    Eastern Church. Akathistos hymnos. English. 1994.
        II. title.
    BT652.R66L56   1994
    232.91′094961′8 – dc20   93–47960

ISBN 0–415–09677–4

To my husband, Paul J. Smith
ἀληθευτής ὁ ἄνθρωπος
and our children, Antigone and Isaac

Contents

Acknowledgments   ix
Abbreviations   xi
Introduction   1

Part I   Mary's introduction to the new empire

1 Greco-Roman civic religion versus "The Kingdom of
  God on Earth"   7
  Constantine's Christianity   7
  The city Constantine inherits   10
  Constantine and the deities of his city   14
  Constantine's Christianization of the empire   21

2 The Theodosians and paganism   30
  Theodosius I and civic ceremony   34
  *Eudoxia, John Chrysostom, and his confrontation with
    civic piety*   37
  Resituating the rubrics of ritual: holidays   40
  Pulcheria, Theodosius II, and paganism   41
  Theodosius' legal proscriptions against paganism   43
  *The traditional civic ceremonies of Constantinople,
    circa 420*   45

3 Theodosius, Pulcheria, and the civic ceremonies   47
  *The welcoming of relics: Pulcheria's appropriation of
    civic ceremony*   52
  *Pulcheria's victory over Nestorius: the Theotokos
    dwells in Constantinople*   53

Contents

4 Imperial cult, panegyric, and the Theotokos   62
   Panegyric in the fourth and fifth centuries   64
   Eulogizing poems   65
   Adventus panegyrics   68
   Panegyrics for other occasions   70
   Christians, rhetoric, and the civic ceremonies   76
   Heresy and rituals of civic ceremony   79
   Hymns to the Theotokos: fruits of the Nestorian crisis   85
   Rhetorical devices used in the Akathistos Hymn   92

Part II   Mary's inheritance

5 The hierarchs' Mary   101
   Pre-Constantinian Mary   101
   Devotions to Mary   104
   Cyril of Alexandria and the Theotokos   107
   Epiphanius and heretical devotions to the Virgin   116

6 Byzantium's bequest to the Theotokos   121
   Byzantium's dual goddess tradition   123
   Tyche   124
   The mother of the gods   133

   Conclusion   143
   Map of Constantinople   148
   Appendix: The *Akathistos Hymn*   149
   Notes   159
   References   187
   Index   195

Acknowledgments

In most books, authors thank their spouses and families at the end of their acknowledgments. I have always found this odd, because in my experience my family has always helped me most. I therefore extend my gratitude to them first. My husband, Paul J. Smith, has contributed countless hours acting in turn as an editor, historical critic, software expert, typist, and child-sitter. As a professor of Chinese history, he knows first-hand the equal share of toil and delight that goes into writing a book. Our small children Antigone and Isaac have been as flexible and light-hearted as ever, spreading their good cheer at moments when it was most needed. I also owe many thanks to Mrs Rabia Aksöy, who has lovingly watched over our children each day, and has generously given me extra time on many occasions.

This study on the rise of the cult of the Virgin Mary in Constantinople is a substantial revision of the dissertation I wrote at Harvard Divinity School under the direction of Professor Helmut Koester. He has always taught his students to approach the study of ancient Christianity in the context of the wider Greco-Roman culture, and his methods of evaluating evidence of the religious cultures in the ancient Mediterranean have proven exciting and innovative. To him I extend heart-felt gratitude.

Professor Kelley McCarthy Spoerl, of St Anselm's College, read the manuscript several times and provided helpful insights and criticism. Her professional opinions and editorial skills were indeed invaluable. But I thank her above all for her abiding friendship and kind support during these many years since Divinity School days.

I thank the Department of Religion of Temple University.

Ms Cornelia Michelle Venable, Ms Irene Riegner, and Mr Paisios Whitesides, graduate students who were in my seminar during the spring 1993, helped hone out ideas about religious culture in antiquity that proved seminal for reshaping this study on the Virgin Mary, Theotokos. Professor John Raines, department chair, came up with time, that most precious commodity, so that I could finish this book. Professors Mahmoud Ayoub, Khalid Blankinship, Lucy Bregman, Katie Cannon, Robert Wright, Shigenori Nagatomo, Laura Levitt, David Watt, and Bibhuti Yadav have provided collegial friendship throughout the endeavor. I am pleased to be a member of a religion department that represents so many different religious cultures from all over the world, and from whom I have learned a great deal.

I thank Professor Joseph Russo of Haverford College for his explanations of the finer points of Greek meter. Professor David Frankfurter's suggestions and criticisms proved most helpful at the very end. I am indebted to my friend, Maureen Tilley, professor of religion at Florida State University, who literally made this book possible. Mr Richard Stoneman, editor at Routledge, has understood the project from the beginning, and I thank him for his help and encouragement.

Finally, I express my thanks to the people at the computer center at Haverford College, and the staff of Canaday Library at Bryn Mawr College. The classics study of Canaday has become my home-away-from-home during the writing of this book. It is a quiet haven, filled with tremendous resources and a wonderful ambiance created by scholars devoted to their work. I appreciate the help that both institutions have provided me.

V.L.
Temple University, Philadelphia

Abbreviations

AJAH	*American Journal of Ancient History*
ANF	*The Ante-Nicene Fathers*
CIG	*Corpus Inscriptionum Graecarum*
CSCO	*Corpus Scriptorum Christianorum Orientalium*
CSHB	*Corpus Scriptorum Historiae Byzantinae*
Cod. Theo.	Pharr, Clyde (trans.), *The Theodosian Code*
DOP	*Dumbarton Oaks Papers*
Eccl. Hist.	*Greek Ecclesiastical Historians*, 6 vols, vols 2–5, respectively, Eusebius, Socrates, Sozomen, and Theodoret
JRS	*Journal of Roman Studies*
LCL	*Loeb Classical Library*
Life of Constantine	*Greek Ecclesiastical Historians*, Eusebius, vol. 1
NPNF	*Nicene and Post-Nicene Fathers*, first and second series
ODCC	*Oxford Dictionary of the Christian Church*
PG	Migne, *Patrologia Graeca*
PO	*Patrologia Orientalis*
RE	*Real-Encyclopädie der classichen Altertums wissenschaft*

Introduction

The subject of this study is how the historical figure, Mary, the mother of Jesus, came to play such a vital role in the cultural and religious life of Constantinople in late antiquity. More specifically, how she is transformed from a humble Jewish maiden of first-century Palestine into a divine figure, intercessor, and the supernatural protector of the city of Constantinople is the crucial question. Mary's apotheosis must be seen in the context of the religious culture of the Mediterranean world, especially during the critical period after 325 when Constantine makes Christianity the official religion of the Roman empire. For with this event two very different religious cultures, pagan and Christian, were united at the most fundamental level: the level of civic religion.

Certainly Christianity had flirted with various aspects of pagan religious culture before, mainly with pagan philosophy. Christianity had been successful in adopting pagan philosophy because it did not involve compromising on matters of ritual or cultic practices. When Constantine made Christianity the state religion of the empire, the Church was suddenly confronted with a deluge of civic religious customs and traditions, some of which honor the emperor or the city of Constantinople. Though not all of the civic rituals detracted from the worship that belongs to the one Christian God alone, Constantine's decision presented the Church with problems and dilemmas of accommodation and acculturation that it had always eschewed. As the official religion of the empire, the Church found itself in an intimate relationship with the emperor and his court, including aspects of Greco-Roman civic religious ceremonies which were utterly alien.

Christians had always refused to participate in the rituals of civic religious ceremonies that were an inherent part of life in Mediterranean cities. Civic religion is the outward performance of cultic ritual required of nearly all – if not all – of the population at a temple or shrine through the mediation of a priesthood for the honor, appeasement, and pleasure of a divinity.[1] Manifestations of civic religion in the Greco-Roman world included public displays of veneration at a designated place centered around prescribed rituals including song, processions, libation and or sacrifice. They usually ended with festive meals and some form of public entertainment like dances, games, or theater. The rituals of civic religion were one instrument by which the Roman state sought to guarantee the *pax deorum* and the loyalty of its citizens.[2] For this reason Roman emperors and the populace in general were usually suspicious of foreign religions, such as the mystery cults of Isis and Dionysus, and the peculiarly exclusivist ones, such as Judaism and Christianity. In Rome's view these foreign religions were potential causes of a host of societal evils, as they competed with the empire for the loyalty of its adherents.

The demands of secrecy and exclusivity exacted by these foreign religions gave the government legitimate cause for concern as to the possibly seditious and even anarchic effects they could have on society. By Roman standards their rites could lead to immorality and even cosmic disruption and disfavor with the gods. Roman tolerance of foreign religions only resulted after a usually hostile waiting period while Roman officials supiciously watched the sect with careful skepticism, making sure the religion was neither politically subversive nor socially disruptive.[3]

Some of the foreign religions, such as Isis, Mithras, and Cybele, readily adapted to the cultural expressions of the dominant Greco-Roman culture. Isis and her consort Serapis lost their traditional Egyptian facial features in sculpture, the cult language was translated into the vernacular, and the thousands of epigraphic inscriptions to her show that those cults became an accepted and acceptable expression of religious life. Most important, devotion to Isis, Cybele, Dionysus, or Mithras did not preclude participation in other gods' cultic rituals as one's civic duty.

But devotion to the Christian God did. Christianity demanded the same exclusivity for its God as its Jewish progenitor, but it

did not enjoy the privileges that exempted Judaism from participation in civic ceremonies, chiefly sacrifice to the gods and
veneration of the emperor's genius.[4] It is precisely the
Christians' refusal to participate in the rituals of Roman civic
religion that cast them as enemies of the Roman state.

For three centuries Christians had been able to survive as a
growing minority movement within the larger Roman society,
successfully forming separate communities. Their strict set of
beliefs that prevented them from fully participating in the cultic
practices of Roman civic religion ironically helped spawn a great
deal of Christian apologetic literature in the second and third
centuries. Such defenses were written with the hope of convincing Romans that Christians were indeed pious, peaceful, law-
abiding citizens.[5] Yet this literature also served to reinforce the
permanent boundary that isolated the Christians from the wider
Roman society, having been erected by the Christians' refusal –
or inability – to comply with Rome's religious observances.
During the Decian persecutions when some weaker Christians
ended up buying "certificates of compliance with the imperial
order to sacrifice to the gods,"[6] this same set of beliefs made it
possible and necessary for the bishops to expel those lax members from full participation in the Christian community, either
by excommunication, penance, or both. In sum, then, it is
apparent that Christianity essentially had formed a sectarian
existence and identity in the Roman world. Thus when
Constantine made Christianity the state religion of the Roman
empire in 325, the Church, although elated at such a gracious
act, had to face all the aspects of Roman civic religion – aspects
that Constantine retained – which had so repelled them for
three hundred years.

The process of the Church's adaptation to its official position,
while the emperors became "more Christian" as they simultaneously institutionalized certain civic religious customs, provided the context for the emergence of Mary as the Divine
Heiress and Theotokos. As we shall see, the Nestorian controversy was the catalyst that united the strands of pagan religious
culture still present in society from 325 to 450. Some "strands"
were instituted by Constantine, such as his statues of Rhea and
Tyche in the Tetrastoön, and his civic religious ceremonies in
the Hippodrome which were continued by the Theodosian
dynasty. The efflorescence of imperial panegyric served as a

vehicle for spreading the themes of imperial cult to the greatest number of people – and to the Church. And other "strands" surface in eccesiastical and legal sources, such as those revealed in Pope Damasus' letter to Bishop Paulinus, and in hymnography and homilies. It is in this initial period that the Church experimented with the cultural forms of Roman civic religion to which it was exposed simply by virtue of its position. It is precisely in this process of experimentation that those strands of pagan religious culture were finally woven into Christianity in the public veneration of the Virgin Mary, Theotokos.

Part I

Mary's introduction to the new empire

Chapter 1

Greco-Roman civic religion versus "The Kingdom of God on Earth"

Barnabas they called Zeus, and Paul, because he was the chief speaker, they called Hermes. And the priest of Zeus, whose temple was in front of the city, brought oxen and garlands to the gates and wanted to offer sacrifice with the people.

Acts of the Apostles 14: 12–13

Constantine's Christianity

In 311 Constantine had just decimated the barbarians along the frontier of the Rhine. By 312 he was ready to march on Rome against Maxentius. The night before the decisive battle, Constantine had a vision. He was told that if he marked his military standard with the Greek letters "chi-rho," which stood for Christ, he would be victorious.[1] Socrates says that Constantine was told, "in this will you conquer" (ἐν τούτῳ νίκα). Liebeschuetz has demonstrated that Constantine converted in a time of great political and economic stress.[2] The imperial tetrarchy which had included his father was disintegrating. Ultimately Constantine waged a campaign against Maxentius after his father had died. He needed "a powerful and effectual aid,"[3] and the Christian God chose him. Constantine accepted the sign from God in a vision; and only long after he was victorious did he slowly begin learning the requirements of the faith. But from the very beginning his chief response to divine help was "placating the Christian God," which "became a cornerstone of his policy."[4]

Constantine's interpretation and response to the aid from the Christian God was completely in keeping with Roman belief about the link between the divine world and the emperor, explicitly enunciated since the reign of Augustus. With Augustus' establishment of the cult of the genius of the emperor, the populace celebrated the divine power residing in the emperor, enabling him uniquely to "guide and protect the Roman people as a father does his children."[5] The extension of the religious policies to emperor worship while Septimius Severus was alive only reinforced these ideas. Constantine as emperor was the source of religious policy, and he took his role very seriously – especially the duties of teacher, patron, and guide.

It was completely within the religious climate of the late third century that Constantine should receive a vision in answer to his prayer, and that he should view his responsibility to the god as one of appeasement.[6] Constantine's recognition and acknowledgment of the Christian God as the supreme deity was also in keeping with the age. Constantine had grown up with an amorphous Greco-Roman henotheism, which had been popular in the army and with his own father, Constantius.[7] Devotion to Sol Invictus as the chief God was common in the ranks of the military. It was also *au courant* to acknowledge that the supreme god could syncretistically be called by other names, and that he ruled over subordinate gods.[8] This religious milieu was conducive to Constantine's new God. His conversion was initially to another form of henotheism, and when he eventually reached the religious position of exclusivity – Christian monotheism – it was not at the expense of civic religion.

After Constantine's military victory at the Milvian bridge in 312, he credited his new god and its cult in the traditional Roman way: bequests of property and money to the Church, grants of immunity from taxes to clerics so that their duties of appeasing the divinity would not be interrupted.[9] He issued directives to the governors of the provinces, setting up a social welfare system for orphans and widows, a system of clerical pay, as well as a food dole for the churches to distribute.[10] Yet he did not withdraw support from the pagan priesthoods or renounce his title of *pontifex maximus*.[11] Constantine was determined to be seen as an adherent of the Christian God – but on his own terms, not the Church's. And in these terms Constantine's imperial actions and religious definitions are entirely consonant with his cultural background. His Christianity, or even his idea of Christianity, was not formed by any contact with a Christian culture. When one reads an account of Constantine's religion by any of the Church historians, the idiosyncratic character of his Christianity stands out. He really does not know very much about Christianity, so what he does know he puts forth through the hermeneutic of his own religious culture, and through the meaning of imperial religion and office he has inherited from the time of Augustus.

In 324 Constantine defeated his last foe, Licinius, in a battle at Chrysopolis, and became sole emperor of the Roman empire. He had come to the east as a liberator,[12] establishing peace for pagan and Christian alike. To celebrate his universal victory, he chose the city of Byzantium as his new capital. Choosing Byzantium as the new imperial city may have been Constantine's way of getting revenge on the Roman senate and the praetorian guard which had supported Maxentius.[13]

The Church historians say that Constantine chose Byzantium as his new capital for a variety of reasons. Zosimus relates that Constantine felt great remorse in 326 after he had his wife Fausta murdered for her alleged infidelity.[14] According to the historian, Constantine asked a pagan priest how he could be absolved from the crime. The pagan hierarch said that he could not be pardoned. Constantine, feeling terrible remorse, was told that in Christian baptism all former sins are forgiven. About this time his Vicennalia took place. On the advice of a Christian priest, Constantine refused to sacrifice at his own celebration, indicating that his commitment to Christianity was certain. Soon after, he moved the capital to Byzantium to "replace Rome." Eusebius mentions very little about the establishment of Constantinople, but he gives the impression that Constantine founded it in order to restore the empire to its former glory. Sozomen gives yet another reason.[15] The emperor, he says, always intended to advance the cause of Christianity. To do this he founded a new city, "to be called by his own name, and to be equal in celebrity to Rome."[16]

The Church historians notwithstanding, there seems to be other evidence that gives clues as to why Constantine chose the city of Byzantium as his new capital. Byzantium was an ideal location for the emperor to craft his new state and his new religion. He could invent his own civic ceremonies there due in part to the city's lack of a strong Christian community. As we shall see, Rome would have been too constricting as his capital for two reasons: he could not have easily coopted Rome's ancient pagan city cults to change their rites, and the Church in Rome, like its pagan counterparts, was too strong and well established to suddenly take orders from an emperor.

The city Constantine inherits

Unlike the cosmopolitan city of Rome, when Constantine arrived in Byzantium in 324 the city was not a cultural hub, nor had it ever been. This is not to deny it the recognition it had always had as a strategically useful town for garnering tribute from busy naval traffic – only by virtue of its geographical position. Legends preserved by historians[17] tell us that a certain Byzas, from either Thrace or Megara, founded the colony on the Bosphorus in the mid-seventh century BCE. In 628 a second colony was sent out from Megara under Zeuxippus.[18] The transmission of the worship of Hera, whose temple both in Byzantium and in Argos was on the citadel, and the tradition concerning Io confirm the general assertion of Hesychius of Miletus that the Argives had a share in the foundation of Byzantium.[19]

According to one myth Byzas' parents are Poseidon and Keroessa, daughter of Zeus and Io. Byzas comes from Thrace and wins as his bride Phidalia, the daughter of Barbysios, king of the Hellespont. Phidalia had already begun building a new city before she married; afterwards she and her husband continued the work. On completion of the city, Phidalia names the Tyche of the city apparently after her mother-in-law, Keroe.[20] Byzas named the city after himself and ruled the city after Barbysios' death. After its foundation, Argos, Athens, and Miletos all vied for the honor of being its founder.

Remarkably Byzantium remained relatively independent during Hellenistic and Roman times. Upon the death of Alexander the Great, unlike many of its neighbors, Byzantium managed to stay free of Seleucus, since it united with Chalcedon and Heracleia in a defensive league. Polybius attests to both the wealth of this city and the high tributes it had to pay various protectors during this period.[21]

Luckily for Byzantium, it sided with Rome during the wars with Greece. As Polybius describes the situation, both the Greeks and the Byzantines benefited financially from the city's geographical position. He calls the city "εὐπορίαν," prosperous.[22] The Byzantines had complete control over the trade of all of the necessary products that the Pontus region produced in "plentiful supply":[23] wine, cattle, olive oil, honey, and preserved fish.[24] Byzantium controlled who sailed into the Black Sea and on what conditions. In fact Polybius makes it quite clear that the Greeks were much more dependent on the goodwill of Byzantium than the other way around.

"They are of great service to other peoples,"[25] says Polybius about the citizens of Byzantium; and the Romans, with their unerring sense of how to make good use of others, did not let Byzantium slip by them. In 130 BCE the Romans built the Via Egnatia from the Adriatic coast ending in Byzantium. The city enjoyed the Roman designation of "free city" and the status of being "ally of Rome." Yet such superior advantages and privilege attracted the negative attentions and jealousy of several emperors. Byzantium suffered under the envious eye of Vespasian (69–79), who revoked her privileged status. However, these privileges were not long afterwards restored. A little over a century later Byzantium found itself again the victim of an emperor, this time Septimius Severus (193–211). Unfortunately Byzantium was supporting Severus' enemy in a war, Pescennius Niger. After a brutal two-year siege of the city, Severus reduced it to rubble in retribution. "He deprived the city of its independence and of its proud position as a state, and made it a tributary confiscating property of citizens," writes the Roman historian, Dio.[26] He demolished the famous walls, which Dio describes with such detail in a tone of horrified awe; "looking as if they had been captured by some other people rather than by Romans."[27]

After five years Severus' anger subsided, and he realized (with remorse perhaps?) the terrible consequences of his rage. He rebuilt the walls, built a theater called the Kynegion, the gates of the Tetrastoön, "the Place of the Four Porticoes,"[28] and the huge baths of Zeuxippus, which he unsuccessfully tried to rename the "Severion." His crowning achievement was the construction of the impressive Hippodrome, resembling the Circus Maximus in Rome.[29] At the request of his son Antoninus-Caracalla, he restored to Byzantium its former rights and privileges, and renamed it "Antonina," but this title did not enter common parlance.[30]

Dagron has pointed out that Severus' magnificent rebuilding projects in Byzantium were not accomplished for purely humanitarian reasons: Severus wanted to throw out or at least neutralize the ancient – and very independent – city cults.[31] He intended to supplant them with his own cult and that of the worship of Rome. His plan was a full-scaled Romanization of a small yet important Greek city. We must note here that the Severans were the ones to introduce the concept of the "deified emperor" throughout the empire.[32] To accomplish this in Byzantium Severus removed the statue of the beloved Thracian god Helios Zeuxippus from the Tetrastoön baths, and unsuccessfully renamed the baths the "Severion." Helios Zeuxippos was banished to the old acropolis, and housed in a small temple to Apollo, next to the original divine dwellers, Artemis and Aphrodite. The temple to Hecate and the cult to the Dioscourii, both so vital to the ancestral memory and traditions of Byzantium, were physically engulfed and overshadowed by the huge Hippodrome, rendering them effectively ornaments of the Roman racetrack. Dagron suggests convincingly that the placement of the Strategion and the Kynegion so close to the temples of Achilles and Ajax, and Aphrodite and Artemis,[33] was Severus' implicit attempt to distract citizens from those cults.[34] Severus' own personal glory and Rome's imperial grandeur were foisted on the city to replace the cults of the local heroes, the Dioscourii, Byzas, and the deities, Hecate and Zeuxippos, whom the Byzantines had honored for eight hundred years.[35]

Even though Severus' encounter with Byzantium may have been a mixed blessing for the city, on the whole the Severan dynasty is remembered in Roman history as one of peace, prosperity, expansion, and even toleration.[36] Under the Severans all free men were declared Roman citizens. Yet the Severan dynasty as remembered by church historians is known as the time of persecutions, sporadic and non-systematic though they were. The fiercest seem to have broken out against Christians in Egypt and in North Africa.[37] Clement, Origen, and Tertullian were all affected personally by the Severan persecutions. Christianity's inability to conform to an urbane, tolerant, syncretistic religious attitude so characteristic of Severus, his wife Julia Domna, and her relatives Julia Maesa and Julia Mamaea, put the religion at a disadvantage in the empire. Severus' desire to be worshipped gave local officials ample opportunities to question, cajole, reason with, abuse, threaten, and finally condemn to death those Christians who would not conform to Roman practice, by proving their loyalty to the the state and worshipping the emperor and the gods.

It is reasonable to assume then that, had there been a Christian community in Byzantium, it is highly unlikely that it would have been able to survive Severus' reign. Even if the Christians had survived the demolition of the city, it would have been difficult for them to escape Severus' notice when he made himself the object of worship for the city, while concentrating his attentions on rebuilding the city. Their inability to comply with his religious decrees would have made them social pariahs, just as it did in Egypt and in North Africa.

Thus there is no evidence for a Christian community in Byzantium before Constantine. It was genuinely considered an out-of-the-way place. As Polybius describes his genuine appreciation of the beauty and lucky geographical location of Byzantium, he must nevertheless concede that "the majority of people are unacquainted with the peculiar advantages of the site, as it lies somewhat outside those parts of the world which are generally visited."[38] We do know from the correspondence of Pliny and Trajan that there were Christian communities in regions adjacent to Byzantium, in Pontus, Thrace, and Bythinia.[39] If there had been a Christian community in Byzantium earlier than the Severan dynasty, it was probably very small, and there are no accounts of it. If it survived the attentions of Severus, it was probably governed by the bishop of Pontus or Thrace, since the church during the third century was "based on strong provincial capitals supervising enormous contiguous areas."[40] Yet when one considers Polybius' description of Byzantium, it is difficult to make a case that Christianity had any sort of presence in the city.

Significantly Eusebius mentions no bishops of Constantinople when he lists the bishops of all the major cities of Christendom: Rome, Antioch, Jerusalem, and Alexandria.[41] How advantageous this would have been for Constantine. At the beginning of his sixth book describing the Church during the Severan dynasty, he states that "Severus was stirring up persecution against the churches" . . . which allows him to discuss all the martyrdoms especially in Egypt. He never refers to Severus' horrifying destruction of Byzantium or to any Christian community in that city. He would probably have done so had Christian martyrs been involved. Socrates is the first Church historian to mention Metrophanes as bishop of Constantinople, circa 317, who was succeeded by Alexander.[42] Theodoret mentions only Alexander as bishop of Constantinople, circa 324.[43] When Sozomen devotes a chapter to the description of Arius' banishment from orthodox territories, he mentions that "Alexander who was then at the head of the church of Constantinople" refused to readmit Arius to communion.[44] The seventh-century *Chronicon Paschale* cites Metrophanes as the "first leader of the church in Byzantium for ten years" (c.314–325),[45] and there are substantial reasons – some of which have already been stated – to believe this is true. First, there is no evidence of any significant Christian community at Byzantium. Second, before Constantine Sozomen tells us that the city's "former population was insufficient for so great a city," so Constantine had to import people. Had there been a pre-Constantinian Christian community in Byzantium, it would have been small and under the jurisdiction of a bishop of a neighboring region, in accordance with third-century practice. Finally, given Severus' policy of persecuting Christians, coupled with his intensified focus on vengefully destroying the city, it is likely that a community of Christians in that city would have at best barely survived, let alone had an occasion to thrive in the glory of martyrdom.

The situation under Severus was unique: the entire population was punished and then exonerated. A century later, when Licinius, Galerius, and finally Constantine arrived, they found a beautiful town, newly rebuilt in the Roman style, strategically situated. For reasons that will become clearer, this lack of a Christian establishment and tradition, in addition to the vivid memory of Severus' brutality in the Byzantines' consciousness, allowed Constantine to inherit the best possible scenario for crafting not only a city in his image, but also an imperial Christianity.

Constantine and the deities of his city

The whole empire now devolved on Constantine alone. At last he no longer needed to conceal his natural malignity but acted in accordance with his unlimited power. He still practices the *ancestral religion*, although not so much out of honour as necessity . . .[46]

The Church historians, Eusebius, Socrates, and Sozomen, lead us to believe that Constantine completely eradicated paganism in all its forms, and would not tolerate any custom or practice that could vaguely be associated with paganism. But we have several other literary sources supported by numismatic and archeological evidence, which paint a much more ambiguous picture of Constantine's "conversion" to Christianity. He retained the forms of Roman civic religion and accommodated them to the ancestral rites of the cults of gods and goddesses important to the founding traditions of Byzantium.

Libanius relates three interesting pieces of information about Constantine's religious activities.

He after overcoming the person who had infused new life into the cities thought it to his own advantage[47] to recognize some other as a god, and he employed the sacred treasures on the building of that city upon which his heart was set. For all that, *he made absolutely no alteration in the traditional forms of worship*, but, though poverty reigned in the temples, one could see that *all the rest of the ritual was fulfilled*.[48]

In 324 Byzantium had a number of operative cults to traditional gods and goddesses tied to its very foundation eight hundred years before. Rhea, called "the mother of the gods" by Zosimus, had a well-ensconced cult in Byzantium from its very foundation.[49] One legend claims that Rhea was named by Byzas as the Tyche of the city in the Basilica.[50] Severus' attempt to overshadow them with his own cult had been unsuccessful. There was a statue of Apollo in the Tetrastoön inscribed to Zeuxippos, but Severus – not Constantine – had removed it to the old acropolis. The memory of connection of the gods to the foundation of the city was perpetuated by Christian Constantinople.[51]

Devotion to Hecate was especially favored by the Byzantines for her aid in having protected them from the incursions of Philip of Macedon.[52] Her symbols were the crescent and star, and the walls of the city were her provenance. By crediting Hecate for their historical victory over Philip – mixing legend and history – the Byzantines essentially escaped the Hellenistic period and its influences. Her title "light bearer" (φωσφόρος) was corrupted into the name of the straits of the Bosphorus.[53] Constantine would also have found Artemis-Selene and Aphrodite along with the banished Apollo Zeuxippus on the Acropolis in the old Greek section of the city. Other gods mentioned in sources are Athena, Hera, Zeus, Hermes, and Demeter and Kore. Even evidence of Isis and Serapis appears from the Roman era on coins during the reign of Caracalla and from inscriptions.[54]

From the evidence of the placement of his building projects, it appears that Constantine basically ignored the oldest part of the Greek city where the temples stood on the acropolis. But the neglect, it can be surmised, was benign, because he did build new temples for Tyche and Rhea at each end of the Severan Tetrastoön. Libanius, who was no friend of Christianity's or Constantine's, certainly seems not to exaggerate when describing the cults as emiserated, yet somehow functioning for the people as they always had. Malalas also states that the three temples on the acropolis were by Constantine's orders "to remain without revenue."[55]

What was most important in crafting his new civic ceremonies was the way in which Constantine set up the physical plan of the city to unite the Great Palace, the Hippodrome, and the Forum. Severus had built the Hippodrome on the model of the Circus Maximus; Constantine only renovated it, embellishing the spina with beautiful Greek and Roman statuary, including the ancient serpent tripod from Delphi. In order to link his private domain with the public, Constantine had the *kathisma*, or imperial box, built at the halfway point of the east side of the Hippodrome. Constantine could make his solemn entry into the public sphere by means of a stairway connecting his palace to the imperial box. This ingenious placement, as we shall see, enabled him to invent a new ceremonial identity for the people, the emperor, and the divine world.

Constantine designed his Forum in a way that would sacralize his own person. Spherical rather than angular, the Forum intersected the Via Egnatia, or the "Mese," as it was called within the new city limits.[56] The main entrance to the Forum was the Old Gate in the Severan Wall. Constantine's Forum was on one of the highest hills in the city.[57] This is significant because the focus of the Forum was the porphyry column in the center twenty-five meters high.[58] Socrates reports that the column was topped by a statue of Constantine's head. Malalas relates even more details: he says that Constantine set up a full-body statue of himself whose head was topped by a splendid crown of seven rays.[59] The crown was unambiguously reminiscent of Helios. Constantine's statue was visible from all parts of the city.

Constantine finished building Severus' public baths, decorating them also with ancient bronze statues of heroes and deities.[60] He too was responsible for the basilica housing the newly established Senate, and two colonnades from the palace called the "Regia." Significantly, he enlarged the Tetrastoön. At opposite ends the new emperor built two temples. And Zosimus relates that "two statues were set up in them, in one Rhea, mother of the gods, and in the other, the statue of Fortuna Romae [Tyche]."[61]

There seem to have been two solemn public dedicatory ceremonies of Constantine's city. One took place in the Forum before the Constantine statue atop the porphyry column and the Tyche statue he put there alongside it. The other took place in the Hippodrome on the day of the consecration of Constantinople, 11 May 330. Philostorgius describes the honorary rites that took place before Constantine's column and statue in the Forum.[62] He says people burned incense, lighted candles, and gave honor to the emperor as a god in the same way townspeople all over the Mediterranean had traditionally honored the "genius of the emperor since the days of Severus."[63] Malalas, the author of the *Chronicon Paschale*, Zonaras, and Procopius all give a more detailed account specifying that, after he offered a "bloodless sacrifice," Constantine dedicated his City to the Tyche and named her "Anthousa," the literal translation of the name of Dea Roma, "Flora."[64] She was soon known as "Tyche Constantinopolis." This Tyche, sharing the Forum with Constantine's statue atop the porphyry column, was the bridge which allowed for the potent transfer of symbols legitimating his city, from the old capital personified in Roma, to Tyche, the "New Rome."[65]

The *Chronicon Paschale* adds a tantalizing bit of information about Tyche Constantinopolis. This account actually allows for the conflation of three goddess legends as the incarnation of the Tyche of New Rome. It says that Constantine secretly stole the Palladium[66] from Rome, and it was this Palladium that he set up in the Forum next to the porphyry column, and named "Tyche

Anthousa." The identities of Pallas Athena, Dea Roma, and Tyche then, according to the legend in the *Chronicon Paschale*, were fused into a rejuvenated goddess. The Palladium legend only strengthens the most salient aspect of the dedication of the city: Constantine established solemn public rites before the statues of Tyche Constantinopolis and himself.

The second half of the public ceremony took place on the joyous day of celebration, May 11, 330, the dedication of Constantinople. The new Tyche also played an important role in these ceremonies. The *Chronicon Paschale* describes the impressive new statue of Tyche Constantinopolis.[67]

> And he [Constantine] made a great festival, and commanded by his sacred decree that the anniversary of his City be celebrated on the same day, and on the eleventh of the same month of Artemisius [May] the public bath of Zeuxippon be opened, which was near the Hippodrome and the Regia of the Palace. He made for himself another gilded monument of wood, one bearing in its right hand a Tyche of the same city, itself also gilded, and commanded that on the same day of the anniversary chariot races, the same monument of wood should enter, escorted by the troops in mantles and slippers, all holding white candles; the carriage should proceed around the further turning- post and come to the arena opposite the imperial box; and the emperor of the day should rise and do obeisance to the monuments of the same emperor Constantine and this Tyche of the City.[68]

The *Chronographia* gives even more specific details about the statue of Tyche. "He [Constantine] had another statue made of himself in gilded wood, bearing in its right hand the Tyche of the city, itself gilded, which he called Anthousa." Malalas also states that the emperor made obeisance to his own image. Significantly these ceremonies were ordered, by imperial decree, to be performed annually thereafter,[69] and one has no reason to assume that they were not. According to this account Constantine, along with thousands of spectators, watched the statue of himself, carrying Tyche perched on his hand, solemnly enter the Hippodrome, the veritable heart of the city where all public ceremonial took place. The statues rode on the "chariot of the sun."[70]

This day of jubilation in honor of Constantine and Tyche

Constantinopolis, celebrated in the magnificent Hippodrome where all interactions between the citizens and the emperor took place, cemented forever two symbolic relationships for the propaganda of Constantine's new empire. The first is the connection between imperial victory and popular prosperity. The second is the figure of Tyche herself, who by acting in her traditional role as Dea Roma symbolizing Rome's powers of overcoming and blessing the world, linked the destiny of the emperor to his people.[71] It also gave the citizens newly approved rites: Tyche and Constantine were to be publically honored yearly in a traditional civic display of reverence, pomp, and patriotism. Constantine himself gave instruction by example.

It is important to remember that, although Tyche was a newcomer with Constantine, her function for the city would not have been an innovation for the populace. He introduced the new deity by venerating the old. One traditional city legend said that when Byzas finished building Byzantium, he honored Rhea as Tyche of the city and queen in the Basilica.[72] Numismatic evidence supports this claim of Rhea as Tyche Poliade.[73] Constantine slightly changed this. By honoring Tyche and Rhea each with their own temples opposite each other in the Tetrastoön, Constantine preserved Rhea's ancient status as "mother of the gods" amongst the Byzantines. Tyche Constantinopolis assumes Rhea's position as guardian and protector of his New Rome, but in Rhea's presence in the Tetrastoön. Constantine reinforced Rhea's "mother of the gods" function when he eventually set up a statue of his mother, Helena, in the Tetrastoön. He then renamed the area the "augusteon" in honor of his mother, Augusta Helena.[74]

Constantine's temples to Rhea and Tyche seem to have invited different interpretations about the significance of the goddesses to the city. Zosimus in his account conflates their symbolism with the Pallas Athena legend. In the *Chronicon Paschale*, on the other hand, "The Tyche of Rome [or New Rome] was assimilated to Pallas of the Palladium, which Constantine had just brought from Rome, and the other Pallas, the other Tyche, was that of ancient Byzantium, Rhea, assimilated to Cybele."[75] Rhea's importance and all she symbolized appears to have been revivified by Constantine's new civic cult to Tyche Constantinopolis.

Constantine merged the symbolism of Helios with his own public person atop the porphyry column and on countless coins, the most effective propaganda medium in the Mediterranean. It was certainly intentional to put his statue as Helios on one of the highest points of the city. The appropriation of the sun god was nothing new for Mediterranean culture; rulers Greek and Roman for centuries had used this image as their own on coins.[76] And the cult of Sol Invictus had been in vogue for a generation or more in the Roman army; Sol was considered the personal companion of the emperors.[77]

If one imagines Constantine's epiphanic entrance as Helios into the Hippodrome, regally descending the winding stairs from the palace to the *kathisma*, one can begin to grasp the method, scope, and impact of his religious program. He imbued the traditional ancestral civic religion with new symbols. Solemnly the assembled people in the Hippodrome watched Constantine watch himself – represented by the statue holding Tyche – ceremoniously ride into the arena on a chariot. And they watched him do *proskynesis* before his statue, as it stopped before the *kathisma*.[78] There was a new meaning to an ancient practice. Constantine had not changed the traditional rituals of Roman civic religion.[79] The Byzantines still had in their collective memory the remembrance of emperor Severus' brutality, and then his renovation projects that had attempted to displace their traditional gods with his own cult. By contrast they found in Constantine a renovator of their traditional institutions and a generous builder. He revived the old religious centers of Byzantium, honoring Rhea by her proximity to Tyche and his mother's statue in the Tetrastoön. The Hippodrome took on new imperial religious significance. To the people Constantine looked like shining Helios Zeuxippos, watching over them from his porphyry column.

Constantine may have embraced a new god and attributed his victory to him alone; but from the vantage point of the Byzantine people, this new god was not yet visible or distinguishable in the public ceremonies dedicating Constantinople. Constantine had banned sacrificial cult by his official decree, but one must remember that animal sacrifice did not constitute the greatest part of pagan Mediterranean religion. Constantine's ceremony with Tyche in the Hippodrome was consonant with the traditions of Mediterranean civic religion. Zosimus reports that Constantine practiced ancestral religion "out of necessity." That "necessity" was to insure that the public knew the proper way to support him and his family so that universal harmony and peace would prevail in the empire. The Byzantines had been introduced to ruler worship from the time of Severus. Constantine resituated the "impressive ceremonies and formulae" of ruler worship to guarantee harmony with the divine world, rather than solely to honor a mortal.[80] He also maintained a balance between the traditional civic religious practices and those of the imperial ruler cult, which focused on his personal greatness – or his genius. But most significantly he recreated for Constantinople the importance of Tyche. She was not just Dea Roma transplanted; rather she was created in Dea Roma's image, just as Constantinople was created in Rome's. And for the townspeople, Rhea, the mother of the gods, continued to be honored through Constantine's efforts.

Constantine could alter the rites to suit his needs and his vision in Byzantium in a way that would have caused social scandal and been nearly impossible in Rome. Rome's impressive continuity of religious/political tradition was most effectively manifest in the established calendar of civic cults that were closely guarded by the ancient institutions themselves. Constantine's innovations would have come up against outcries from the Senate and the hierarchies of the various state cults.[81] In their view, Rome was the center of the powerful civic cult whose responsibility was the entire empire. To innovate upon that could cause cosmic as well as civic strife. Byzantium, on the other hand, was a typical small city in the Mediterranean: syncretism without a politically rigid civic cult prevailed. Constantine could easily mould his own religion there – and did.

Constantine's Christianization of the empire

It is not improbable that his henotheism led Constantine to his personal distaste for animal sacrifice and the trappings of temple cults. It was a common position among many pagans, especially those who were attracted to philosophical religion.[82] His repulsion for bloodshed went so far as outlawing gladiator games in the Hippodrome.[83] Constantine himself refers to Christianity in philosophical terms; it is a result of a logical quest for knowledge.

Whatever is comprehended under the sovereign laws of nature, is capable of conveying to all men an adequate idea of the forethought and intelligence which characterize the arrangements of God. Nor can any, whose minds are directed in the true path of knowledge to the attainment of that end, entertain a doubt that the just perceptions of sound reason, as well as those of the natural vision itself (the true perfection of each faculty having one and the same tendency), lead to the knowledge of God.[84]

It seems that Constantine's distaste for temple ritual and animal sacrifice led him to take upon himself the role of "teacher" to the populace about giving up their cultic practices of animal sacrifice. Sometime after 324 Constantine apparently consented to the request of the citizens of Hispellum (now Spello, Umbria) that they build a temple to honor his family, the *gens flavia*.[85] His only stipulation was that it be free of the defilement "of the evils of any contagious superstition."[86] There is little doubt that this meant sacrificial cult. His refusal to sacrifice on the occasions of both his Decannalia (316) and Vicennalia (326) was remarkable for a Roman emperor, and probably was central to his decision not to make Rome the capital or his residence.

In his role as teacher Sozomen recounts, people were "clinging to their ancient customs and manners and feasts of their fathers."[87] In a brilliant political move as pedagogue for the new state religion, as he understood it, Constantine issued edicts to instruct the governors to suppress their superstitious rites of worship. Unaided by the military, Christian men went from city to city ordering the people to obey the emperor's decrees. Constantine attacked only sacrificial cult; since he replaced it with the new state religion, Christianity, he was able to put social pressure on the pagan priests to give up the wealth of their temple treasuries. "The priests and those in charge of the temples, *being unsupported by the multitude*, brought out . . . their most precious treasures," relates Sozomen.[88] And the "governors and priests of Christ strictly enforced the injunctions contained in the letter."

Constantine's acting on his imperial duty to promote and teach the new state religion is illustrated by Sozomen's account of the people's response to the imperial edict: the emperor had always had the right to dictate on matters of religion. Sozomen says that on hearing the decrees ordering them to give up their "superstitious rites of worship," the people were induced to remain passive from the *fear* that, if they resisted these edicts, they, their wives, and their children would be exposed to evil.[89] When they saw that the emperor had given authority to his governors to seize their images and other cult objects, then cast them down and stuff them with hay, they naturally were "led to despise what they had previously venerated, and *blamed* the erroneous opinion of their ancestors." Finally, "Others, *envious* at the honour in which Christians were held by the emperor, deemed it necessary to conform to the imperial institutions."[90] Imperial authority induced the universal motivating forces of fear and public pressure through the humiliation of temple statues and objects, and most potent of all, imperial coercion unleashed envy amid the population to make them adhere to the religion. Constantine's persecution of paganism was selective;[91] he maintained civic religion.

Constantine reinforced his edicts against pagan cult through his nearly ubiquitous building of churches in the empire, but especially in the cities of the eastern Mediterranean.[92] People had new, grand places to worship as the emperor instructed. He materially replaced the old cults with the new. Eusebius especially devotes a great deal of his accounts to the details of Constantine's churches. Finally, coupled with the legal and financial benefits previously mentioned, Constantine's efforts to promote his new god were successful in keeping with those of a victorious emperor.

All this imperial attention and recognition took the Church hierarchy by surprise, delighting the bishops with regard to financial, legal, and construction matters. Yet it was Constantine's role as teacher and initiator of religious policy that dismayed the bishops. From their perspective Constantine's egregious theological errors were an embarrassment to himself, and a delicate situation for them to handle. Yet Constantine's greatest concern, as was every emperor's before him, was to keep the relationship between the divine world and the empire harmonious.

Constantine had never dealt with the clergy of the Church before, and it seems that because the institution he found himself involved with "was nothing like numerous or influential enough to be a source of political power,"[93] the Church had to tolerate some of the meddlesome, interfering actions of their new patron. Initially, his most bothersome interference was in the Arian controversy. On the model of the Senate, Constantine convoked the first Ecumenical Council at his palace to solve the dispute that was bitterly dividing the Church and now his empire. The proceedings followed Roman law.[94] Constantine eagerly shared his naive theological points of view and confirmed episcopal decisions. Obviously bishops had to endure the emperor's avid involvement – which was unprecedented in their three hundred year old tradition. As Straub laconically points out, Constantine was not even baptized.[95]

Constantine believed himself to be the "civic Bishop."[96] Eusebius quotes Constantine with this claim, "You are bishops whose jurisdiction is within the Church. I also am a bishop, ordained by God, to overlook whatever is external to the Church."[97] Constantine's claim is a prime example of his own theological *gnome* – his opinion which really did not need the approval or benefit of Christian clerics.[98] He interpreted his episcopal office as divinely ordained and sealed through his military victory on the Milvian Bridge. Constantine could claim the office of bishop just as he and his imperial predecessors held the office of *pontifex maximus*. He interpreted the office of bishop this way: the *pontifex maximus* presided over the state cult as head of the whole state clergy, exercising disciplinary function over some of them.[99] Hence Constantine's letters to Arius and Athanasius. Thus he was bishop of the state religion, which was now Christianity.

Eusebius has to do his best to make sense of Constantine's claims. It is Eusebius who is forced to make a distinction between bishops "within" the Church and those "without" – between the secular and the sacred. Constantine would not have been able to with his Greco-Roman frame of reference. He imbued the Christian office with imperial meaning: it was his duty to act as chief priest of the state religion of the empire, and that was now Christianity. Eusebius and the other bishops had to find a way, while not offending the emperor, to limit his sphere, so that their traditional domain and authority – and, from their perspective, the Faith – would not be impaired.

Describing the beginning of the council, Eusebius betrays the reason the bishops had to restrain themselves:

Constantine is the first prince of any age who bound together
such a garland as this with the bond of peace, and presented it
to Christ his Saviour as a thank-offering for the victories he
had obtained over every foe, thus exhibiting in our own times
a similitude of the apostolic company.[100]

Straub has shown that even though Eusebius was embarrassed,
he dealt with Constantine's intrusions probably more fully than
any other Church historian. Eusebius was not an intimate of the
imperial court.[101] He visited Constantinople on ecclesiastical
business only four times.[102] Thus he ended up constructing a
political philosophy for the Church which seems to reflect
neither Constantine's belief about his role as Roman emperor
devoted to the Supreme Being, nor his actions. Eusebius promoted a political philosophy which was foreign and new for the
Roman empire. He tried to harmonize Constantine's actions
with the Biblical concept of kingship.[103]

Eusebius' theory of separate spheres of kingship and episcopal authority apparently did not have influence over
Constantine. The emperor considered himself the "bishop," or
"overseer," of all dwellers of the empire, Christian and pagan
alike.[104] He envisioned the bishops as taking care of cultic
matters only. His own sphere was the public domain, to which he
was appointed by God. For Constantine this included putting
himself in the center of theological disputes because they not
only threatened the unity and harmony of the empire, they
could displease the Supreme Deity. And the maintenance of
ecumenical peace Constantine took seriously, since it was the
primary responsibility given to him by God.[105]

Yet Eusebius did not concur: he designated Constantine,
"like a bishop," to those on the "outside." In reinterpreting
Constantine's robust claims assigning separate spheres of influence for bishops and emperors, Eusebius created a manual for
future emperors that was meant to curtail the power they would
wield in the Church. No future emperor should be allowed the
wide parameters Constantine had naturally assumed by the very
traditions inherent in the Roman imperial office. Eusebius had
to channel the emperor's enthusiasm for the faith. He contex-
tualized it in two ways: in the perspective of Biblical kingship
and as enthusiastic convert. In both cases Eusebius chose to
ignore – in fact he had to ignore – Constantine's continuity

in religious policy with his imperial predecessors, his continuity with his Greco-Roman civic religious culture. Eusebius and Constantine represented two very different cultural traditions.

It is *precisely* in the realm of civic religion that Christians for three hundred years had never been able to participate in the wider Greco-Roman culture. From the perspective of the Church hierarchy, Constantine and his benefices were an embarrassment of riches. There are two other places in Eusebius' meticulous recounting of the miracle of the Constantinian peace for the Church which belie his discomfort with the emperor's religion and patronage of the Church. First, Eusebius chose to completely ignore and exclude the foundation of Constantinople and the building restoration of all the civic buildings in the capital. All the fine ancient statues of gods and heroes that Constantine brought were a chagrin to Eusebius.[106] Of course he never mentions the dedicatory ceremonies of the city, the statue of Tyche, or the statue of the emperor with the crown. For him Constantine's building projects were sufficiently recounted in his descriptions of churches built mostly outside the capital,[107] since the emperor only built two churches there, St Irene and the Holy Apostles, and only laid the foundations for Agia Sophia.

The second area Eusebius finds problematic concerned Constantine's grandiose plans for the Church of the Holy Apostles in Constantinople, which was finished in his lifetime. Eusebius could not avoid dealing with the fact that Constantine had it built as his future mausoleum. This purpose defied two ancient customs: it allowed for burial inside the city limits, against Roman custom, and it broke with Tetrarchic custom of imperial burial inside the royal palaces.[108] Constantine required that the liturgy be celebrated over his tomb; and, because "according to his wish," says Eusebius, he wanted to "share the honor with the Holy Apostles,"[109] literally. Eusebius necessarily distances himself from the claim by saying it was Constantine's wish. The bishops would have been shocked.[110] This claim for honor is not extraordinary from the viewpoint of Greco-Roman religious culture, since Constantine, as a responsible emperor, did his best to keep harmony between his new deity and his people. What Eusebius is balking against is precisely Constantine's success at merging Christianity and the Roman ideology of the emperor as *pontifex maximus*. Constantine's new imperial Christianity succeeded despite Eusebius' attempt to correct Constantine's actions for future generations of emperors as he reinterprets them in his account of Church history and in his panegyrics of Constantine. Eusebius' subtext is always prophylactic *propaideia*.

Constantine succeeded in making Christianity a Greco-Roman civic religion; and Eusebius and the hierarchy, although genuinely thankful and relieved at his patronage, were not quite ready for either his expansive intrusions into ecclesiastical politics or what they regarded as his naive attempts at doctrine. Until Constantine's time, custom was the real reason why Christianity had been hated.[111] Christians had always stayed away from the "ancestral religion, the rule of custom, and the role of tradition."[112] It is difficult to know whether Zosimus knew the depth of his statement when he said Constantine did practice "ancestral religion." All the aspects of religious culture that the Christians had successfully eschewed for three centuries were suddenly merged with Christian belief. Constantine built churches, he allowed tax exemptions to clerics, gave generously to bishops for charity distribution,[113] and rescinded the old Roman laws against virgins and celibates. Yet he maintained civic religious temples to Tyche and Rhea, instituted public ceremonies that celebrated him and Tyche Constantinopolis, issued his coins with Helios and other pagan symbols.[114] The citizens of Constantinople venerated Constantine's Helios image in the Hippodrome each year, and had occasion to venerate Tyche and Rhea even daily if desired. And according to Libanius pagan temples, although poverty stricken, continued to function. Finally Constantine was buried according to his wishes as "isapostolos" in the Church of the Holy Apostles, his mausoleum.[115]

Constantine was able to accomplish this in Constantinople because the Byzantines had had an amorphous, highly syncretistic pagan tradition without civic cults as strong as those in the city of Rome, such as the Vestals and Flamens.[116] When Constantine set up his Tyche as Tyche Constantinopolis as a parallel to the Dea Roma (whether she was the Palladium or not), the Byzantines took on Roman civic religion, mediated through the new emperor, who now resided there. When he imbued the religious culture further with his version of

Christianity, again they were receptive at his instruction of the "new" imperial religion.

It has already been mentioned that Constantine could not have accomplished what he did in his new city in Rome because of the strength of the ancient civic cults. Yet there is another reason. The Church in Rome was almost as ancient as the empire itself. The hierarchy, cult, community, and entire administrative institution were powerful, with customs long established. It is highly unlikely that Constantine could have merged his idiosyncratic version of Christianity with the Church or the civic cults there. Neither the Roman Church nor the traditional city cults could have tolerated the abomination of innovations upon each other's "ancestral rites" and traditions from a new emperor. It would have been very difficult for Christianity to emerge as the civic religion of the empire in the city of Rome.

Through Constantine's efforts the Church was literally "publicized" – even politicized. Christianity had become the the state religion of the empire, with civic ceremonies enacted in Constantinople. Because of this the hierarchy of the Church had to cope with the traditional Roman concept that society – both religious and secular – was a unity headed by the emperor himself. In some respects, the Church adapted quite well. In the administrative organization it soon began to mirror imperial bureaucracy, based on cities, provinces, and dioceses.[117] Through Constantine's church building, the plans of the traditional imperial basilica were realized as magnificent new churches, announcing in various cities the arrival of an imperially honored cult. Yet the focus was not so much how the institutional church reacted and changed under Constantine, but rather what Constantine and the pagan converts brought to Christianity, first in attitude towards the divine and then in ceremony.

Once converted, or brought into the fold, through social pressure, envy, fear, or genuine conviction, people did not give up their original attitudes to the divine world any more than they gave up their culture. Most scholars have held that paganism – or the old religion – was very tolerant. This simply means that the Mediterranean religious culture was quite elastic and adaptable. It is this very adaptability that was bound to find an outlet of expression in Christianity, since fundamentally Christianity could not be made non-exclusive – or tolerant.

Although there are few and fleeting references to common people's attitudes to Constantine's edicts on his new religion, it is not impossible to construct a tableau of religious attitude as more and more pagans from all social classes began to publicly profess Christianity and leave testimony to it in ways that betray a less-than-orthodox belief. Legislation from the reigns of his sons, Constans and Constantius, reflects this spirit of civic religion which their father had initiated. Constans allowed the temples outside the walls of the city to remain, because some of the spectacles, theater, and contests for the Roman people had always been provided by them.[118] Constantius issued a law that distills the essence of what was culturally immutable in civic religion.

> To insist upon the ancient customs is the discipline of future times. Therefore, when nothing that is in the public interest interferes, practices which have long been observed shall remain valid.[119]

To fit together this scant information, it is necessary to turn to the post-Constantinian emperors to sketch the next stage of Christianity's adaptation to her new status as the civic religion.

Chapter 2

The Theodosians and paganism

When Gregory Nazianzus reluctantly came to Constantinople in 379 as the elected bishop, he remarked several times about the religious situation in the city. As bishop of the minority Christians in the city, the orthodox, he was actively involved with the Arian controversy that was still raging. His friend Gregory Nyssa had even noticed that shopkeepers and ecclesiastics alike were noticeably preoccupied with the questions of how the Son relates to the Father.[1]

Yet the new bishop saw evidence for two other kinds of religious activity in the city. Apparently the citizens of Constantinople had taken Constantine's example of Christianity as the new imperial religion seriously.[2] The new churches and the ceremonies in the Hippodrome were the *loca religionis* for Constantinopolitan Christianity, an amalgam of official state ceremony and Christianity.[3] But neither Arianism nor the civic ceremonies seem to have irked him so much as the paganism he found in the capital. In his quieter moments he bemoans the fact that Christians wasted so much time fighting each other rather than paganism.[4] He wistfully writes that he dreamt of "converting the pagans in the city."[5] From Gregory's point of view, paganism was a viable religious presence in the capital. And it was terribly bothersome to him that paganism was not labeled the "enemy," rather than heresy.[6]

The many gradations of Arian heresies, and the divisive effects of Donatism in the west, allowed the Church to exercise its power as the state religion. As the Church put all its energy into battling the number one enemy of the state, heresy, there was less focus on paganism's continued presence. Pagan philosophers still played a role at court. But when confronted with the overt operation of pagan rituals or temples, the emperors were quick to act against them.

Socrates gives an interesting detail exemplifying this situation. Emperor Valens (364–378) battled long and hard against the homoousion position in the Arian controversy, taking on even Basil, bishop of Caesarea. Thanks to Valens, the greatest number of churches and sees in the east were in Arian hands. He actively persecuted the Homoousions so much that it took the rhetorical expertise of a pagan philosopher, Themistius, to persuade him to mitigate his zeal. Themistius exhorted Valens with three points to adopt a policy of greater toleration. First, he used a comparison with the number of pagan opinions on the Godhead. Since they amount to more than three hundred, and the ones held by the Christian are so few, "the discrepancy is trifling."[7] Then God would actually be "more glorifed by the diversity of sentiment,"[8] since finally the Godhead is essentially inscrutable.[9] Unfortunately Themistius did not completely convince Valens, but the emperor did stop executing bishops. He did continue to exile them, however.[10]

In the meantime Valens brother, Gratian, was proving himself an able emperor in the west. Zosimus reports that Gratian was the first emperor to refuse the title *pontifex maximus*, creating a precedent for future emperors.[11] Consistent with his aversion to the cults of the city of Rome, he removed the Altar of Victory from the Senate.[12] Because of Valens' policy favoring the Arians, and the bishops on both sides wrangling over creeds and property, when Valens died in 378 Gratian was left with an officially Arian capital city. The Great Church had been handed over to them.[13] Gratian was orthodox.

The political situation was just as precarious. Barbarian raids threatened the empire on all fronts. Socrates apologizes for his intermingling war events with ecclesiastical affairs."[14] But he insists that he must do this because the Church and State were inextricably woven together: disturbance in one created havoc in the other.[15] And he blames the bishops for their constant conniving against each other.[16] Socrates then goes on to say that he must review the actions of the emperors because once they began professing Christianity they "exercised a powerful influence on the affairs of the Church."[17]

Although Gratian took his faith seriously, he did not prohibit the continued operation of pagan temples, nor did he exclude

pagan philosophical discourse. During Gratian's reign a prominent philosopher, Theon, taught and interpreted the astrono-
mical writings of Hermes Trismegistos and Orpheus.[18] In 379
Gratian's former tutor, Ausonius, wrote a panegyric to him in
thanksgiving for appointing him as consul. Although both of
them were Christian, Ausonius compares the emperor to the
pontifex maximus who randomly chose the priests to fill the college. His chaste way of life he compares to the "altar of Vesta."[19]

In 378 the Gothic raids on Constantinople demanded that
Gratian act quickly. A young soldier from Spain, named
Theodosius, caught Gratian's attention. He promoted him to the
rank of general to help him stave off barbarian attacks. Their
military efforts were so successful that Gratian made Theodosius co-emperor of the east. Soon after, Theodosius was baptized in Thessaloniki, because he thought his death was
imminent. When he entered the Arian capital city in 380, he
made it publicly known that the Catholic Church meant
"homoousion."[20] He was greatly outnumbered.

Theodosius called the Council of Constantinople in 381, soon
after his arrival. His primary goal was to "restore concord
among the churches."[21] Theodoret devotes several chapters to
describing the council. The letter of Pope Damasus to Bishop
Paulinus of Thessaloniki which he preserves includes a fascinat-
ing clue about the religious culture.

Pope Damasus begins his defense of the homoousion position
against the Arians by condemning the Pneumatomachians, and
continues for several pages to list all the variations of the Arian
heresy by anthematizing them. Finally he ends with the condem-
nation of those who would divide the Trinity into three separate
Gods, or who would claim that the Father alone is God, "putting
aside the Son and Holy Spirit." He then explains why.

> The name of *gods has been given by God to angels and to saints.*
> But the Father, the Son, and the Holy Spirit are not called
> gods but God, because of the oneness of their divinity, and
> because they are co-equal.[22]

The point of Damasus' arguments is that Christians can only
worship the *one* God, so by necessity the Son and Holy Spirit
must be united in divinity with the Father. Saints, archangels,
and angels he calls "gods," yet because of their very separateness
Christians cannot and do not worship them. Their salvation lies

in unity of power, divinity, and substance. Pope Damasus' calling
saints and angels "gods" is striking for several reasons. First, the
bishop of Rome uses the appellation to distinguish the importance of the unity of the Godhead. But his intended argument
may have been lost on people just entering the new religion of
the empire for the many less-than-pious reasons that Sozomen
cites. Instead of focusing on the unity of the Trinity, people
easily could have asked, "If angels and saints are gods, how does
one honor them?" And Pope Damasus' appellation is an indi-
cation that the Church's process of experimentation has begun,
as it accustoms itself to the wider culture. The Church starts
addressing the contingent of holy beings, "saints and angels
called gods," with the influx of pagans as it begins to realize and
enjoy its privileged position as the Roman state religion.

When emperor Gratian died in 384, Theodosius embarked on
a campaign to close all the pagan temples in the empire. He had
already destroyed the three ancient temples on the acropolis in
Constantinople. After he had it converted into a courtyard
surrounded by houses, Theodosius donated the temple of
Helios to the Great Church.[23] The temple of Artemis became a
gambling den for dice players; and the Aphrodite temple was
made into the carriage house for the praetorian prefect.[24]
Alongside it was constructed a shelter for destitute prostitutes.[25]

Reactions to the emperor's policies were fiercest in Egypt.
When Theodosius ordered the temple of Bacchus converted
into a church, the imperial enforcers publicly humiliated and
ridiculed the statues of the old cult.[26] Pagan reaction was so
violent that imperial troops had to restore order to Alexandria,
which was devastated by the riots.[27] The temple of Serapis was
relinquished only after a military siege.[28]

Yet Theodosius was successful in prohibiting the "centuries-
old sacrifices and ancestral rituals" from functioning.[29] By 391
Theodosius' edict against paganism reached into the private
realm of domestic deities. Not only was it illegal to attend temples, every form of cult practice was forbidden, "from public
sacrifices to venerating lares with fire, venerating a genius with
wine, or a penates with fragrant odors. No incense, lamps, or
wreaths were permitted."[30] Zosimus, who never disguised his
antipathy for Theodosius, laments that it was unsafe for anyone
to believe in the gods, "or to look up to heaven and worship what
he saw."[31] According to Sozomen, however, temples in the less

important cites of Petraea, Raphi, Hieropolis, and Apamea remained open, despite the edict.[32] He relates that Theodosius did not want to persecute his subjects; his overriding concern was "the enforcement of uniformity of religion through the medium of intimidation."[33] The policy obviously worked in the east. Since pagans had nowhere to worship, they began to go to the churches, not daring to perform their rites clandestinely, on penalty of confiscation of property or death.[34] But most other ancient historians argue that Theodosius not only closed the temples, he demolished most of them.[35]

There is other evidence that supports Sozomen's view pointing to the difficulty of eradicating pagan cult. Legislation from the period shows that Theodosius came up with penalties which, in some respects, were even stiffer than death. From five laws enacted from 381 to 391,[36] there is evidence that not only were pagan temples still in operation, Christians were "going over" to their altars and temples. For this reversion to paganism Theodosius' first law declared that people could not make wills.[37] Yet the punishments in the next four laws become progressively harsher, suggesting their ineffectiveness. In 383 not only were these people prevented from making wills, they could not inherit. The next one states that they would be banished with no hope of restoration. And finally those of eminent social position, those of "splendor of rank," would be stripped of their status and "be branded in perpetual infamy."[38]

In Rome Theodosius met with stronger pagan tradition and resistance. When he proclaimed his son Honorius emperor of the west in Rome in 393, the senate was summoned. When the emperor urged the senate to abandon their rites which had protected Rome for over a millennium, the body refused. Theodosius then lectured them on the superiority of his religion. All the senators still refused.[39] For their punishment and "his greediness," Theodosius absconded with their treasury, leaving the Roman senate and their cult impoverished.[40]

Theodosius I and civic ceremony

Yet Theodosius' zeal for the faith apparently did not mitigate his passion for the visible trappings of civic religion. Zosimus claims that Theodosius' love of ostentation, luxury, extravagance – as well as the frequent occurrence of war – forced him to overtax

the population.[41] In 387 a riot broke out in Antioch because of
new tax levies. The statues of the emperor and his wife Flacilla
were thrown down and dragged through the streets.[42]
Theodosius retaliated, threatening to burn the city to the
ground. In the version told by Zosimus, the great sophist
Libanius was chosen as the envoy to Theodosius, successfully
assuaging his anger.[43] Sozomen and John Chrysostom both
write that it was Bishop Flavian of Antioch who gently calmed
the emperor enough to avert his anger.[44] Considering what
statues represented, Theodosius' reaction in some respects was
not excessive. Since the reign of Severus imperial statues were
not only greeted by the people as if it were the emperor himself,
they were revered as an epiphany of a god.[45] Constantine had
retained this ceremonial propaganda of imperial images and
statues modifying it slightly. Imperial statues were received by
the townspeople as if they were the emperor himself, not a
god.[46] When one venerated a statue it was believed that the
prototype was also honored. This explanation had justified the
practice of venerating statues in Greco-Roman society since
classical antiquity.[47] The ceremonious welcoming of imperial
images had become a civic obligation.[48] Zosimus recounts that in
386 Theodosius sent imperial images to Egypt to replace pagan
religion,[49] obviously intending to replace pagan cults with civic
cult.

Nothing in the ancient historians suggests that Theodosius
changed any of the civic ceremonies Constantine had initiated.
In fact, Zosimus leads us to believe that Theodosius reinforced
existing civic rituals, since he adored public processions, shows,
and all events in the Hippodrome.[50] Socrates laments that it is
customary to address the emperors as "lords" and "most divine,"
although he cannot bear to do so,[51] even Theodosius. A law
issued under his reign specified that judges could attend spectacles only on the emperor's birthday or on the anniversary of his
imperial accession.[52] And the judges were only allowed to celebrate until noon, since they were obliged to return to work.
Otherwise they were prohibited from taking off work to go to
the shows. In other words, if the celebration was specifically to
honor Theodosius, he would make great concessions to allow all
to pay him their respects. This indicates that even though he
eradicated paganism and he is considered the first "Christian"
emperor, his idiosyncratic love of pomp kept the civic ceremony

intact, and that he loved the laudes of Tetrarchic days, praising him as "divine.'

Another incident shows how unclear the lines were dividing the spheres of Church and State in Constantinople, at least from the Church's perspective. In 393 the people of Thessaloniki wanted the release of a charioteer from prison, whose presence was required for their celebration.[53] This criminal had been incarcerated for his "declaration of obscene passion" to Buthericus, the commanding general of Illyria. When the man was not released, a mob killed Buthericus. Theodosius was so outraged that he required that a certain number (7,000 people, quotes Theodoret) be killed. The slaughter proceeded. Afterwards when Theodosius continued his journey to Milan and tried to go into the church, Bishop Ambrose prevented him from doing so. Ambrose shamed the emperor publicly for his vengeful murder of so many innocent people and forced him to do penance. When the bishop finally allowed him back into the church, Theodosius was chastised yet again.

It had been the imperial custom at Constantinople for the emperor to sit in the altar during the divine liturgy with the other bishops and priests. Theodosius was only acting on that custom. Ambrose, on the other hand, motivated by the clear divisions of authority that were typical of the Church in the west, would not tolerate this; and he sent him back outside the altar in front of the people.[54] According to Theodoret, he stood with the rest of the laity.[55] Ambrose reportedly said, "The priests alone are permitted within the altar, all others must not approach it, a purple robe makes emperors but not priests."[56] Sozomen relates that Ambrose considered that the imperial "custom had originated either from subserviency or from want of discipline."[57] Theodoret defends the imperial custom further by stating that Theodosius had not done this out of arrogance, but "because such was the custom at Constantinople."[58]

According to these historians, the emperor humbly accepted Ambrose's instructions, but this did not change the custom in Constantinople for quite some time.[59] The incident only points to Constantine's innovative practice of imperial Christianity. Bishops of ancient sees with long established traditions like Ambrose were unable to tolerate invention of Christian traditions such as this in the imperial name. Although Theodosius bowed to Ambrose's wishes, the bishop's influence did not reach

to Constantinople. The practice admirably illustrates Constantine's vision of the emperor as head of the state religion, which
ran counter to the Church's tradition and the bishops" definition of their own role.

Eudoxia, John Chrysostom, and his confrontation with civic piety

Theodosius died in 397, leaving his sons Arcadius and Honorius
as emperors. Arcadius resided in Constantinople with his wife
Eudoxia and four children, Pulcheria, Marina, Arcadia, and
Theodosius II. Arcadius ruled for only eleven years before his
death. Although his reign was short, it is remembered in part for
the controversial conflicts Eudoxia encountered with John
Chrysostom, bishop of Constantinople from 398 to 404. The
empress Eudoxia was not only the recipient of John's golden-
mouthed invective against her and her statue, she ended up in
the middle of a political/ecclesiastical power struggle. For our
purposes here, however, what is most interesting are Sozomen's
descriptions of the ceremonious dedication of the silver statue of
Eudoxia, and the cursory description of Chrysostom's arguments against it.

Sozomen relates that a silver statue of the empress was set up
on a prophyry column, just south of the Great Church.[60] From
his account, it seems, the statue survived Chrysostom's haran-
gues. The bishop not only disapproved of the statue of the
empress, he was equally distraught by the boisterous celebrations that accompanied the dedication. Sozomen says that
there was "dancing, games, and other manifestations of public
rejoicing" at the dedication.[61] It is significant that Sozomen
states that all of this celebration was "customary on the erection
of the statues of emperors."[62] Among other vituperations,
Chrysostom hurled the epithet "Herodias" at the empress, in
retaliation for her hubris in setting up the statue. This was his
last public display against her, however; Arcadius banished him
from the capital in 404.

Chrysostom's opposition to the statue and the festivities is
symptomatic of his visceral antipathy to Constantinopolitan
Christianity: the incarnation of Christianity as the civic religion
of the Roman empire. Chrysostom feared the real connection
between festival celebrations and pagan cult. Arcadius and

Honorius issued a law in 399 which acknowledges this ancient traditional connection, by distinguishing civic religion from temple sacrifice and ritual.

> Just as we have already abolished profane rites by a salutary law, so we do not allow the festal assemblies of citizens and the common pleasure of all to be abolished. Hence we decree that, according to ancient custom, amusements shall be furnished to the people, but without any sacrifice or any accursed superstition, and they shall be allowed to attend festal banquets, whenever public desires so demand.[63]

John Chrysostom represents perhaps the most pristine, unacculturated Christianity of the fourth century. He was born in 347 in Antioch, the most ancient of the Christian sees outside of Jerusalem. Antioch is where the name "Christian" was first used. His vision of Christianity shows that he shunned the influences of cultural norms of Greco-Roman society. Chrysostom's homilies and commentaries indicate a fundamental dependence on the preaching styles of early Christianity, rooted in conservative Biblical exegesis, from a period long before Constantine.[64] It made no difference to him that there was a civic tradition from the time of Constantine dedicating statues. He is the one who pits Church attendance against attendance at public shows and processions.[65] It is telling how he deals with the topic of statues.[66]

In Constantinople the emperor and his household held a religious office and function of the sort that Augustus and his family instituted. Constantine had kept this same form and definition of religion: all that he had done was change the deity to the Christian God. And he had expected and demanded the Church to follow suit and cooperate. More importantly, it was in these traditional Roman terms of religion, responding to the religious function of the imperial household, that the population of Constantinople understood Christianity. Stated in other terms, the people of the capital did not dichotomize religion. They stood riveted at Chrysostom sermons for hours and followed his political and ecclesiastical fortunes avidly,[67] without disavowing their civic religious duties at the Hippodrome.

John Chrysostom was indeed in foreign territory in the capital, precisely because he was from Antioch. Like Ambrose of Milan, Chrysostom came from an ancient episcopal see that acted on its own ecclesiastical authority. He was not about to change ecclesiastical tradition and bow to the novelties of the imperial household as it constantly intervened in Church affairs. Since Constantine's time, the Church in Constantinople had been made to accommodate imperial guidance and the civic religious ceremonies. Like Ambrose, for Chrysostom to submit to such imperial policies would have constituted a serious breach of his vows. Assuredly he was popular with the people,[68] they flocked to the church to be captivated by his stunning rhetoric. Yet he could not wrest them from their traditional displays of civic piety that merged veneration of the emperor, worship towards God, and festive city celebrations. He could not tolerate any vestiges of paganism. For his way of thinking, a statue left as decoration in the public baths was a potential occasion for idolatry just as scandalous as animal sacrifice.

On the other hand imperial policy on statues was much milder and more nuanced. A law of 396 read, "Just as We forbid sacrifices, so it is Our will that the ornaments of public works shall be preserved."[69] And although their father's policy called for the demolition of temples, a law of 399 shows more leniency on the part of Arcadius and Honorius. If a temple stood empty of idols and cultic objects, it was illegal to raze the building.[70] Chrysostom could not allow for gradations of paganism in the wider culture which was now declared to be "Christian."

Yet he alone was not strong enough to transform the citizens into the kind of Christian society he envisioned.[71] Chrysostom's belief that the imperial office be subject to the sarcedotal in all matters appears in many of his treatises.

> The one appointed to the priesthood is a more responsible guardian of the earth and what transpires on it than one who wears the purple, and . . . the magnitude of priestly power is not to be diminished but one's life is to be surrendered sooner than the authority which God has assigned to this office from above.[72]

As a master of rhetoric, Chrysosotom knew the power of allusion in his sermons. When referring to the imperial household, he judiciously chose to tread the middle ground. His references were clear, precise, short, devoid of both flattery and criticism.[73]

In Constantinople Chrysostom discovered that the bishop was expected to defer to the emperor.[74] But the reason for this

was not some sort of anachronistic caesaro-papism; rather
Chrysostom and the imperial court found themselves in a conflict over models of religion. The model of religion Chrysostom
represented was sectarian. His Christianity, as received from the
Antiochene Church, was a highly independent institution, re-
quiring its adherents to obey its clergy and laws before all other
institutions', and that included the government's. Chrysostom's
Christianity, however elaborate in hierarchy and doctrine, was
still based on the model of a sect.[75]

When Chrysostom arrived in Constantinople, he found a very
different kind of Christianity based on the model of civic religion. Constantine had assumed the role of *pontifex maximus*,
chiefly responsible for the religious well-being of the empire, as
had all his predecessors. Christianity suddenly was co-opted by
him into the model of Greco-Roman civic religion, becoming the
only state-approved cult of the empire. Even though Gratian
renounced the title, all the succeeding emperors continued to
function as Constantine had as the head of the state religion. A
law of 396 revoked the privileges that had been accorded by law
to "civil priests, ministers, prefects, or hierophants or the sacred
mysteries."[76] They had been replaced by the Christian clergy.
The imperial court understood the position and function of the
bishop of Constantinople as an office of the state religion, with
all its extra-ecclesiastical ceremonies. Chrysostom did little to
hide his antipathy to such a model of Christianity. It is no
wonder that his tenure in the capital was stormy, or that his view
of the Church ultimately lost.

Resituating the rubrics of ritual: holidays

Anti-pagan legislation continued to be a strong policy under
Theodosius and Arcadius. One of the ways these emperors
reinforced this legislation was to redefine the rules for celebrating Christian holidays and those for celebrating civic holidays.
These laws concerned the proper celebration of the emperor's
birthday and the proper treatment of his image in public spaces.
They show consistent reinforcement of Constantine's civic religious ceremonies that centered around the imperial dignity.

Under Theodosius I several laws reinforced what had been
legislated under Constantine in 321: the day of the Sun was a
holiday, and no litigation except manumission could take place,

as well as on the fifteen days after Easter.[77] It seems that it was necessary to define how the "day of the Lord," Sun day, was to be observed. Theodosius legislated against holding circuses, contests, and spectacles on Sundays, excepting of course the imperial birthday.[78] His sons" decrees further define this. No spectacles were allowed on Christmas, Epiphany, or on the fifteen paschal days.[79] A law issued in 409 indicates that these restrictions were not being followed or enforced. It emphatically states that "absolutely no amusements were to be produced."[80] It would have been difficult to hold a spectacle in secret.

Special ritual was forming around images of the imperial family. A law issued in 394 shows that there is a qualitative difference between imperial images and those of celebrated entertainers. If pictures of actors, charioteers, or mimes were posted in "public porticos" or elsewhere in the city where imperial images "are usually consecrated," the law required that they be torn down.[81] The reason for this was that those of the performers were "disreputable"; they could not be hung in "reputable places." Rather, they were only to be hung in the circus entrances or in the theater. By posting them in proximity to the imperial image, they dishonored both the image of the emperor and his person.

Another law of 406 describes the conditions for removal of imperial images from buildings needing repair.[82] Images of present and past emperors could be removed "with due reverence, even without consulting Our Clemency," when building restoration commenced. The final provision of the law stipulates that the images be returned to "the proper places" on completion of the project. These laws indicate that a code of ritual behavior was developing around imperial images. They were not posted, they were "consecrated" in public places. They demanded special treatment in removal and replacement. And above all, they could not be dishonored by the propinquity of pictures of common entertainers.

Pulcheria, Theodosius II, and paganism

Arcadius outlived the empress Eudoxia, who died in childbirth in 404,[83] by four years. When the emperor died, he left his four young children in the care of of the eunuch Antiochus, the *praepositus sacri cubiculi*, who provided for their education.[84]

Although the empire was technically to be ruled by Theodosius II when he would come of age, his older sister Pulcheria exercised such profound influence over him all his life that she must be considered the co-regent of the empire until her death in 453. In fact it can be said without exaggeration that Pulcheria gave the identity to her brother's reign.[85] She presided over all the political and ecclesiastical events of the first half of the fifth century, events crucial to the formation of Christianity as the civic cult.

When she was fifteen years old Pulcheria quarreled with Antiochus and convinced Theodosius to dismiss him. Sozomen attributes these occurrences to "the design of God."[86] She also took it upon herself to educate her brother in the imperial responsibilities and customs.

> She caused all affairs to be transacted in the name of her brother, and devoted great attention to furnishing him with such information as was suitable to his years. She employed masters to instruct him in horsemanship and the use of arms, and in literature and science. But he was taught how to maintain a deportment befitting an emperor by his sister; she showed him how to gather up his robes, and how to take a seat; and taught him to refrain from ill-timed laughter, to assume a mild or formidable aspect as the occasion might require, and to enquire with urbanity into the cases of those who came before him with petitions.[87]

But above all Sozomen stresses that Pulcheria taught her brother "piety and the life of prayer.[88] Pulcheria had taken her instructions seriously in her own life. At this very age of fifteen she compelled her sisters, Arcadia and Marina, to join her in dedicating their virginity perpetually to God.

> She devoted her virginity to God, and instructed her sisters to do likewise. To avoid all cause of scandal and opportunity for intrigue, she permitted no man to enter her palace. In confirmation of her resolution she took God, the priests, and all the subjects of the Roman empire as witnesses of her self-dedication, and presented a table, elaboratedly adorned with gold and precious stones, to the church of Constantinople, in token of the life of virginity to which she and her sisters had devoted themselves.[89]

Pulcheria's vow enabled her to escape the bonds of marriage which would have removed her from her position of power. Socrates states diplomatically that life at the imperial palace in most respects resembled a monastery.[90] Fasts were observed on Wednesdays and Fridays. Pulcheria required that the household rise early, pray together at regular intervals, and chant hymns antiphonally.[91] When the time came for Theodosius to marry, it was Pulcheria who found him an appropriate bride, a young woman from Athens, named Athenais, daughter of the philosopher Leontius.[92] She was baptized, took the name Eudokia, and was married to the emperor. Their only daughter was named Eudoxia. It is no wonder that under this religious climate cultic paganism was vigorously opposed. The empire during the next fifty years became recognizably Christian. The key to that transition was Pulcheria's leadership of the Church in its appropriation of the forms of civic cermony for its own use. It is Pulcheria who transforms the locus of civic cult from the Hippodrome to the Church.

Theodosius' legal proscriptions against paganism

Theodoret reports that Theodosius had the "ruins of idolatrous temples removed, and their very foundations destroyed.[93] The reason he gives is that Theodosius wanted to insure that future generations would have no vestiges of pagan cult to corrupt them. What is strange, however, is that legislation decreed during his reign reveals that the pagan temples still continued in operation in some capacity. A law was issued right before Arcadius' death that "income from taxes in kind shall be taken away from the temples" for the benefit of the military.[94] Temple buildings should not be destroyed according to the law, but confiscated for public use, after the altars were destroyed. Banquets for the dead held at cemetaries were also prohibited by this law, as well as "celebration of any solemn ceremony."[95] Finally, the law gave bishops the right to interdict these practices, and fined civil judges "twenty pounds" of gold if they were caught overlooking occurrences of these kinds. Because pagan cult was still a presence in the empire, imperial authority began to enlist the power of bishops to enforce their decrees, since the civil judges were failing to do so. Clearly previous laws were not having the desired effects.

In 415 Theodosius had to address paganism again, in a very detailed law.[96] Carthage in particular was singled out. Pagan priests were ordered to leave that city, or suffer "proper punishment." It seems from the wording of the law that these pagan priests were flocking to large cities, because they were ordered to "return to their ancestral municipalities." This applied to all cities in Africa. The law also stipulates that pagan property be confiscated "to the property of Our privy purse," especially those places formerly possessed by the "Frediani and the Dendrophori."[97] Representing a clear break from past legislation, the next section declares that statuary used for decoration in "baths and favorite haunts" be removed.[98] The "Chiliarchs and Centenarii, or any other persons who are said to appropriate to themselves the distribution of the common people" were disbanded, on pain of death. Finally, that same year it also became illegal for any pagan to "be admitted to imperial service, nor be judge or adminstrator.[99] This law would have been easy to enforce, and apparently was. Dagron showed that most of the prefects of Constantinople before 415 were pagan.[100] After 415 this abruptly stopped, and accusing an official of "Hellenism" was a way to force him out of office.

In 438 a famous incident concerning the prefect Cyrus took place, and he was exiled for his "Hellenism."[101] Cyrus held two offices, the praetorian prefect and the city prefect. He fell victim to Theodosius' envy and jealousy at his popularity with the people. According to Malalas, Cyrus was responsible for the tremendous rebuilding and restoration of city buildings. They acclaimed him in the Hippodrome in front of Theodosius, chanting "Constantine built, Cyrus rebuilt, put them at the same level, Augustus.[102] Furious, Theodosius deposed him, confiscated his property, and exiled him, all on the charges of paganism. It does not seem to have mattered that Cyrus built a church to the Theotokos in Constantinople, or that at his banishment, he took refuge in the Church, which soon made him a bishop.

One of the novels of Theodosius II, issued in 438, follows up on this theme of excising pagans from the empire – in fact it seems to speak specifically to the case of Cyrus. Yet it adds as a reason for it an ancient justification for imperial religious policy: appeasement of the deity. The law begins by stating that the emperor has done everything in his power "to scare pagans from desisting, even exile.[103] The novel continues by stating that even if the emperor wanted to forget the pagans, he would not be able to do so. More importantly, heaven is manifesting its anger in poor crops and bad weather. Thus "the venerable majesty of the Supernal Divinity must be appeased." Theodosius saw it as his duty to placate God, it was not the Church's responsibility.

The traditional civic ceremonies of Constantinople, *circa* 420

It is important now to articulate just what constituted civic religious ceremonies from the time of Constantine. All the public festivals including games, theater, and circuses were from their origins religious festivals.[104] Their celebration had formed the very heart of civic religion in the Greco-Roman world. In the fourth century no matter how disengaged a festival became from its original purpose to honor a specific god, the essentially religious and ceremonial character of the civic celebrations remained.[105] Constantine's innovative Hippodrome ceremonies, which were celebrated annually, honoring himself, Tyche Constantinopolis, and the foundation of the City did not rupture the age-old customs of civic religion.[106]

Constantine's civic customs were consistent with the traditional ceremonies of Roman civic religion, the most important of which were veneration through *proskynesis* to the emperor, on his arrival either in person or in image.[107] The act included kneeling and kissing the royal purple robes.[108] Processions including lamps or torches, rhythmic acclamations (or denunciations) by the crowd often sung in chant, and exchanges between the emperor and his people at the Hippodrome were all vital parts of civic ceremony.[109] It was the Church's task to come to terms with the meaning of civic religious ceremony, especially since Christianity was now officially the state religion. We shall see that, as the Church begins to become accommodated to its official status, it begins absorbing some of the rituals and forms of civic religion.[110] One of the clearest ways to understand civic ceremonies of Constantinople as they merge with the Church's is to look at the office of the prefect of the city. One of the prefect's major duties was to control the population of the city for the emperor.[111] In order to accomplish this he was responsible for upkeep of public buildings and spaces, water supplies, the bread dole, and fire prevention.[112] Equally important to the maintenance of peace in the city was the prefect's duty of organizing public ceremonies.

Public games and events in the Hippodrome, as well as processions[113] in the streets and fora, were also the prefect's responsibility. He designed them to please the citizens, honor the emperor, and celebrate the city, keeping all parties content. It was also the prefect's duty to crown emperors. Theodosius II was crowned by Prefect Ursus "in accordance with custom" in the Theodosian Forum – this usually took place in the Hippodrome – after a glorious procession from Heracleia.[114]

The Hippodrome, in some sense, was the city prefect's "office." Administrative sessions took place there, as well as flagellations, executions, acclamations, and of course all the entertainment spectacles.[115] The Hippodrome was the locus for the day-to-day governing of the city, as well as the locus for ceremonial control and organization of the people. The prefect oversaw all events in the Hippodrome, including "the deeply religious atmosphere" of the civic ceremonies.[116] In Constantinople city government was theater for a society so dependent on ceremony for its order and its meaning.[117] Thus with this in mind, it is most interesting to note an augmentation in the prefect's duties after 415. Those in office after this date take on the organizing of the reception of the relics of saints.[118]

This is significant because it points to the merger of public Church rituals (reception of relics) with the duties of the city prefect, who was responsible for all civic religious activities. The State, the Church, and the public were connecting Church ritual with civic ritual. Theodosian legislation betrays the insuppressible tenacity of pagan cult, and the more stringent methods the imperial court needed to use to eradicate it. Yet it also equally points to the imperial courts' delight in maintaining the Roman practice of venerating imperial images. These emperors continued Constantine's practice of dictating on religious matters for the empire. The Church's ambiguous position in this state of affairs comes to the fore when we examine more closely the role civic ceremony, imperial precedent, and imperial privilege played in empress Pulcheria's defeat of bishop Nestorius, the enemy of the Virgin Mary, Theotokos.

Chapter 3

Theodosius, Pulcheria, and the civic ceremonies

Under the Tetrarchy the arrival of the emperor, or his image, was received and understood as the *deus praesens* amongst his people.[1] In portraiture the Tetrarchs are presented as gods. With Constantine there was a break with this tradition in the understanding of his portraiture and *adventus*. Constantine's identity, represented in panegyric and in images, has not yet reached deification. Rather, he is depicted as uniquely chosen by the god or close to the deity.[2] Constantine is linked to Sol-Apollos in his medallions and statues. The people would see him not as a god, but as a specially chosen human being, often receiving divine epiphanies which would enable him to carry out God's will,[3] and which no other mortal was privy to.

Constantine's statues, representing the emperor as one divinely inspired, became the model for imperial images during the rest of the fourth and early fifth centuries.[4] By the time of the Theodosian dynasty, imperial images no longer detail historic military deeds of victorious emperors;[5] rather they depict an idealized, still presence of the emperor that evokes the imperial ideology of his universal dominion.[6] On both the base of the obelisk of Theodosius I and the column of Arcadius, what is celebrated is ahistorical and non-specific, it is a universalized Christian victory.[7]

What are important for our purposes are three points. Theodosius II continued to celebrate the Constantinian anniversary of Constantinople in the Hippodrome. Second, with regard to imperial images, although it is important that the evolution of imperial ideology begins to represent a Christian empire, what is especially significant is that images of the imperial families continued to be made. Finally that the populace continued to

receive and use the imperial images in much the same way as
they had for centuries – in the context of civic religious ceremony – is important. Statues and images functioned in the civic
ceremonies of the city alongside Christianity. The people continued to honor the imperial statues and images as if the
emperor were a superhuman being, by veneration through *proskynesis*.[8] The laws that Arcadius issued concerning imperial
portraiture fit within this context.[9] Imperial images were not
mere pictures, they represent the divinely chosen imperial dignity. And their treatment was governed by the traditions of civic
piety and ceremony.

In 425 Theodosius II issued two laws which speak to the use
of statues. The first orders that when any imperial image is
erected, a judge must be present,[10] pointing to the solemnity of
the occasion. His presence was required to "grace the day, the
place, and Our Memory."[11] It also indicates that statues were
usually erected on festival days, but the event could also occur
on "ordinary days."

From what the next section of the law addresses, it appears
that veneration of imperial statues was popular and had become
excessive for Theodosius' sensitivities. Another reason for re-
quiring a judge's presence was to mitigate "vainglorious heights
of adoration."[12] The law asks that "worship in excess of human
dignity" for the imperial statues present at the theater or games
cease. It should be given to God, "the Supernal Deity."[13]
Speaking through the law, Theodosius nevertheless concedes
that "Our divinity and glory" should "live only . . . in the hearts
and secret places of the minds of those who attend." Apparently
the townspeople were all too eager to venerate his statues.

The second law is more a request than a command. It deals
with public spectacles held in honor of the emperor. The
emperor asks that people not worry if they "show less devotion"
to him "than is customary," at a game or at the theater. The law
states that if they should skip a public show in order to attend a
church service, due reverence is paid to the emperor when God
is worshipped. Conversely, however, people ought never "to
neglect the divine religion" in order to "give attention to such
spectacles."[14] The law overtly positions the two forms of religion
in a competition. Former laws had spoken before to the problem
of competing religious activities, by prohibiting festivals from
occurring on Sundays and Christian holidays. Theodosius rele-

gated divine worship to a higher position than the honor paid to him in civic religion, yet he positioned himself – not a bishop – as unique arbitrator of religious affairs on earth. It was his duty as God's chosen ruler, like a *pontifex maximus*, to dictate on religious matters. By declaring that when God was honored in divine liturgy, most certainly the emperor was honored too, he subordinated civic ceremonies to ecclesiastical ones. In this respect the person of the emperor was bringing the two forms of religion of the city, the civic and the ecclesiastical, closer than they have ever been. Worship in church counted as respect paid to the emperor. An interesting coalescence was beginning to take place.

This is not to say that the imperial household was in any way disinterested or uninvolved in civic ceremony. In 415 a gold statue of Theodosius was dedicated in the senate by the praetorian prefect Aurelian.[15] Pulcheria's own bust was also set up in the senate. Like his predecessors, the emperor undertook building projects which facilitated civic ceremony. Theodosius built colonnades, public arenas, as well as public baths; a harbor, and new walls were finished under his reign.[16] Hence his jealousy that Cyrus was proclaimed the great builder. Theodosius continued to take great pleasure in the celebrations in the Hippodrome. Yet he introduced something new. When he felt that human exigency dictated that the divine will be placated, he took it upon himself to lead the people in Christian worship. Acting as a *pontifex maximus*, not consulting a bishop, he turned the Hippodrome and the streets into a church. His sister Pulcheria, we shall see, did just the opposite. She used the church as her public arena. The Great Church of Constantinople became her Hippodrome.

Since Pulcheria had taken a vow of perpetual virginity, and she lived a monastic life, she did not participate in civic ceremonies the way former Augustae had. Pulcheria exercised her power and presence in the city in ways that befitted a wealthy Christian woman of the early fifth century.[17] She owned so much property in Constantinople that the area became known as the "Pulcherianiai."[18] Sozomen writes that it would take too much time to describe all the churches Pulcheria built,[19] as well as hospitals and inns for the poor. Her zeal for her faith caused her to be a constant presence in ecclesiastical affairs. Under Bishop Atticus (406–425) it became practice in the Great Church that Pulcheria's robe was used as an altar covering during the divine liturgy.[20] Pulcheria's most potent presence in the city, however, was the image of herself painted above the altar in the Great Church "to instruct the faithful."[21] Either Bishop Atticus or his successor Sissinius agreed to this. With this image Pulcheria succeeded in taking a token of civic religion and resituating it in an ecclesiastical context. By this action there is a convergence of two systems of ritual, one civic, one ecclesiastical. We do not have any sources relating the people's reactions. But it is not untenable to think that people venerated her portrait in the Great Church as they would have in any other situation. Pulcheria transferred part of civic ceremonial into the ecclesiastical sphere, to which she had dedicated her life. She did not, however, change any of the rituals connected with her image to accommodate the Church. It is significant that she acted in her imperial role to do this. She chose to retain this symbol, her portrait, to gain honor, not in the outside world of the city, but in her chosen sphere, the Church. Of course she did take part in civic cermonies, but ones having to do with dedications of churches and the arrival of holy relics. Before we deal with these, we shall discuss evidence for Theodosius' role in processions and acclamations – both civic ceremonies.

In the *Chronicon Paschale* Theodosius reputedly had Constantine's column repaired in 416.[22] Soon after theater performances and chariot races were held in celebration of his military victory over Attalus. On another occasion at the death of the barbarian Ataulph, Theodosius ordered a thanksgiving procession with lamps, ending in a chariot race the next day.[23] Theodosius seems to have enjoyed his obligation of presiding over the civic festivals. The *Chronographia* mentions that Theodosius favored the faction the Greens,[24] giving them a better location to sit in in the Hippodrome, opposite the *kathisma*, so he could literally see their support for him.

Some of Theodosius' actions in the Hippodrome betray the spirit of his law passed in 423 and his sister's coalescence of the civic and ecclesiastical forms of religion. Socrates reports that once in the Hippodrome Theodosius became particularly fearful of the bad weather during the show,[25] and the storm was becoming worse. So Theodosius, acting as head of the religion, ordered the show to stop. He took off his imperial robes, descended into the midst of the people, and led – like a bishop –

the entire population in prayer and hymns to God, "that we may be preserved from the impending storm."

In another instance Theodosius received word while attending festivities in the Hippodrome that John the tyrant who had usurped control of Ravenna, had been defeated. The emperor ordered the games to stop, and everyone to proceed to the Great Church "to offer thanksgivings to God."[26] Malalas records that when Constantinople suffered an earthquake, Thedosius continued barefoot in a procession of prayer for days with the "senate, the people, and the clergy."[27] Again, we have example of Theodosius changing the character of the events in the Hippodrome. Yet the *public ceremonious* form does not change. In these cases he acted as a chief religious officer in order to appease the Divinity.

Panegyric was a central feature of the *adventus* ceremony in honor of the arrival of an emperor.[28] Panegyric, as an ancient rhetorical form, was intended originally to praise the emperor's virtues and deeds. As MacCormack has shown, in Late Antiquity panegyric evolved into a description of ceremonial, it "articulated the modes of contact between the emperor, his subjects, and the gods," or god.[29] Audiences responded to panegyric speeches as they would to the emperor.[30] Panegyric was expected by emperors and subjects alike, as a highly stylized discourse that enabled them to communicate in a formulaic manner. It is in this context that the extraordinary hymns to Pulcheria can be understood.[31] Proclus, a presbyter in Constantinople in the 420's, wrote rhyming verses in praise of Pulcheria's virginity.[32]

> She confesses that the tomb is the treasury of salvation. She finds her glory in the cross, through which the old covenant was torn up. She embraces the death that sets us free from bondage. She proclaims the Resurrection, the greatest gift of the Crucified One. She wonders at the baptismal waters, virginal though mother of so many, from which the bright ones rise. She marvels at the mystery by which the devil suffered unexpected shipwreck. Such are the gifts of the Crucified One.

During the late 420s when Proclus was preaching his very popular Marian sermons, a memorial for the Virgin Mary was instituted for virgins on December 26.[33] Pulcheria and the many other women like her participated in the "celebration of virginity."

The welcoming of relics: Pulcheria's appropriation of civic ceremony

It is the rapid arrival of saints' relics that is one of the most striking characteristics of the first half of the fifth century. The remains of the apostles Andrew, Luke, and Timothy had already been transferred to the Church of the Holy Apostles early in Constantius' reign.[34] In 392 the head of John the Baptist was taken to Constantinople.[35] Theodosius I had it deposited in a new church near the Hebdomen, on the outskirts of the city. Theodosius, Pulcheria, and their sisters presided over the arrivals of Sts Samuel, Joseph, and Zechariah, and the building of the martyrium of St Anthimius.[36] Princess Arcadia built the church of St Andrew.[37]

Pulcheria began to craft her pivotal role in the public ceremonies welcoming relics in the early 420s. When the relics of St Lawrence and the Prophet Isaiah arrived, she built churches for them "to live amid the populace," close to her own palace.[38] When war was threatening to break out against Persia, Pulcheria made sure that supernatural intervention would aid the campaign. Thus "in imitation of his sister" (ὁ εὐσεβῆς κατὰ τῆς Πουλχερίας) Theodosius sent a great deal of money for the poor and a large gold cross encrusted with precious stones to the Jerusalem patriarchate. In thanks and exchange, the Bishop sent the relics of St Stephen back to the capital.[39] St Stephen had informed Pulcheria in a dream to meet him in Chalcedon. She arose, took her brother, and there they met. Once the relics arrived in Constantinople in a grand *adventus* ceremony, Pulcheria built a structure as a proper repository for them. Holum gives evidence that Pulcheria's interest in St Stephen's relics was to bolster morale for the war against Persia. St Stephen was associated with the "crown of victory"; the saint would provide further assurance for a Christian victory.[40]

Furthermore Holum gives convincing evidence that Pulcheria played the most important role in the *adventus* ceremony to Constantinople, not her brother. In the ivory relief sculpture called the "Translation of Relics" in the Trier Cathedral Treasury, Pulcheria is the focus of the scene.[41] She holds a cross, is dressed in full imperial regalia, and welcomes the relics as they enter the city.[42]

Pulcheria took the lead in the ceremonies of adventus of other saints as well. When Proclus was bishop of the city (434–436) Pulcheria was led by means of a dream to the place where the forty martyrs were buried.[43] Putting their bones in a beautiful vase, she had them placed "with the utmost pomp and ceremony besides the remains of St Thrysus."[44] Sozomen himself claims to have been present at the "gorgeous spectacle," and reports that many others can speak to the magnificence of the "festival." Pulcheria was obsessed with immortalizing the intimacy between herself and the holy dead in civic ceremony.[45]

In 438 Bishop Proclus persuaded Theodosius to bring back the bones of John Chrysostom. Theodosius and Pulcheria presided over the relic *adventus*.[46] Theodoret's description suggests the public excitement at the public ceremony welcoming the saint to "live" in the city.

A great multitude of the faithful crowded the sea in ships, and lighted up parts of the Bosphorus near the mouth of the Propontis, with torches.[47]

Pulcheria's victory over Nestorius: the Theotokos dwells in Constantinople

They make Him (Christ) second to the blessed Mary, and they set the mother against the divine demiurge of time. For if her is not the nature of man, but God the Word, just as they say, with regard to her, then she is not the mother. For how can someone be the mother of a nature completely other than her own? For if she be called "mother" by them, he is of human nature not divine. For like bears the same essence of every mother. . . . In his nature and essence the Son is the Essence and nature of God the Father, but in flesh his nature is human from Mary.[48]

Woven into the demise of Nestorius, bishop of Constantinople (428–431), is the fierce opposition Pulcheria mustered against him, during his tenure in office. Nestorius was a Syrian, born in Germanicia. He entered a monastery in Antioch where he was steeped in the theological principle associated with that city, especially the theological methodology of Theodore of

Mopsuestia.[49] Nestorius' fame as a great preacher spread throughout the empire. Going against the judgment of his ecclesiastical advisors, in 428 Theodosius II invited Nestorius to accept the episcopacy of Constantinople. A few months after his arrival, his presbyter, Anastasius, who had accompanied him from Antioch, began to preach against the use of "Theotokos" as a title for Mary.[50] Nestorius applauded him, yet the faithful were not so receptive.

> These words created a great sensation, and troubled many both of the clergy and laity; they having been heretofore taught to acknowledge Christ as God, and by no means to separate his humanity from his divinity on account of the economy of incarnation.[51]

Nestorius also set out on a campaign against all heretics. He attacked Arians, Novatians, Borborians, and Manicheans.[52] What had become custom during other bishops' tenures Nestorius sought to change. The Quartodecimani were no longer able to celebrate Easter on the Jewish Passover. Arians, many of whom were German soldiers and generals in Theodosius' army, set fire to their own church in the suburbs when Nestorius tried to seize it.[53] Theodosius admonished him for this, but Nestorius was not deterred. Moreover he insulted Cyril, bishop of Alexandria, by not sending him the customary gifts at his own accession.[54]

Apparently Nestorius did not realize how much power Pulcheria and her entourage of virgins had. He would not allow them to come to vespers or to wakes, charging that when women were out at night it inevitably lead to "promiscuity with men."[55] Nestorius took specific action against Pulcheria. He implied that she had enjoyed illicit sexual relations with at least seven lovers.[56] He also would not accede to her demand that she be remembered in prayers as the "bride of Christ" since she had been "corrupted by men."[57] Most egregious of all, he effaced her image which he had removed from above the altar; and he refused to use her robe as an altar cover.[58] When she attempted to receive communion on Easter in the altar, Nestorius barred the royal doors and exclaimed that no women could enter. She insisted by proclaiming that she had given birth to God.[59] This statement announced her personal belief that her identity was one with that of the Theotokos. Nestorius countered by charging that she had given birth to the devil.[60] Nestorius wrote in the *Bazaar of Heracleides*:

> You have further with you against me a contentious woman, a princess, a young maiden, a virgin, who fought against me because I was not willing to be persuaded by her demand that I would compare a woman corrupted of men to the bride of Christ. This I have done because I had pity on her soul and that I might not be the chief celebrant of the sacrifice among those whom she had unrighteously chosen.[61]

Late in 428 and early 429 Nestorius began preaching sermons against "Theotokos." In his view no creature could give birth to the Godhead; Mary bore a man, the "vehicle of divinity" but not God.[62] He preferred the title "Theodochos."[63]

Nestorius' restrictions on Pulcheria's imperial "customs" during the divine liturgy enraged her as much as his sermons against the use of the title "Theotokos" for Mary. There is little doubt that Pulcheria understood attacks on the Theotokos as a personal affront.[64] She had patterned her life from a very early age on the model of the Virgin Mary. Thus, not only was the use of the title "Theotokos" the issue of the Nestorian controversy for Pulcheria, it was also the Augusta's own imperial dignity, now merged with supernatural power, which gave her authority to dictate in matters of religion. Pulcheria's closest allies, Proclus and Eusebius, a court official and later the bishop of Dorylaeum, soon rallied the people in her favor.[65] Eusebius was responsible for posting an anonymous document – presumably in one of the fora or the Hippodrome – condemning Nestorius as a heretic.[66] Proclus, readily assenting to Pulcheria's demand, delivered a sermon on December 26 at the Virginity Festival, countering Nestorius' view in the Great Church, in Nestorius' presence. Not only does he vindicate the title "Theotokos" for Mary, he praises all women because of her example.

> The Virginity Festival (παρθενική πανηγύρις) brethren calls our mouths for prayer. And the present festival becomes the patron assisting those who have gathered here, and certainly this is suitable. For the celebration has the purpose of purity, and is the perfect boast of the society of women, and glory of the female sex, because of the occurrence of the Mother and the Virgin. This gathering is the most exalted and extra-

ordinary. For behold earth and sea bear gifts to the Virgin, the sea spreads her back calmly under ships sailing across, the earth dispatches unhindered those people traveling by foot. Let nature leap about, and let the human race exult in joy, because women are honored. Let humanity dance, because Virgins are glorified. "But where sin increased, grace abounded all the more" (Romans 5: 20). For this reason the Holy Virgin Mary Theotokos called us now together.[67]

Meanwhile Cyril of Alexandria, after hearing about Nestorius' replies to Proclus from some of his informants in Constantinople, began to send letters to Nestorius admonishing him, but to no avail. Cyril alerted Pope Celestine who tried to listen to both sides. Theodosius remained a staunch supporter of Nestorius, who was nevertheless condemned by Pope Celestine in 430. Cyril, ever vigilant in his campaign against Nestorius, had written three long treatises to Theodosius and his wife Eudokia, and to the princesses Pulcheria, Marina, and Arcadia,[68] and one to Eudokia and Pulcheria. They were an attempt to convince them that his doctrine was correct. Pulcheria needed no convincing. Her task was to pressure her brother for her cause, and to rally support from the populace.

Nestorius wanted a council to decide on the orthodoxy of his position; by November 430 Theodosius sent out the letters to bishops for the convention in Ephesus that following June. Cyril controlled the council from the beginning. The council was weighted heavily in favor of the Cyrillians, since they had "planted" uncouth Alexandrians to heckle the Nestorians. They drove the emperor's ambassador and the Nestorian bishops out of the session, and then declared Nestorius a heretic.[69] A counter-synod was convened a few days later, and Cyril was himself deposed.

Realizing that everything depended on the emperor's decision, both sides tried to persuade Theodosius, especially Pulcheria. The restive citizens of Constantinople packed the Great Church and began their chants calling for Nestorius' deposition.[70] Conversely, the crowd shouted acclamations to Pulcheria as the champion of orthodoxy and their guide in religious affairs. Under such public pressure Theodosius succumbed to Pulcheria's demands and had Cyril's decree deposing Nestorius read in the Great Church. Nestorius was sent back to his monastery in Antioch, and the aged man Maximian was consecrated the new bishop.[71]

Although the Council of Ephesus assured that the title "Theotokos" was orthodox, doctrinal debates concerning the two natures of Christ continued unabated. The situation came to a head by the late 440s. What is important here is not the details of the Christological controversy, but how Pulcheria acted to resolve the crisis.

In 450 Theodosius died after a riding accident. Pulcheria assumed the position of running the empire; but to maintain the imperial tradition that only males could rule, she married Marcion.[72] He respected Pulcheria's vow of virginity and, on matters of ecclesiastical politics, deferred to her judgment and experience.[73]

To quell the disturbance in the Church caused by disagreement as to the two natures of Christ, Pulcheria and Marcion called for the convention of a council at Chalcedon in 451, despite the protests of Pope Leo.[74] In an unusual move, at the end of the council Pulcheria took her place before the bishops. They repeatedly showered her with acclamations, praising her as the "protectress of the faith," and "the light of Orthodoxy," while giving similar lauds to her consort, Marcion.[75]

The Council of Chalcedon was the last occasion for Pulcheria to instruct on religious matters for the empire. She had devoted first her private life, then her public one, to the Theotokos. She would live only two more years. Yet there is one other way that she truly accomplished the establishment of the cult of the Theotokos in Constantinople.

In the last decades of her life Pulcheria crowned her life-long devotion to the Theotokos by building three churches dedicated to her in Constantinople. They were the churches Hodegetria, the Blachernae, and the Chalkoprateia.[76] In fact it was due to Pulcheria's efforts that the Theotokos came to "reside permanently" in the city, in the form of her shroud, her cincture, and an icon of her painted by St Luke.[77]

Pulcheria originally built the churches to honor the Theotokos. But when Eudocia, Pulcheria's sister-in-law, traveled with Melania to Jerusalem, Nicephorus Callistus reports that she returned with the icon of the Virgin painted by St Luke. She gave it to Pulcheria who then ceremoniously housed her in the

Hodegetria. At her request, a vigil was held for the Virgin there every Tuesday evening.[78]

Pulcheria built the church of the Blachernae, but her successors completed the Soros chapel which actually housed the shroud when it arrived in 473.[79] The Blachernae was the church most dear to the Constantinopolitans; its fame spread from Crete to Cherson in the Crimea,[80] where other churches were named "Blachernae" in its honor. Remarkable for its rich multicolored marbles, it was probably finished under the rule of Leo I (457–474) and his wife Verina. According to the legend[81] the shroud of the Virgin was discovered by two aristocrats, Galbius and Candidus, in a small village in Galilee. They were Arians, but they had converted and were on a pilgrimage to the Holy Land. One night they stayed at the home of a very old Jewish woman. She was quite dignified and ascetic. They discovered that she possessed the Virgin's shroud and kept it in a small chest. According to the legend, the old woman was a descendant of Mary's, and the robe had been passed down in her family for generations. Galbius and Candidus stole it from her and took it back to Constantinople. With the advent of the shroud, the Virgin Mary was believed to reside in Blachernae.[82] Unfortunately, the church was completely destroyed by fire in 1070.[82]

Pulcheria's single-minded efforts to spread the veneration of the Virgin appear in a later legend as well. In one of his homilies on the Dormition, John of Damascus (d. 789) recorded that Pulcheria sought the coffin, presumably carrying the corporeal remains of the Theotokos, to bring to Constantinople. At the Council of Chalcedon (451) Pulcheria and emperor Marcion reportedly approached Patriarch Juvenal of Jerusalem and asked him for the remains of the Virgin, who, they understood, was buried in her church in Gethsemane. Juvenal replied that indeed Mary was buried there, but three days after her death when the coffin was opened, only the fabric of her garments and shroud were there. John of Damascus ends the story by relating that Pulcheria gladly took those remains and "put them in the Blachernae quarter in Constantinople."[84]

Pulcheria had the Chalkoprateia church built on the site of a synagogue which Theodosius bought from the Jews. He then constructed a new synagogue for them outside the city.[85] When the Virgin's cincture arrived several decades later, the

Chalkoprateia became its residence. According to Nicephorus Callistus, Pulcheria instituted a vigil there each Wednesday for the Theotokos with candles, hymns, and a procession.[86]

Pulcheria achieved two things by building these churches. She brought the Theotokos "to dwell" in the city precincts. Her personal vow to the Virgin became an imperial act of beneficence, insuring the protection of the Theotokos over the capital. Second, as a member of the imperial house, she introduced a new supernatural person to the city – with new ceremonies – and instructed the people on her proper veneration. Pulcheria had taken the Church's more private devotions to the Theotokos that she had learned as a girl[87] and opened them up to the public, transforming the veneration to the Virgin into a civic religious ceremony. By building these three churches she set the location for the public veneration of the Theotokos and instituted weekly liturgies with processions, images, candles, and chanting of hymns. No doubt Pulcheria led the processions or had a place of honor at the vigils. She not only acted as a *pontifex* to the people, she instructed the ecclesiarchs.

As a young woman Pulcheria had taken the Virgin Theotokos as the model for her life. Her daily routine in the palace took on the air of a Christian monastery, which indeed was unprecedented for a Roman Augusta. Yet when Pulcheria had to leave the Palace for public duties, she merged her zeal for the Christian way of life with the traditional forms of civic religious ceremonies, which looked remarkably like those of her imperial predecessors.

Pulcheria actively sought out relics of saints – those particularly Christian *sacra* – for Constantinople, and then organized the ceremonies for their arrival on the model of an imperial *adventus*. The relics themselves were venerated in the traditional Roman fashion. She instituted religious processions with all the accoutrements familiar to the people. Pulcheria also took from the Hippodrome the importance of controlling the *vox populi*, which proved crucial for her during the Nestorian controversy. Above all else, she brought the Theotokos to dwell in the capital. The three most famous churches to the Virgin in Constantinople Pulcheria built so the people could venerate her properly. All of Pulcheria's efforts to establish public veneration of the Theotokos in Constantinople she accomplished as an Augusta creating new civic religious ceremonies. In addition by

doing so she created new ecclesiastical rituals based on traditional civic ceremonies. Pulcheria's special attention to the
creation of public ceremonies for distinctively Christian celebrations gave those celebrations an unprecedented imperial sanction. Essentially the Church was instructed by Pulcheria to
imitate rituals of civic ceremony.

Pulcheria made the battle against Nestorius her personal ven-
detta. Her behavior – like that of all her imperial predecessors –
displayed her firm conviction that she had the imperial right to
dictate on matters of religion. She fought not only to keep
Mary's title as "Theotokos," but also was unrelenting in her
campaign to keep the imperial customs honoring herself which
she had established in the church since she was quite young.
Pulcheria seems to have expected the accolades given to her
publicly by Proclus' hymns. It befitted her imperial dignity to
have the people see her image above the altar and venerate it.
Honor was given to her when her imperial cloak covered the
altar. And it certainly was her imperial right to be allowed
unlimited access into the altar to receive communion with the
priest and bishops. Pulcheria, as an Augusta, demanded nothing
new; she simply had changed the customary locus for these
activities from the foras and the Hippodrome and put them in
the church. But for the Church hierarchy this indeed was new.

What is unique about Pulcheria is the extent to which she took
her claim to "be the Virgin."[88] When she began to institutiona-
lize her personal piety to the Virgin during the Nestorian crisis,
the Church and the citizens had already become accustomed to
venerating the Augusta in Church. It was a very slight change
for the Church and people to begin an institutionalized public
veneration of the Theotokos when Pulcheria deemed it both
politically and personally necessary. When she claimed that her
identity was the Virgin's, suddenly the identity of the Theotokos
was merged with the imperial power Pulcheria held as Augusta.
As one of imperial rank, the Theotokos required the public
ceremonies reserved for such dignitaries.

Finally Pulcheria's claim to the Virgin's identity was a great
factor in making the Theotokos divine. Not only were imperial
persons publicly praised in panegyrics and hymns, venerated in
images, and celebrated in ritualized ceremonies, so had the gods
of antiquity been praised. Pulcheria's claim that her identity was
the same as the Virgin's was a claim to supernatural power. It

sounded vaguely like the Tetrarchs' claim to divinity. Pulcheria was the first imperial person since 325 to claim a supernatural identity and demand public acclamation for the belief. In many ways she had undone what Constantine had established in civic ceremonies honoring him as the one "chosen by God." Second in the minds of the people an Augusta could only claim an identity greater than her own, and that could only be a divine being, not a humble maiden of first-century Palestine. As we shall see in the next chapter, Pulcheria's devotion to the Virgin was a superior precipitator for the Church to develop its traditions about the Virgin in the context of civic religion.

Chapter 4

Imperial cult, panegyric, and the Theotokos

We have seen that the Christian imperial courts from Constantine to Pulcheria managed to retain a great deal of Roman civic religion as they molded a new imperial identity with a new religion in Constantinople. Although this phenomenon appears paradoxical – even contradictory – its explanation lies in two areas: the nature of ritual and the nature of the retainable part of the Roman civic religion – the imperial cult. The clearest example of the merger of imperial cult and Christianity is the rise of the cult of the Theotokos under Pulcheria. It is specifically in the new hymns to the Virgin, written on the model of imperial panegyric, that we see the convergence. The most influential hymns to the Theotokos are from the orations of Proclus and the anonymous *Akathistos Hymn*. These works exhibit how the Church appropriated a genre from civic religion to fight the Nestorian heresy, and in so doing grafted an imperial identity onto the Theotokos.

Ritual has been shown to endure over centuries and cultures, paradoxically somehow remaining unchanged yet indubitably powerful and central to the changing society it is serving.[1] On the analogy of a kaleidoscope, whose beautiful geometric shapes are shifted to form a new, equally beautiful pattern, the rituals and ceremonies from the imperial cult were reincorporated into Late Antique society in a new configuration. Like the pieces in the kaleidoscope, as ritual gets used by both the court and the Church, it is transformed, yet remains observable and recognizable.

Although until this point we have implied the specifics of the emperor cult, it is worthwhile now to examine what made the rituals of imperial cult transferable to both the Church and the

Christian court. The Roman ruler cult since the time of
Augustus was one part of Roman civic religion, yet by Roman
practice and definition it was distinguishable from the individual
Roman city cults to the gods. The Roman cults to the gods were
ancient institutions organized into *collegia*, the most important of
which were the *collegium pontificum* and the augurs. Significantly,
the Romans believed that the deities were specifically interested
in the affairs of Rome itself, as a "chosen city."[2] The ruler cult,
which was a much younger institution evolving from the time of
Augustus, spread all over the Mediterranean and has a long,
complex history with many variations over three centuries, but
three things can be distilled:[3] it never functioned as a replacement or competitor to the worship of the gods;[4] its rituals and
ceremonies on the whole mimicked those of a god's cult;[5] and
finally, the prescribed rituals included a ceremonial procession
carrying a statue or image of the emperor that was venerated by
the people, a sacrifice or supplication (offerings of incense and
wine), acclamations, and panegyrics, all culminating in feasts,
games, and/or the theater.[6] It is important to note that supplication became more frequent as the empire expanded, and as the
calendar became more crowded with expensive festivals.[7] Few
officials could afford the rising costs of animal sacrifices.
Supplication began to replace sacrifice at festivals. Hence it is
much less remarkable than is usually recounted that Constantine
did not allow animal sacrifices at his ceremonies.

What is most striking about imperial cult is the way it
extracted all the ritual, pomp, and *gravitas* from the cults to the
gods and explicitly fused them to the political world. Imperial
cult bore all the significance of religion for the populace without
challenging or threatening the *pax deorum*. Constantine knew
well that the rituals of the emperor cult belonged alongside the
proper worship of the deity. It was the ecclesiarchs – like
Eusebius, John Chrysostom, and Ambrose – who took issue with
this. How these rituals began to enter the Church is the question
we must address. Indeed many scholars have noted in hesitant
language that rituals of the imperial cult "seem to have had an
influence on the growth and adoration of Christian icons, relics,
and saints."[8] But they have not addressed the reasons directly.
Such reasons will begin to emerge with an investigation of the
encomiastic poetry and panegyrics of the fourth and fifth centuries that played such a central role in ceremony. Both of these

genres, but especially panegyrics, were the vehicles that linked pagan ritual of the emperor cult with the Church.

Panegyric in the fourth and fifth centuries

According to the *Progymnasmata* of Nicolaus Sophistae, a teacher of rhetoric around 430, the plan of exercises he used to teach epideiktic oratory was as follows:[9]

1 ekphrasis – description
2 ethopoiea – the presentation of imaginary actions of persons or things
3 encomium – praise, and its opposite, invective
4 synkrisis – comparison

Of these the encomium was the most popular and important form of oratory. There were three kinds of encomiastic speeches which varied according to the occasion.[10] On religious occasions hymns –praises to a god – were delivered. Informal speeches at schools were simply labeled "talks" (λαλία). And for secular festivals panegyrics, eulogizing speeches, were given. By the fifth century, the term "panegyric" was used interchangeably with "encomium," and generally meant an epideiktic speech.[11] Panegyric itself was divided into ten categories.[12]

1 speech to an emperor	6 speech for a dignitary
2 speech to an official	7 speech at a feast
3 speech for an arrival	8 farewell speech
4 speech for a birthday	9 funeral speech
5 speech thanking the emperor	10 wedding speech

When rhetors prepared a panegyric for the emperor, they were obliged to follow a set outline. After an introduction, the emperor's birth, ancestors, and natal country had to be extolled, then came the manner in which he was raised and educated.[13] Following this, his virtuous accomplishments in soul, body, and fortune were praised. The panegyric charactertistically ended with an epilogue including a prayer.[14] There were slight variations in this order if the speech was for an arrival of an emperor, but these elements remained the prescribed outline.

In the fourth century panegyrists followed the rules of encomium quite closely.[15] However, panegyrics to the emperor did change their focus slightly during this period. The descriptions of the emperors' virtues and deeds became a description of imperial ceremonies and court rituals.[16] Rhetors gradually replaced accounts of emperors' virtues with long details of processions, regalia, and images. In some respects panegyric collapsed into ekphrasis during the fifth century.[17] Verbal images became paramount.

For many reasons, the popularity of panegyrics grew in the fourth and fifth centuries.[18] Their popularity was also probably linked to the simultaneous surge in interest in literature, learning, and the rhetorical arts. In 356 Constantius II established a scriptorium in Constantinople, where classical texts continued to be copied. Valens maintained it.[19] The University in the capital was started in 425; and Theodosius II himself, quite a fan of panegyric,[20] commissioned a life of Christ based on Virgil, the *Cento Probae*, in calligraphy.[21]

The sheer volume of classical poetry copied during this period shows that there was a renewed interest in this form, which undoubtedly had influence on the rhetoricians.[22] Yet influence went both ways. The poetry of Late Antiquity exhibits strong rhetorical topoi characteristic of epideiktic prose. From the mid-fourth century onward, encomiastic poetry becomes as popular as prose encomia.[23] Writing in metrical verse, empress Eudokia, the prefect Cyrus, and Eusebius Scholasticus are only a famous few who in the early fifth century experimented with encomiastic verse.[24] The Theodosian court may have resembled a monastery, but it was also filled with poetry, oratory, and the attendant pomp of ceremonial. It is in this imperial milieu that the Church was most exposed to the current trends in encomiastic poetry, epideiktic poetry, and the ceremonial enactment of panegyrics. We shall now explore the elements of the poetry and panegyrics that were directly to influence Christian literature praising the Virgin.

Eulogizing poems

In a thorough study of encomiastic poetry of this period, Toivo Viljamaa concludes that there are three groups: actual rhetorical encomia containing all the formal parts of encomia; eulogizing poems that are not formally encomia but have rhetorical comparisons; and some poetry that is not entirely eulogizing.[25] Almost all of this poetry was written in hexameter and in iambic trimeter.

Although it is not possible here to analyze individual rhetorical encomia, some of their most important features will be discussed. The long, strictly encomiastic poems, those rhetorical encomia written in verse, began with a prologue. Most of the authors used certain rhetorical devices to create a desired mood in the audience. These devices are food and feast metaphors and similes; nature metaphors, the reemployment of old familiar maxims; and finally four figures of speech, asyndeton, antithiesis, pleonasm, and paranomasia.[26] These are important to highlight for two reasons: they were very much in vogue, and audiences grew to expect the certain kind of rhetorical entertainment they produced when a great person was being publicly praised. These devices could obviously be manipulated to suit the intention of the rhetor. Christians and pagans alike learned this kind of poetry at schools, and could craft their desired effects.

Encomiastic poems exhibit the most important characteristics of the genre that the long encomia do; their brevity makes it possible to look at five in some detail. According to Viljamaa's conclusions, they fall within the category of "eulogizing poems." The first poem, written by Cyrus of Panopolis, praetorian prefect and city prefect under Theodosius II, is a short poem praising the emperor. Cyrus displays his skill at Greek verse as he compares Theodosius to Teucor, Agamemnon, Odysseus, and Nestor so that none of their foibles are his, only their virtues.[27] This is one of the most important devices of the genre. The author took familiar mythic characters and their feats and made sure that his subject bettered the god or hero in every category. Most comparison in encomiastic poetry relied on mythological background of gods, heroes, and deeds.[28]

The second poem is anonymous, reportedly found on a stele. Like the first poem, it praises Theodosius I as a man of heroic proportions, contrasting him to "mortals," without mentioning a specific myth.[29] And in this example we find use of another important device: celestial and astral metaphors for the emperor.

From the east shines forth another light-bearing sun,
Theodosius, while amongst mortals, he is in the center
of the axis of the celestial sphere, gentle-natured,

> At your feet you have the ocean in the midst of the limitless
>   earth,
> From every side radiant, helmeted while the noble and
> eager horse easily, great-hearted one, you restrain.[30]

It is significant, too, that the word "μεγάθυμος," "great-hearted,"
would undoubtedly have been recognized by the audience as the
word used describing Achilles in the Illiad, and Athena in the
Odyssey.[31]

The third example is a much less refined poem by the poet
Palladas to the famous and unfortunate Alexandrian philosopher, Hypatia. He probably wrote it in the 420s. The comparisons are with astral bodies.

> When I look at you, I fall down in veneration, and at your
> words, as I regard the astral dwelling of the virgin, for your
> things are celestial, Revered Hypatia, the beautiful form of
> your words are the undefiled star of wise education.[32]

Her purity, virginity, beauty, and wisdom are worthy not only of
praise, but of something even higher: veneration. It is significant that Hypatia is "revered." Although the term simply may be
hyperbole, it shifts the focus of the praise. In this succinct poem,
Palladas has moved from a simple ekphrasis – a description – to
a prayer.

Poems four and five are clearly Christian. They are both
anonymous, but the first one is plagiarized from one of Gregory
Nazianzus' poems to Christ.[33] The first one praises Christ, the
second one empress Eudokia's piety.

> O one (Christ) who is from beyond everything, by what else
> shall I celebrate you in song? How shall I name you, you who
> are above all else in everything. How can I sing with words
> about the one who is not comprehensible by words?[34]

The poem evokes the paradoxical greatness of the story of
Christ being both man and God. In other words it does praise
Christ while relying on the myth – or story – of who Christ is.
The poet skillfully uses word plays to create the proper attitude
of praise with awe.

In much the same way the poem to Eudokia contrasts her
august station with the piety she rightly shows at holy shrines.
There are really two subjects of praise in this poem: Eudokia

and Christ. Both are subject to paradoxical contrast, but only Christ's myth is referred to.

> The wise mistress of the world enflamed by a
> pious love, appeared as a servant, falls down
> and venerates a tomb of one man.
> She, who is bowed down to and venerated amongst
> all human beings; for the one who gave the throne
> and marriage died as a man, but lives as God.
> Below he was human, but above he became as he was.[35]

These encomiastic poems present a glimpse of the high degree of praise rhetors were expected to produce for the imperial court. They are compact versions of the long panegyrics, displaying the most important devices of the genre: astral and/or celestial metaphors, comparisons with gods or heroes, and the adroit use of paradox to heighten the sense of awe.

Adventus panegyrics

Panegyrics were at the heart of civic ceremony, lending a studied spontaneity to a carefully orchestrated urban ceremony. The populace was given the chance to participate physically, visually, and emotionally – even sometimes vocally. The rhetors' words both spoke for the people, and inculcated the proper way to respond to the imperial presence which was utterly foreign to the mundane. Panegyric defined the parameters of the public relationship between the people and the imperial household. Besides praising the emperor, the chief reason for panegyric was to teach the populace to respond to the imperial household with the attitude and actions of divine awe.

The ceremony of the emperor's arrival, *adventus*, was the most frequent occasion for panegyrics to be delivered. The speech could emphasize his arrival, the gift of his presence to the city, or simply mark the occasion of the civic ceremony during which he was visible to the people.[36] Under the Tetrarchy panegyric had extolled the emperors as visible gods on earth. [37] Menander, the famous author of rhetorical handbooks in the third century, had taught rhetors to welcome the emperor as a "ray of the sun."[38] The emperor renewed the seasons on arriving.[39] Menander's welcoming panegyric to the emperor shows how this civic ceremony united the people to the emperor in a display that visually realized the ecumenical propaganda of the empire: unity, peace, victory, blessedness by the deities.

> [You say] for instance, we have all gone out to meet you for your welcome, with our whole families, children, old men, and men in their prime, and priestly families, the city council and the people at large. We were all glad in our hearts [and expressed it] with acclamations calling you our savior and our wall, a most radiant star, and children call you nourisher, and savior of their parents, sweetness on the day, light more radiant than the sun.[40]

This emphasis on the epiphanic qualities of the emperor changed in panegyrics to Constantine. Panegyrics reflected the same change in focus that was occurring in imperial statues and art.[41] Instead of praising the emperor as a manifestation of a god on earth, the panegyrics extolled Constantine as the "one chosen by God." During the fourth and fifth century *adventus* panegyrics most consistently praise the emperors not for their divine qualities, but for their universal victory.[42] The arrival panegyrics represented the emperors as physical symbols of their imperial authority, grandeur, and benefaction.[43] Yet for both the Tetrarchs and the fourth century emperors, the panegyrics were based on actual deeds that had brought about victory. By the time of Arcadius, praising the emperor's deeds became unnecessary. Imperial victory was still the theme, but it was greatly abstracted. These emperors rarely went on military campaigns, they neither left nor arrived. Therefore celebration of imperial victory in panegyric had no reference to historical fact; it was a quality tied to the imperial dignity and office itself.[44]

As was pointed out in the last chapter, the Church absorbed the rituals of imperial *adventus* in the celebrations for the arrival of saints' relics.[45] By means of this ceremony, the Church, under Pulcheria's direction, gave imperial welcome to the sacred remains in order to establish sacred spaces in Constantinople. Panegyrics for these occasions would have been written for the specific arrival ceremony. Hence they would have been used less frequently if at all during the liturgical year. Yet it is on the model of imperial panegyric for other occasions that the church patterns its hymns to the Theotokos. And these become integral parts of the liturgical cycles.

Panegyrics for other occasions

Five panegyrics to emperors and to one empress from the fourth century provide excellent examples of the genre. They are Nazarius' panegyric to Constantine (321); Julian's to Constantius; Julian's to empress Eusebia, Constantius' wife; Ausonius' to Gratian; and finally Pacatus' to Theodosius I. Bishop Eusebius' panegyric to Constantine will be discussed later. There are four aspects in these works that must be explored: the nature of the deeds that are praiseworthy, characteristics attributed to them in similes and metaphors, the pace of the language, and the nature of the benefit for the people brought about by the emperor or empress.

Nazarius composed a long panegyric in Latin for Constantine on the occasion of his Quinquennalia, in 321.[46] Although the panegyric is long, the praise is comparatively restrained. Nazarius follows the traditional outline of panegyric, giving long details of Constantine's military victories. Nazarius moves back and forth between lavishly recounting and praising Constantine's marvelous victories on the battlefields to detailing his personal virtues of wisdom, generosity, and clemency,[47] patience, moderation, dignity, and nobility.[48] These give Constantine his divine quality; Nazarius refers to him as "our divine emperor."[49] All his victories show divine inspiration. Although he gives Constantine divine titles, Nazarius is restrained in likening him both to specific gods and heroes, and in his lack of astral metaphors, both common features of imperial panegyrics. Although Nazarius portrays Constantine as quite exceptional, he calls attention to the emperor's human qualities by his frequent digressions addressing the emperor's young sons. This technique allows a tender, mortal vulnerability to creep into the panegyric's depiction of Constantine, moving the audience to a kind of pathos.[50] Nazarius is also not above a backhanded criticism of the emperor. At the very end he begs the emperor not to abandon Rome for a new city.[51]

Nazarius' panegyric would have skillfully controled the emotions of the crowd both by his personal attention to the young caesars and by his series of rhetorical questions and exclamations. "What triumph is more brillant? What spectacle more beautiful? What procession is more fortunate?"[52] And "What conveyances have jolted you, powerful Africa? What an excess of joy! Nothing is more luxurious than a sudden joy after a long affliction!"[53]

In a string of short terse sentences, he lists the ways in which Constantine's reign benefits the people. With this style, the panegyric allows no time for anyone to disagree – it becomes a statement of fact. "Peace reigns in the exterior parts, in the interior abundance of goods, harvests are plenteous."[54]

Finally Nazarius devotes a considerable amount of the work to the wondrous benefices Constantine has brought to the entire world. Freedom and peace have brought great joy to all inhabitants.[55] Rome has beautiful new buildings and renovations, especially the columns at the Circus Maximus.[56] Above all Constantine restored the moral fiber to the Roman Empire, through his example and through new legislation.[57] People had not lived so well as this before Constantine.

Julian's panegyric to emperor Constantius, delivered in 355 when Constantius raised Julian to the rank of caesar, illustrates just how purely formal the genre of panegyric could be. By following Menander's rules of panegyric very carefully, Julian managed to hide his understandable hatred for both of his cousins, Constantius and Constantine. Constantius had murdered Julian's father, brother, and cousins in 337 to secure power for his immediate family. The panegyric mechanically proceeds from one prescribed topic to the next, praising the emperor according to the guidelines and masking Julian's visceral antipathy.

Julian spends a great deal of time describing – rather than extolling – Constantius' military victories. In fact he uses very few words of praise; he lets "the facts speak for themselves." Summing up the long catalogue of the emperor's military maneuvers ending in peace, Julian abstractly exclaims, "Long may we continue to enjoy it (peace), O all-merciful providence."[58] When he arrives at the section which must discuss Constantius' personal virtues, his evasive phrasing is brilliant. He never calls Constantius "temperate," "wise," or "brave." Rather, since rules dictate that he must mention the emperor's virtues, he writes, "A few words about your temperance, your wisdom, and the affection that you inspire in others,"[59] as if all people have these virtues in some quantity, and they can be duly commented upon. Nowhere in the panegyric does Julian address the emperor with sincere praise. The panegyric is contrived; the language is plodding and pedantic and seems designed to bore an audience rather than rouse or entertain it. Since the panegyric is formulaic, he refuses to create overt similes and metaphors for Constantius. Ultimately Julian neglects to give clear reasons why the citizens should publicly acclaim the emperor. The oration was an academic exercise for Julian.

This is not the case for Julian's panegyric to empress Eusebeia, Constantius' wife. When Julian was sent to the court in Milan around 353, he felt awkward and mistreated, since his unfortunate rebellious brother, Gallus, had just been murdered by Constantius. Empress Eusebeia protected Julian at court, encouraging him to pursue his academic interests. This panegyric, written to thank her, reflects the sincerity and spontaneity the other one lacks. He defends his praise of a woman by stating that virtue also belongs to that gender. He bolsters his claim with the example of Athena herself, who sang an "encomium to queen Arete."[60] He continues by saying that as Athena praised Arete, "as no other woman in the world is honored," so shall he praise Eusebeia.

Eusebeia's native land, Macedonia, and her family are extolled in the conventional way. Julian continues to follow the rhetorical outline by praising her obedience to her husband, her virtue of modesty, her generosity to her family and relatives. Then Julian leaves the outline and gives specific instances of her trust in him, and her advocacy on his part. She knew of his love of philosophy and sent him to Greece to study. She "defended me and warded off those false and monstrous suspicions." And "when I had departed from this interview, I felt the deepest admiration and awe, and was clearly convinced that it was Modesty (σωφροσύνη) herself I had heard speaking."[61] Throughout the oration Julian compares Eusebeia to Penelope. In his strongest metaphors he says Eusebeia became his "zealous aid" (βοηθός), an "averter of evil" (ἀλεξίκακος), and "my savior" (σώτειρα).[62] She displays goodness (ἐπιείκειαν) and temperance (σωφροσύνη), and wisdom (φρόνησις).[63] He gives by way of example that, at an imperial arrival ceremony in Galatia, all the people went out to welcome her as befits an empress. Yet rather than participating in the lively festival for Eusebeia, Julian preferred to sit quietly in his study and write this panegyric in her honor.

Julian's panegyric is based on personal experience, but he

implies that Eusebeia's virtues benefit the populace by her status as empress. Rather than using stimulating short statements and questions, Julian prefers to draw people slowly into his own story, so that they will end up as captivated by the empress as he was.

Ausonius wrote his panegyric to emperor Gratian sometime soon after 379. He had been the young emperor's tutor and had known him since 364. Ausonius wrote the panegyric to thank the emperor for elevating him to the rank of consul.

Above all else Ausonius concentrates his praises of Gratian for that one deed only, the gift of the consulship to him who was by then an old man. Ausonius nevertheless finds it difficult to express his gratitude, so overwhelmed is he by Gratian's graciousness, kindness, bounty, valor, and august imperium.[64] Ausonius seems worried about the charge of flattery, so he leaves Gratian's personal qualities and moves to a description of his military prowess. Because of his victories on the northern frontiers, all people "can rest easily in their beds."[65]

Ausonius never refers to Gratian as divine, but says he is guided by the heavens and Fortuna.[66] He is the one "who stands next to God."[67] In a belabored metaphor, Ausonius says that Gratian's actions happen more quickly than people can initially conceive of the idea of them. And thought, Ausonius says, "claims to be something divine."[68] As *pontifex maximus* (this was before he gave up the title) Gratian is "participator in the designs of God."[69] That is the most explicit reference to the emperor's superior nature. Otherwise he lauds Gratian with the usual valor in battle, comparing him more favorably to Menelaus, Ulysses, Nestor, and emperor Antoninus (138–161 CE).[70] Ausonius tortures another metaphor when he over-analyzes Gratian's name, trying cleverly to point out that his name suits his natural virtues.[71]

Gratian gave Ausonius the consulship as a repayment of a debt to him. This overwhelmed the old tutor. And he breaks into a litany of praise.

> Oh how that sentence is overlaid with the
> gold of your nature!
> How sustaining is the milk of these words springing
> from the sincerest breast!

> Is there anyone who shrinks so modestly from
> arrogant display of his generosity![72]

Ausonius gives two references to the emperor cult and civic ceremonies. The foras and basilicas which were once filled with the sounds of legal business are now, since Gratian, busy with the "taking of vows for your well-being."[73] In another section Ausonius says that he ranks Gratian above emperor Antoninus. In an awkward fashion without further explanation, he goes on with the following passage, probably referring to anniversaries celebrated in Antoninus' honor.

> It is true that all the world over, every city which lives under our governance observes the annual days of festival, Rome as a matter of custom, Constantinople out of imitation, Antioch out of love for indulgence, as also do degenerate Carthage and Alexandria, the gift of its river; but Treves is enabled to do this by the kindness of our prince, and will do so in company with the author of that kindness.[74]

Ausonius' speech, although unremarkable in style and content, does reveal that panegyrics were the popular and appropriate way to address the emperor. The poor quality of the speech mattered little because the institution of emperor cult in civic ceremony was so much a convention of court and society that the ritual itself could overshadow the actual poem. Significantly Ausonius' panegyric itself explicitly refers to the very popularity – and spread of the civic ceremonies to outlying western cities.

Pacatus' long Latin panegyric to Theodosius I (circa 389) varies slightly from the rules of the genre because he is less concerned with biographical details and more concerned with recent events.[75] The last third of the panegyric is devoted to Theodosius' heroic defeat of the usurper, Maximus. Pacatus' unrestrained language for the emperor in the elaborate oration shows that lavish praise on the emperor within the context of civic ceremonies was still a vital part of life in the empire.

The most striking feature of the panegyric is the unambiguous language describing Theodosius as divine. Theodosius possesses "divine beauty"[76] which the entire Roman populace had prayed to have lead them. In conformity with the rule of the genre, Pacatus praises Spain, the birthplace of the emperor, as it was Trajan's and Hadrian's. With short choppy sentences he builds to a climax contrasting the mythological traditions of the birthplaces of the gods Jupiter, Romulus and Remus, and Hercules. Dismissing them he ends dramatically, "We know nothing of the authenticity of these sayings, but Spain gave us a god which we see."[77]

Theodosius' uncanny memory is a quality only possessed by gods; even the famous abilities of Hortensius, Luculus, and Caesar paled by comparison.[78] Pacatus' most blatant statement about Theodosius' divinity require him to speculate about the gradations of godliness among the souls of human beings. The "more majesty a face possesses, the more his beauty came from the heavens."[79]

Conceding that even though these are divine mysteries, Pacatus can safely state that Thedosius is privy to these mysteries since he has more divine soul than other human beings. All that the *hoi polloi* understand is this: Theodosius' kind of divinity "is the type adored by nations, it is the kind that the whole universe addresses in prayers, the kind sailors turn to to ask for good weather, and from which soldiers expect felicitous predictions."[80]

Pacatus highlights this imperial divinity by employing the device of antithesis. Theodosius is eminently human. The emperor does not just appear in the crowd during ceremonious occasions; he frequently mingles with the people.[81] Theodosius "introduced friendliness to the court."[82] His simplicity, clemency, modesty, self-restraint, generosity, and beneficence were incomparable. His generosity was such that he made the beneficiary feel that the gift was his due.[83]

Theodosius was the cause of the common happiness of all people in the empire. Even barbarians recognized him as the one "seen on their sun."[84] The Persian king came to venerate him.[85] Speaking again of the conjunction of Theodosius' divine qualities made manifest in his magnanimity, Pacatus compares the emperor to the ocean which gives back much more than it takes.[86]

Pacatus lauds Theodosius' military acumen, crediting his victories to his divine nature, and crediting his victories for the exceptional prosperity enjoyed by all. Alexander, Hannibal, and Africanus no longer set the standard for military excellence.[87] His victories are as worthy of immortalization by artists and poets as the feats of Hercules and Bacchus.[88] Neither was any emperor as lawful as he was.[89]

Pacatus' panegyric is so long that he has time to punctuate it periodically with emotional language, stirring the crowds by pithy rhetorical questions and cavalcades of replies. Typical of this he writes:

> To my way of thinking, if the divine and sacred law author-
> izes mortals to judge heavenly things, then we should have as
> emperor the most felicitous emperor who creates happiness,
> combats misery, tames fortune, and gives humanity a new
> destiny.[90]

For Pacatus, Theodosius is capable of incredible, destiny-shaking activities. For the most part, however, Pacatus allows the audience to relax and listen to the accounts of the brilliant military campaigns.

Pacatus also includes information about civic ceremony honoring the emperor. He refers to the *tensis*, the chair in which the emperor was carried.[91] The same chair was used to bear the gods' statues in processions.[92] Pacatus writes that it is customary on entering large cities to make a visit to the sanctuaries and temples dedicated to the "supreme deity," then to admire the public spaces: fora, gymnasia, and their promenades. On finishing the tour, one then is obliged to pay homage to the "sacred rites of your palace and to the honorable custom which are equal to the ceremonies of old."[93]

Pacatus' panegyric is a rich source of history, bits and pieces of evidence for civic religion, and evidence for unmitigated praise for Theodosius. There is no doubt that he considers Theodosius in some way divine. The panegyric does not appear stilted or archaic; to the contrary, it is chock full of up-to-date descriptions of the emperor's most recent victories. This is all the more telling because it presents civic ceremony and emperor cult squarely within the life of the Christian imperial court, not on the periphery as part of some dying vestigial custom of the past.

Christians, rhetoric, and the civic ceremonies

As we have seen, the calendar of civic ceremonies and court rituals, established and maintained by the Christian emperors, continued the practice of panegyric and praise to the deity. No longer was it up to the *theologoi* of old to compose a hymn for the deities. It was now the Church's duty to present the public praises to the deity who protected the empire. It is important to remember that as a rhetorical exercise the encomia to the gods, or hymns, were not uniformly included in the curricula of the school of rhetoric. Rather, hymns emerged from a long tradition within specific cults, and some teachers of rhetoric reluctantly included them in their pedagogical exercises.[94] Thus, unlike other encomia, hymns had no set canonical list of forms, so rhetors were able to experiment with them during this period.[95] Because hymns to deities were connected to the individual cults, Christian ecclesiarchs would have had little if any exposure to them in that context.

Yet hymns to protecting gods had always been an integral part of the *civic ceremonies* honoring the emperor. Whenever an imperial occasion was to take place, the court would hire a *theologos* or *hymnologos* to compose and deliver the sacred hymn for the civic ceremony.[96] The public thus heard hymns *outside* of a cultic context. In the fourth century even though Church officials were now responsible for the praise of the deity in civic ceremonies, both lay people and clerics would still have been exposed to occasional encomia to the gods in the setting of a civic ceremony.

Yet fourth-century hierarchs were still uncomfortable and ideologically conflicted about the civic rituals that continued unabated the Roman ruler cult. They had not yet found a *modus vivendi* between their exclusivist views of Christianity and the civic religion of the Greco-Roman world. With regard to the Church's public role in the ceremonies specifically, and their relationship to the state generally, the ecclesiarchs were still "confused and evasive."[97] Athanasius had nothing but contempt for the emperor cult. In *Against the Heathen* he writes that the Senate deifies popular emperors; the hated ones remain mortal.[98] The most ridiculous aspect of the emperor cult, in his opinion, was that the Senate was composed of mortal men, and "the strange thing is this, that they themselves, by dying as men, expose the falsehood of their own vote concerning those deified by them."[99] Athanasius is representative of a most uncompromising Christian position. As Price has pointed out, Christian hierarchs on the whole grudgingly ignored or accepted the "legitimacy of the imperial honors" after the Constantinian settlement.[100] The Christian protestations against emperor Julian's duplicitous attempts to slip in a few statues of gods next to his image for the purpose of veneration are the most telling proof of this.[101]

Even though Eusebius was utterly against the imperial cult, he was able to appropriate the genre of imperial panegyric for his own tastes and purposes. Eusebius delivered a panegyric to Constantine for the celebration of his Tricennalia.[102] His pan-egyric would have been one of several heard at the festival.[103] Eusebius uses the occasion to give a theological treatise on the proper woship of the Supreme God and the nature of salvation history, not to praise Constantine according to the traditional format of a βασιλικὸς λόγος. When he does digress from his theological exposition on God or the Word he praises Constantine in relationship to God.[104] Because Constantine worships the true God, he is emperor. Eusebius engages in a few rhetorical questions directed against paganism: "For how should he whose soul is impressed with a thousand absurd images of false deities be able to exhibit a counterpart of the true and heavenly sovereignty?"[105] He answers this farther down: "He is indeed an emperor, who calls on and implores in prayer the favor of his heavenly Father night and day, and whose desires are fixed on the celestial kingdom."[106]

Not surprisingly, Eusebius does not follow the traditional plan for panegyric. He does not praise the emperor's family or home-land, nor does he describe his virtuous upbringing. His praise of Constantine is a thinly disguised pedagogical exercise to instill theological truths. Constantine's virtues are those of a Christian philosopher: temperance, modesty, serenity of spirit.[107] He is powerful only by paradox – or grace: he is utterly dependent on God, and for this he is called "noble-minded." Eusebius has created his own version of panegyric with this work.

Yet Christian reaction to the emperor cult and the civic cere-monies is not the central issue. What is important is that the Church was suddenly thrust into a very public position by hav-ing to perform at public civic ceremonies run by the court. At the same time a tremendous change was going on *within* the Church. As the Church was now responsible for the spiritual life of the majority of the population – at least nominally – suddenly its own liturgical rituals and responsibilities were much more public and exposed. And its theological crises became political issues. It is during this period of accepting new public duties while fighting off heresies that the Church begins to form its own hymnography befitting its status as the state religion of the empire.

Heresy and rituals of civic ceremony

It bears stressing that nearly all the leaders of the Church in the fourth and fifth centuries were formally schooled in the rhetorical arts. Gregory Nazianzus, for example, attended university with Julian in Athens. He wrote fine panegyrics to his family members and friends on various occasions. And his poetry in iambic trimeter rivals that of any of his contemporaries. Yet none of the many bishops who made any contribution to doctrinal definitions during the Arian crisis took up writing poetry, panegyrics, or hymns for use in Church liturgies. Nazianzus wrote poems lauding Christ, but none was intended for use in churches. These educated bishops would have been aware of the experimentation going on in rhetorical circles – especially in the writing of hymns. And likewise the potent pedagogical quality of hymnography would not have escaped them. As Ramsay Macmullen put it so well:

> the literature of religion par excellence was hymns, in every century; and hymns present a world of ideas quite cut off from higher criticism.[108]

It is with these two points in mind that we shall look at the liturgical situation in Constantinople.

In book five of his *Ecclesiastical History*, Socrates devotes a great deal of space to the description of the lack of uniformity on the Christian calendar of festivals and liturgical practices throughout the empire. Even Easter, the major feast of the year, was subject to conciliar dispute. Fast days and periods varied from city to city, as well as the lists of foods the faithful should avoid. Socrates' bewilderment at the situation is obvious from these quotes.

> In short you will scarcely find anywhere among the sects, two churches which agree exactly in their ritual respecting prayers.

It would be difficult, if not impossible, to give a complete catalogue of the various customs and ceremonial observances in use throughout every city and country.

This diversity was occasioned, as I imagine, by the bishops who in their respective eras governed the churches; and those who received these several rites and usages, transmitted them as laws to posterity.[109]

This lack of consistency was in some respects fortunate for the Church in Constantinople, since it had no strong apostolic traditions to bind it, and since it was called upon by the court to serve in public ceremonies. This is not to say that the Church in the capital was quicker to welcome liturgical innovations than in other cities. The Church in Constantinople had a "great liturgical puritanism" that characterized all the other large sees.[110] It simply had less august liturgical precedents to invoke in case of indecision or ambiguity. Even before the Constantinian peace, the Church had struggled with what rituals and kinds of hymns were allowable in the liturgies and which were not. By 325 the fact was that the Church had few set hymns and a simple liturgy; yet an entirely new sector of the population was filling the new churches, expecting ceremonies, music, and singing, which had played a large role in pagan cults to the gods.[111] The hierarchy not only found themselves in the position of needing to provide services at state functions, within their own realm they needed to ward off Arian competition and to prevent "nostalgia for pagan ceremonies."[112]

At the beginning of the fourth century the Church in Constantinople had very little official hymnography.[113] With the advent of the Arian crisis, hymns, poetry, processions, and acclamations became a way to sway the crowds. This was not new. Heretics had always been open to writing catchy hymns in Greek verse to promote their cause. Paul of Samosata, Marcion, Valentinus, other Gnostic sects, the Syrian Bardesanes, and of course Arius all chose to put their theology into verse to capture the imaginations – and souls – of the people on the streets. Arius' verses, the *Thalia*, were famous because they were popular, and thus dangerous, and eventually all but a few lines were written out of history and memory by the Fathers. Written in brachycatelic verse (didactic verse),[114] his poems had dockworkers and churchmen alike singing. The Church was never slow to condemn the heretical hymns, but it was slow to fight the enemies with the same weapon.

Some of the bishops' hesitancy began to change when after fifty-five years into the battle with Arianism the latter still possessed most of the churches in the capital. Gregory Nazianzus, bishop of Constantinople in 380, wrote of the tortuous sieges he and his small Orthodox congregation endured to wrest back control of the capital. Although he never used his poetic compositions on Christ to rally his followers, he shared the responsibility of repossessing the capital for the Orthodox with emperor Theodosius I. They both commandeered a long triumphal procession back to St Anastasia church amidst the unruly crowds of the city.[115] When they finally arrived at the church, the bishop, exhausted and unwilling to speak, shared the altar with the emperor and relied on his presence for authority and direction.[116] From there Gregory could quiet the crowd in the church.

Socrates and Sozomen give a slightly different version of the incident.[117] They hardly mention Gregory's role in the siege; rather they credit Theodosius alone for the victory. Both of these historians relate that Theodosius had just had spectacular military victories defeating barbarians in Illyria. As the emperor made his way to the capital, he stopped first in Thessaloniki. There he heard of the intractable Arians still in control of the churches in Constantinople. The emperor sent out a rescript to the citizens of the capital informing them that everyone must conform to the Orthodox faith. Theodosius, thus prepared for his entry into the city, headed the procession that resulted in ousting the heretics. At this point the historians do not go into detail. Sozomen relates that "He expelled the Arians after forty years." Socrates says, "He called for the return of the faith."

It is important to note that in Gregory's account, as well as in the two histories, Theodosius had masterminded the entire event. Socrates drops one hint when he relates that since Theodosius had just recovered from a deathly illness in Thessaloniki he was "all the more triumphant on entering." Although the historians do not describe the details of the festival, it can be safely assumed that Theodosius entered Constantinople with the triumphant fanfare of an arrival ceremony. He had just defeated barbarian hoards. Theodosius obviously used imperial *adventus* ceremony as further clout to purge the city of Arian heretics. The church historians relate that the entire city was in an uproar. Gregory Nazianzus, unaccustomed to having religious disputes settled in the noisy streets and public places, willingly went along with the emperor's public siege of the Arians, using the imperial procession of civic religion to regain Orthodox dominion in the capital. Theodosius obviously used the occasion of the imperial arrival to maximize his authority. The Arians could not stand up to the power of an awe-inspiring imperial procession. Gregory, even as bishop, appears retiring and dependent on the authority and power that Theodosius commanded by using the age-old elements of civic religion for his own purposes. Significantly Sozomen ends the description of the incident by saying, "When Demophilus (the Arian bishop) had left the church, the Emperor entered therein and engaged in prayer." Gregory Nazianzus' role is not mentioned; we can imagine Theodosius commanding the faithful from the altar.

A few years later John Chrysostom would not hesitate to "fight fire with fire." The Arians, still powerful in 395 despite the Council of Constantinople, were in the habit of holding night vigils on the first and last days of the week. At dawn the crowd would process to their churches singing wonderful hymns.[118] John Chrysostom countered by staging even more elaborate vigils. He composed his own responsive chants to fight the Arians in the fora and at the city gates.[119] The Orthodox had imperial patronage and wealthier citizens in their group; and consequently they had much more elaborate processions, especially with the silver candle holders and the silver cross that empress Eudoxia had provided.[120] Chrysostom's retaliatory vigils and chants provoked the Arians to attack physically, causing some deaths. As a result emperor Arcadius forbade Arians to chant in public.[121]

What Chrysostom was forced to do was take the battle out of the physical confines of the churches and put it on the street. He took up the challenge of the Arians and met them in a way the Church had never before done. He adapted his theology to popular responsorial verse – although we do not know if it was in Greek meter. The vigils and processions in the public spaces were a radical venture for the conservative bishop. Both of these were elements of civic ceremony, which Chrysostom tailored, out of exigency, to his own purpose.

The Church's greatest fear about introducing new hymns and rituals into its services was that they could corrupt the faith and collapse the discipline needed for moral training. Seven of the canons from the Council of Laodicea (c.360)[122] betray the problems it was having with innovations in hymnography and conflicts with cultural customs. It appears that since 325 some seemingly innocuous customs which Christians had avoided before began to confront the heirarchs with ambiguous, difficult situations.

Canons 15 and 59 explicitly forbid the chanting of anything but the canonical psalms in church.[123] Canon 59 prohibits "individual songs as well as readings from uncanonical books." There also seems to have been some concern about the way psalms were chanted. Canon 17 says it was not permissible to chant them in rapid succession so that they became utterly indistinguishable. Each psalm ought to be recognizable. By virtue of these canons we know there was a great deal of innovation going on in liturgical singing.

With the establishment of Christianity as the state religion came a host of smaller problems having to do with general cultural conventions. When people began to join the Church at the command of the emperor, they obviously were not changing their customary ways of celebrating weddings, births, engagements, or other special familial holidays. Thus there are references in canons 39, 53, 54, and 55 to weddings, dinners, and parties. The verb "συνεορτάζειν" "to join in keeping the festival" also occurs. Canon 39 declares that no one was allowed to join in celebrations with pagans (ἔθνη) or eat with them at their "ungodly" (ἀθεότητι) affairs.[124]

Although the wording in canon 53 leaves room for interpretation, Christians do not seem to have been prohibited from attending weddings. Rather the receptions afterwards were the cause for the Church's concern. In fact, the canon may be directed at Christians who hosted these events. It even may have been intended to change their customary banquets. In any case "bouncy dancing" (βαλλίζειν) as well as "line dancing" (ὀρχεῖσθαι) were out of the question.[125] At weddings Christians should eat modestly, as befits them.[126] Canon 54 implies that priest and clerics would be present at weddings and dinners, but they should excuse themselves before the theatrical entertainment begins.[127] Finally, canon 55 does not allow for any reason that a priest or cleric or laity should attend a symposium, a party.[128]

Although these last four canons do not address changing liturgical practices directly, they richly illustrate the process by analogy. The Church had a growing problem as Christianity was absorbed into the larger culture. Customs from the wider society began to impinge on the Church on all sides.

The Church was in the midst of fighting innovations from inside the institution as well. With Constantine's tremendous building projects in Palestine came many pilgrims and the need for organized, liturgical "sightseeing."[129] The Spanish pilgrim, Egeria, wrote about her pilgrimage to the holy land. She describes how lay people, monks, nuns, and clerics would gather before dawn at the cave of the Anastasis. While they waited for the sun to rise they "joined in the singing of hymns, psalms, and antiphons."[130] She gives the impression that each day this event was a combination of spontaneity of the people and control by the clerics, since she is careful to note that each day a priest and deacon is present to say the prayer between the hymns. By contrast Gregory Nyssa did not share Egeria's enthusiasm for the popularity of pilgrimage. He wrote a burning attack on the practice.[131]

Syrian hymnographers wrote hymns for the new demands and for other holy occasions, and their work began to spread through the monasteries westward.[132] Most of the higher monks governing the monasteries put up resistance to the new hymns.[133] The ancient churches in Egypt and in Asia Minor were the most opposed to the new hymnography. But the Cappadocian churches, whose hierarchs were so influential in Constantinople in the late fourth century, accepted the new antiphonal chanting popular in the Levant.[134] St Auxentius, a native of Syria, was remembered as having advised people in the capital to stay away from the theater and be content with the singing in church.[135] He was also famous for the hymns he was in the habit of composing on the spur of the moment to entertain people.[136] His spiritual son, Anthemius, would later introduce choirs of men and women in the *pannychides* in the capital.[137] Grosdidier de Matons has pointed out that this musical activity was mentioned in the Auxentius' *vita* because it was "original, new, and popular."[138]

The Church then was responding to innovations in hymnography from within its own ranks and from heretics as the need for set liturgical forms grew. While pagan cults and hymns to specific gods posed no threat to the Church, the ritual customs of civic ceremonies honoring the emperor were a vital part of life, and the Church was called upon to play a role in them. Throughout the fourth century the Church in the capital was slowly absorbing hymns which were filtering in from Syria through the monastic network. Yet in response to Arianism and other crises, the Church began to use forms of civic ceremonies, chants, processions, and outdoor vigils to battle the enemy. And above all, the hierarchs accustomed themselves to the emperors' involvement and sponsorship of these activities. They also got used to seeing the emperors use altars of churches and the *kathisma* in the Hippodrome alike to sit in solemn majesty, receive acclamations, or spontaneously lead the populace in prayer if the need arose. It was during the next crisis, the Nestorian controversy, that the Church proved it had observed and learned well the power of rhetorical panegyric in state ceremonies.

Hymns to the Theotokos: fruits of the Nestorian crisis

We have seen in Chapter 3 that Empress Pulcheria took the campaign against Nestorius quite personally, because of his "slander" against the Virgin Mary. We have also seen how Pulcheria's position and skillful use of her imperial tradition to direct matters pertaining to divine worship brought the cult of the Virgin to the public foreground.[139] We must now analyze some of the most popular hymns of the period that so effectively fixed the Theotokos' identity as a cosmological power. Given this imperial context to sponsorship of the devotion to the Theotokos, it is not coincidental or surprising that these hymns were modeled on imperial panegyric.

There are seven hymns to the Theotokos written by prominent ecclesiarchs between 430 and 470. Six of them are embedded in polemical sermons in defense of the Theotokos against Nestorians. These hymns are written in the style of acclamation, greeting the Virgin either with "Hail, full of grace," or "Hail, Bride, unwedded." The genre became so popular that they are known as "χαιρετισμοί." They are the works of Proclus of Constantinople, Basil of Seleucia, Cyril of Alexandria,

Chryssipus of Jerusalem, and Theodotus of Ancyra.[140] Because they are all quite similar to each other, the only one to be introduced here will be Proclus," the most influential of all of them. We shall also examine some of his other hymns to the Virgin written in a different style. The anonymous *Akathistos Hymn*, whose style is so close to that of Proclus, will be examined after these.

Proclus

Proclus angered Nestorius in 428–429 when he delivered his three famous orations on the Theotokos.[141] Not long into the first oration, which was written for celebrating the Virginity Festival instituted by Pulcheria (the παρθενική πανηγύρις), is this litany to the Virgin Mary.[142]

> For this reason we now call Mary Virgin Theotokos.
> She is the unstained treasure of Virginity
> She is the paradise of the second Adam.
> She is the workshop of the union of natures,
> the festival of the covenant of salvation.
> She is the bridal chamber (πάστας) in which the
> Logos wedded all flesh. She is the living bramble
> bush of nature, which the fire of divine labor pains
>   do not burn up,
> She is the true relieving cloud, the producer of him
> in the body, higher above the Cherubim.
> She is the purest fleece of the heavenly rain from
> which the shepherd clothed the sheep.
> Mary, the servant, and mother, virgin and heaven,
> The only bridge from God to humanity,
> The awe-inspiring loom of the *oikoumene*,
> in which the robe of unity was woven inexpressibly.[143]

A few years before he had praised Empress Pulcheria with these verses.

> I am amazed at the great generosity of the Empress,
> which is the spring of spiritual blessings to all. . . .
> The virgin [Pulcheria] dedicated herself to Christ;
> She both empties and exhausts her wealth through
>   pious discretion.

She killed her mortal fleshy dwelling through suffering,
She wedded the crucified one in her soul,
She beautified the earth to be a visible heaven.[144]

Proclus' orations on the Virgin show that he knows how to control a crowd masterfully. The long sermons contain dialogues, exegeses of Biblical texts, hymns, and acclamations. These praises to the Virgin differ very little in form or content from his panegyric to Pulcheria. In each case he praises the subject's deeds and virtues. Pulcheria is praised as a "spring of spiritual blessings," she does good works with her wealth, yet she is the epitome of discretion. And the Virgin changed the status of women from "cursed" to "blessed" as she neutralized all the female troublemakers of the Bible: Jezebel, Dalila, and the archetypal enemy – Egypt.[145] Proclus uses Biblical stories much as panegyrists used mythological characters to highlight their subjects. None of the potential weaknesses of Mary's character or human nature ever come to light in Proclus' hymns. Pulcheria's praises have little mythic comparison. Yet when Proclus calls her the spouse of Christ, mythic themes are introduced. Both hymns praise Mary and Pulcheria by use of paradox. Mary is higher than the angelic cohorts yet remains a servant. Empress Pulcheria mortifies her flesh through suffering.

Proclus makes good use of the devices of rhetoric: repetition, questions, acclamations, and word plays. In another hymn to the Theotokos he says:

Women ran, not because the woman displayed the plant of
    death, but she bore the fruit of life.
Virgins ran along, because the Virgin gave birth but did
    not shame virginity, but sealed incorruption.
For the baby came, and he left the womb with inviolate
    garments.
Mothers ran, because the Virgin Mother reconciled the
    rule of disobedience, now the obedience of the
    daughter is vindicated.
Fathers shall run, because the father is renewed through
    a new age.
The baby shall run, because the baby was swaddled in the
    manger.

And shepherds shall run because the shepherds came
     to the one from the Virgin lamb.[146]

In other places Proclus' language is reminiscent of titles used
for Greek goddesses. He calls out to the Theotokos, "O Virgin,
inexperienced girl and mother not born in a natural way."[147]
"κόρη" is Demeter's daughter Persephone, and "ἀλόχευτος" is the
rare adjective used to describe Athena's springing from the head
of Zeus.

In another oration Proclus says he struggles to find the right
words and "colors" to praise the Theotokos as he develops his
ekphrasis.

> With what colors of an encomia shall I use to paint the
> virginal image? With what words of praise can I illuminate
> the stainless character of purity?[148]

What is exceptional about Proclus is that in his work we have
evidence for the merger of imperial panegyric and hymns to the
Theotokos. His orations to Pulcheria praise her as the genre
demanded. All audiences would have expected the kind of
panegyric of praise he delivered in honor of Pulcheria and
would have been accustomed to the speeches' lofty metaphors.
In contrast what the people may have been startled by were
Proclus' lauds to the Virgin Mary, which echoed so closely those
of imperial panegyric. Proclus' dramatic delivery of his panegyrics to the Theotokos would have changed the interior of the
church into a politically charged, public forum. One must
remember that the orations were delivered at imperial request
to fight against the bishop of Constantinople, Nestorius.
Pulcheria's over-identification with the Theotokos facilitated
Proclus' panegyrics to the Virgin. Proclus' hymns force the
congregation to leave the staid world of conservative psalm
singing in a liturgical setting and transform the entire event in
the church into a festival for the Theotokos, much like imperial
ceremonies in the Hippodrome. After all the church was
empress Pulcheria's public space.

Probably the bishop's most famous hymn is the "χαιρετισμοί,"
embedded in a Christmas oration.[149] Proclus, like the other
ecclesiarchs, weaves the Lukan greeting of Gabriel to Mary, "
Hail, full of grace," with startling metaphors. The verses take on
the rhythm of an acclamation.

Hail full of grace, unreaped soil of heavenly grain.
Hail full of grace, undeceitful Virgin Mother of the true vine,
Hail full of grace, unfailing net of the immutable Godhead.
Hail full of grace, wide open field of the undivided nature,
Hail full of grace, oh unstained bearer, bride of the bereaved
   world.
Hail full of grace, the weaver of the crown, which was not
   braided by hand, and was made for creation,
Hail full of grace, the house of holy fire,
Hail full of grace, you are the return for those who fled the
   world.
Hail full of grace, You are the undepletable treasury of the
   world.
Hail full of grace, The joy from you, Holy Virgin, is infinite,
Hail full of grace, You are adorned with many virtues,
   you are the torch-bearing light,
and the inextinguishable light brighter than the sun.[150]

The last two lines are one of the many places where Proclus
compares the Virgin, like all imperial panegyrics do, to light,
stars, and the sun. Although the phrase "χαῖρε κεχαριτομένη" is
from Luke, to greet a god or emperor in poem or panegyric with
"hail" was a common occurrence in epideiktic poetry. Prokne,
Aphrodite, Hermes, Mithras, and Demeter were all greeted this
way.[151] The most famous hymn to the Virgin, the *Akathistos
Hymn*, too, is a "χαιρετισμοί."

The Akathistos Hymn

Although this famous Marian hymn has been traditionally
thought to be composed by Romanos Melodos in the sixth
century, Grosdidier de Matons, as well as Trypanis, have shown
it to be an earlier composition, and without a doubt, anonymous.[152] Even though Grosdidier de Matons posits the hymn's
date of composition between 475 and 525, there is no convincing
evidence that it was not written anytime after the Council of
Ephesus. In style and content it is very similar to the "χαιρετισμοί" of Proclus.

   Liturgically the *Akathistos Hymn* is the oldest continuously performed Marian hymn used in the Eastern Orthodox Church.
And it is among the most widely known and popular with the

laity. Yet it has continually baffled scholars and theologians alike. The exalted position in the role of the sacred economy which the hymn gives to the Theotokos is explicit, uncompromising, and unambiguous. Her powers encroach on those of the Trinity. Most historical theologians scarcely mask their discomfort over the august theological claims for the Virgin. One scholar contextualizes the metaphors for the Vigin as "poetical exaggerations that cannot be taken as exact theological statements," and as attributions to the Virgin "that strictly belong to God."[153] Another scholar rationalizes the robust language in the *Akathistos* as "springing from the mental categories of Byzantium [which are] more ample in its assertions."[154] Yet rather than passing the shocking language off as some kind of idiosyncratic thought process characteristic of the Byzantines, we shall see that the hymn fits squarely within the traditional imperial panegyric. Before we look at the hymn itself, it is necessary to describe its unique form.

The *Akathistos Hymn* has had two prooimia (prologues) attached to it, one from the late fifth century and one dating from the seventh. The body of the hymn consists of twenty-four verses, which by their initial letter form an acrostic of the Greek alphabet. Each strophe is five lines long. They are separated in alternate fashion by a refrain: the long one consisting of thirteen lines, and the short one only one line. The long refrain is what characterizes the hymn to the faithful as "οἱ χαιρετισμοί τῆς Θεοτόκου," for the lines are constructed as salutations in praise of Mary. Each one ends with "χαῖρε νύμφη ἀνύμφευτε," "hail bride, unwedded'.[155] The short strophes end simply with the refrain "Alleluia." In all the strophes lines one and five are identical metrically. There is a deliberate use of rhyme in the poem; but it is not the device of rhyming ends of lines, *homoioteleuton*, common to most Byzantine religious poetry.[156]

The first twelve strophes depict a dramatic narrative between Gabriel and Mary. The Annunciation and Infancy narratives are retold with a unique emphasis on Mary. The last half of the hymn turns to the theological issues concerning the two natures of Christ, and in so doing praises Mary as Theotokos, God-bearer. Almost all scholars have noticed that the hymn is two in one, praising the Annunciation as well as the Nativity. Tradition has always held that it was a hymn composed for the Annunciation, established as a holiday by Justinian about 540.

But a closer examination of both the hymn and historical data by Krypiakiewicz shows that there was originally a double holiday celebrating Jesus Christ and Mary as the "New Eve" on December 26.[157] Since the Annunciation story also appears in prose sermons for the Nativity before 530, and does not appear after 550,[158] the "double holiday" view for the *Akathistos* is further supported.

Byzantine philologists have agreed in identifying the *Akathistos* as a superb, very early example of a kontakion, a poetic homily. It is a new form of rhyming poetry emerging in Christian literature in the fifth century.[159] In form, however, a kontakion looks very much like an encomium of the Second Sophistic.[160] Most scholars, nevertheless, have posited that the form arose from Syriac poetry which was just entering Greek churches. Scholars have traditionally credited the hymns of Ephraim the Syrian (d. 373) with the greatest influence on Greek hymnographers, whose works were just emerging.

Ephraim the Syrian, whose prolific poetic hymnography began to be translated into Greek in ecclesiastical circles in the late fourth century, wrote elaborate dialogues between Mary and Gabriel in his hymns to the Virgin.[161] Dialogues, too, show up in Proclus' hymns. Yet Greek epideiktic poetry is also filled with conversations between deities, mortals, and a combination of the two.[162] Acrostics, too, are characteristic of Syriac poetry. Yet they are not unknown in Greek poetry and inscriptions.[163] Nevertheless the undeniable difference between the two poetic traditions is this: the use of rhyme separates Syriac poetry from classical Greek verse.

But Grosdidier de Matons has shown convincingly that Ephraim's influence on Proclus is limited. Proclus is concerned with rhyme above all else; Ephraim's poetic concern is isosyllables.[164] Thus Ephraim's influence is limited to form. Moreover, Grosdidier de Matons believes that there is much more influence from Greek secular poetry than from Syriac ecclesiastical poetry. The devices so common in Ephraim's poetry – antithesis, assonance, anaphora, and the isocolon – are "identical with figures of speech in classical rhetoric."[165] The popular pagan encomia and poems of the fourth and fifth centuries, written "κατὰ στίχον," that is, the verse built on the repetition of a line, had more influence on the very early kontakia, one of which is the *Akathistos*.[166] These poetic trends of giving rhythmic period endings and using isocolons were formative influences on Christian hymnography, culminating in the new genre of the kontakion.[167] The *Akathistos* itself displays internal rhyme in both the long and short verses which is closely related to the isocolon, and is really a precursor to the true kontakia of the sixth century.[168]

Thus even though the *Akathistos* is not written in iambic trimeter, the repetition of verse, the encomiastic theme, the use of rhyme, and the fact that it is not really a "homily" (a conversation) point to the fact that it is not truly yet a poetic homily – what would later define a kontakion. This also shores up the hypothesis that the hymn was written in the first half of the fifth century. It is a eulogizing poem in the earliest version of a kontakion[169] which was just beginning to emerge as a poetic form.

In fact in style and content the *Akathistos Hymn* is closest to Proclus' works, especially his sixth oration to the Virgin.[170] Part way into this oration is an elaborate annunciation scene, in which Gabriel and Mary engage in an extended dialogue. Wellesz has pointed out that when the narrator's words are deleted the text becomes a "dialogue in distichs," forming an alphabetic acrostic to the letter "M."[171] All of this points to the fact that the fluidity and experimentation so characteristic of what was going on in the rhetorical schools of this period was also affecting Christian orators and bishops writing the hymns.[172] "Influence" did not come exclusively from within the ranks of the Church. We shall now examine how closely the *Akathistos Hymn* parallels the themes of imperial panegyrics.

Rhetorical devices used in the *Akathistos Hymn*

Given the experimentation in poetry and rhetoric, it is not so shocking that the *Akathistos* displays five out of six topoi of poetical encomia.[173] As outlined by Menander they are as follows:

1 the prooimion emphasizing the importance of the subject;
2 the praise of family and nation (this is not present in the *Akathistos*);
3 presentation of education;
4 the deeds of the person in war and peace;

5 the comparisons;
6 the epilogue, containing a prayer to a deity;

As Viljamaa has pointed out, there was "great freedom" in the use of the topoi,[174] so it is not so exceptional that the Virgin's family and birth are omitted.

In the prooimion of the *Akathistos*[175] the audience is confronted immediately with the importance of praising the Virgin, who is informed by the Archangel that she shall bear the "bower of the Heavens." Even the Archangel is amazed at her, and begins what will be the familiar refrain, "Hail, bride unwedded." The first strophe of "hails" goes on to confirm the greeting of the Incarnation.

The theme of the hymn skips the praise of ancestry and homeland, and moves to the topic of the Virgin's education. The author obviously has stretched the original Lukan story and the themes of encomia; nevertheless verses 2 and 3 explain the Virgin's incredulity at the message, then her quick transformation to *knowledge*, not to her faith and obedience to divine will. In the hymn she "yearns to know the incomprehensible knowledge;" then she is praised as a "knower" or an "initiate" (μύστις) of the ineffable will. She taught no one about the mystery, since she is personified "knowledge superseding the wise." The author shaped the Lukan story to fit more nearly with a wise thoughtful Virgin. This is in direct contrast both to Ephraim the Syrian's depiction of the Virgin, and the later Romanos Melodos'.[176] For both of these authors Mary is rather slow and dull-witted about the Annunciation, as she is eminently human with all the mortal failings.

When in verse 7 Christ is born, the hymn begins to extol the Virgin Mary for her deeds. She is not honored because of her motherhood, but because of her warlike deeds.

> Hail, defense against invisible foes . . .
> Hail, invincible courage of the martyrs . . .
> Hail to you, through whom Hades was despoiled
> Hail to you, through whom we are vested in glory.

In verses 9 and 11 the hymn continues to praise her for her accomplishments, some of which require military acumen, or the power associated with the emperor establishing right religion.

> Hail to you, who has removed the inhuman tyrant from
>   his rule.
> Hail to you, who has redeemed us from pagan religion.
> Hail to you, who has rescued us from the mire of
>   transgression,
> Hail to you, who has ceased the worship of fire.
> Hail to you, who uplifted humankind,
> Hail to you, who refuted the fraud of idols,
> Hail O sea, which drowned the symbolic Pharaoh.

It is at this halfway point of the hymn that the author chooses to praise the Virgin for her peacetime deeds. Verses 13, 15, 17, 19, 21, and 23 are filled with praises of her ongoing virtuous deeds. Here are but a few examples from verse 13.

> Hail, O well-shaded tree, under which many find shelter.
> Hail, O forgiveness of many transgressors,
> Hail, the crown of self-restraint,
> Hail, O robe for those bare of courage.

Verse 17 heaps line after line of praises to the Virgin for her sophistic skills. It begins with

> O Theotokos, we see most eloquent orators mute as fish
> before you . . .
> Hail to you, who extricates us from the depths of ignorance.

From verse 19:

> Hail, O leader of spiritual remaking,
> Hail, O bestower of divine beneficence.

From verse 23:

> Hail to you, through whom trophies of victory are assured,
> Hail to you, through whom enemies are vanquished,
> Hail to you, who are the healing of my body,
> Hail to you, who are the salvation of my soul.

Throughout the hymn the Virgin's deeds, whether in battle or during peace, display the necessary virtues of courage (ἀνδρεία), justice (δικαιοσύνη), prudence (σωφροσύνη), and practical wisdom (φρόνησις).

The author takes particular license in the hymn with the encomiastic theme of comparison. This "license" enables the author to use Bible accounts in the same way that panegyrists were required to use Homeric myths: as a point of comparison. Throughout the work there are allusions to Biblical events and stories, either by comparing the Virgin more favorably either to the event or by showing that she is a more profound recapitulation of the event by use of personification. Thus she redefines the original Biblical dramas. This is apparent in the following lines.

Hail O nourishment succeeding the manna, land of promise.
Hail to you, from whom flows milk and honey.
Hail to you, who has quenched the furnace of error.
Hail, O tabernacle of God the Logos.[177]

There are many other comparisons that give the Theotokos qualities which were up to that time unprecedented. They are clearly reminiscent of abilities that pagan goddesses possessed.[178]

Finally the hymn ends with the prescribed epilogue. Throughout the last half of the hymn the happy state of the world has been stressed in keeping with the rules of panegyric. The Theotokos is both the subject of praise and the subject prayed to. Three lines before in verse 23 she was glorified as the "healer of my body" and "salvation of my soul." The prayer begs her, "release us from future punishment."

The *Akathistos Hymn* is filled with the literary devices so popular among contemporary rhetors. Metophors liken her to feast, food, and nourishment.[179] Comparisons with nature abound. The metaphor constantly used in panegyric for emperors appears in this hymn, too: shining astral bodies. Antithesis and paranomasia both play the most prominent role in creating the quick images in the encomium. An example of the latter is "γνῶσιν ἄγνωστον γνῶναι." The entire theme of the incarnation lends itself to antithesis, which ultimately leads to paradox. Just the refrain "Hail, bride unwedded" (χαῖρε νύμφη ἀνύμφευτε) is both antithesis and paranomasia. This refrain even suggests that the author combined the rules of encomia with some of the rules of epithalamia, or wedding speeches. Classic epithalamia kept repeating a verse of praise. Blending epithalamic forms into a hymn to the Virgin with a refrain so obvious as "Hail, bride unwedded," heightens the theological paradox all the more.

In a technical sense then the *Akathistos Hymn* can be called a panegyric, because it contains five of the six themes prescribed for a complete encomium. According to meter, however, it does not qualify. Nevertheless it is a poem, albeit corresponding to a different scan. By fifth century standards it may have qualified because in the fourth century accentual rhythm had become more common.[180] What is more important, however, is that the hymn's comparisons are similar to those used in imperial panegyrics.

Like imperial panegyric the *Akathistos* is a praise of victory celebrating the wondrous feats of the Theotokos. She completely redefines all wondrous Biblical events of old, not unlike the comparisons made by Cyrus of Panopolis when he likens Theodosius II to Agamemnon, Teucer, and Odysseus. Nor is it unlike the anonymous poem to Theodosius I who was a second sun shining from the east. Although among mortals, Theodosius I had the ocean at his feet and was the axis of the celestial firmament. Like Achilles and Athena, he was "great-hearted." Julian praises Eusebeia as a "savior" and an "averter of evil." The philosopher Hypatia's qualities required astral metaphors and utter veneration, not unlike the Theotokos in Proclus' orations and the *Akathistos*.

Most noteworthy are the identical words in the *Akathistos* that Menander used to illustrate a proper imperial panegyric. The Theotokos is a "wall" (τεῖχος), a "star" (ἀστέρα) revealing the sun, and "nourishment" (τροφέα).[181] There are also slight variations on the theme of brightness, shining forth, and rays of light, all metaphors in Menander. It is obvious that the author of the hymn remained close to the intent of Menander's instructions.

Proclus' work, the *Akathistos*, and the two Christian poems all display the current fascination with paradox.[182] Eudokia is called the "wise mistress" and "servant," as the Theotokos is called in the *Akathistos* and by Proclus respectively. The authors constantly play with the themes of august greatness and humble servitude. But this would not have been strange for audiences: Pacatus lauded Theodosius as one who mingled with the people yet had a divine nature. Rhetorical influences affecting pagan discourse in this period were equally affecting the Christians.[183]

The hymns to the Theotokos, so akin to imperial panegyrics, were intended to call up the same public emotions in order to rally the people against the perfidious Nestorius. There can be little doubt that they furthered Pulcheria's cause of defeating

Nestorius and establishing the Virgin as an object of cult in the capital. And it is apparent that the Constantinopolitan Church, led by Proclus, gave their wholehearted effort to implement her cause.

This intentional modeling of Marian hymns on imperial panegyrics had significant effects on the identity of Mary. Through these hymns she was invested in "the royal purple." Like all the Augustae she enjoyed favorable comparisons to myths and celestial bodies alike. Yet members of the imperial household were not the only ones lauded in panegyrics, so were the deities praised in hymns. The emerging identity of the Theotokos was being shaped, layer by layer, by the institutions unique to Constantinople: the imperial court, the Constantinopolitan Church, and the Byzantine goddess traditions surviving in statuary and religious cultural traditions. We shall now explore who Mary was in Church tradition on the eve of her transformation into an object of public veneration for Constantinople.

Part II

Mary's inheritance

Chapter 5

The hierarchs' Mary

It is probably not a coincidence that Chrysostom shows no signs at all of veneration for the Virgin Mary. Rather the reverse. He stresses her humanity and human weaknesses, such as vanity.[1]

Pre-Constantinian Mary

If the spread of Christianity had been left only to Paul, Mary's name would never have been known. In Galatians 4: 4–5 Paul only says that Jesus was "born of a woman." Only in Luke's gospel does there appear the kernel of the drama that provides for the most intimate conjunction of the divine and human world, revealing the ultimate plan of the divine economy. The Lukan story of the Annunciation and birth of Christ was perpetuated in two very different kinds of Christian literature: apocryphal stories and patristic expositions. We shall give a brief synopsis of how Mary was viewed and remembered before Constantine in both sectors of Christian literature, and then describe the scant evidence for devotions to her and reverence for her.

None of the extra-canonical literature contemporaneous with the Gospels mentions Mary. The first person to name her is Ignatius of Antioch. In the Epistle to the Ephesians (*c*.110) there appears a small creedal formula concerning Christ's humanity that helps his anti-docetic arguments; Christ is "of Mary."[2] The next patristic reference to her occurs fifty years later in Justin Martyr, who sets out the theological arguments that become the foundation and justification for the Church to praise her. He calls her "parthenos" (virgin), she is the new Eve, rectifying by obedience the existential havoc caused by Eve's disobedience.[3] Starting with Justin, the Fathers base their defense of Mary on close adherence to the Lukan text, investigating the theological ramifications of her actions, given the imperilled status of humanity after the Fall.

Although the Father's refined arguments describing if and how Mary was a virgin during every stage of her life are out of the scope of our discussion, suffice it to say that these concerns began early in the second century. Irenaeus of Lyons echoes the second Eve theme, and even stresses Mary's human faults and shortcomings.[4] Tertullian, not surprisingly, gives graphic details why Mary could not be a virgin *in partu*. His pronounced interest in her physical state illustrates that the themes from apocryphal literature were entering theological circles.[5] In general he has little toleration for Marian veneration. Clement of Alexandria (*c*.200) also deals with themes in the Apocrypha, referring to the *Protoevangelium of James*, agreeing that Mary was a virgin *in partu*.[6] Clement's student Origen (*c*.230) did not agree with this, but he is credited as the first Father to call Mary "Theotokos," and "ever-virgin."[7] Nevertheless he tempers his high praise of her with his description of Mary's doubts and inability to grasp the cosmic significance of the divine economy.[8] From Origen to the last persecution in the early fourth century, speculations about Mary in the liturature subside.

Although the early Fathers were slow to venture far from the gospel of Luke, Mary's life and power captured the hearts and minds of many other faithful people. This phenomenon manifested itself during the second century in the spread of creative "popular" liturature that facilitated the crystalization of special beliefs about Mary. The apocryphal stories, written around 140–160 CE, fueled the imaginations of popular piety, and helped make Christianity understandable to a greater sector of Greco-Roman society. The stories about the Virgin formed the "real world of Christian belief."[9] In the *Ascension of Isaiah* Mary is wholly ignorant of the entire birth event, and of course she remains a virgin.[10] The popular *Odes of Solomon*, on the other hand, represent Mary as a powerful being in her own right. She is "like a man" who brought Christ forth of her own will "openly, with dignity, in kindness."[11] By far the most important tract of the Apocrypha is the *Protoevangelium of James*. Mary's life is recounted from childhood, and all the themes of sanctity, virginity, and being singled out by God are developed and given texture. The theme of Mary's perpetual virginity and the focus on Mary alone as a holy person worthy of veneration come from the *Protoevangelium of James*.[12] This text is the source of speculations about the degree of her powerful sanctity, speculations which soon begin to seep into the elevated expositions of the Fathers.

In the early fourth century Peter of Alexandria called Mary "ever-virgin."[13] Athanasius used the terms "panayia" (all-holy) and Theotokos to refer to Mary.[14] In a text called *On Virginity*, attributed to Athanasius, Mary is depicted as a fourth-century nun.[15] She becomes the model of modest behavior for women wishing to retire to the ascetic life. Eusebius, too, called Mary "panayia."[16]

Ephraim the Syrian's hymns translated into Greek were crucial in spreading both devotions to Mary and deep speculations about her prominent role in the sacred economy. According to Ephraim Mary was the "bride of Christ," the conception of Christ occurred through her ear, and Mary was cleansed of the sin of Adam by the Holy Spirit before she conceived.[17] It was Mary who then imparted immortal flesh to Christ.[18]

The Cappadocians did not write a great deal about Mary, but their writings significantly advanced her status. When they do speak of her, it is within the context of Biblical exegesis for theological proof against heresy. There is no speculation from apocryphal texts. Basil believed she was "ever-virgin" and "Theotokos."[19] Gregory Nazianzus has few references to her, but he does call her "undefiled" (ἄχραντος), "Theotokos," and he believes she was virgin *in partu*.[20] Significantly, Gregory makes Mary the test of orthodox belief. He writes, "If anyone does not accept Mary as Theotokos, he is without Godhead."[21]

Gregory Nyssa's support of Mary lies consistently within the tradition of Biblical exposition. He elaborates on the "second Eve" theme, and uses the title "Theotokos." Yet he does venture something different. Well within the realm of theological speculation, he moves slightly away from the theme of Christ alone destroying death; through a kind of *communicatio idiomatum* Gregory implies that Mary too defeats death by her virginity.

> If then death cannot pass beyond virginity, but finds his power checked and shattered there, it is demonstrated that

virginity is a stronger thing than death. But those who by virginity have desisted from this process [procreation] have drawn within themselves the boundary line of death, and by their own deed have checked his advance; they have made themselves in fact a frontier between life and death, and a barrier too, which thwarts him.[22]

And a few paragraphs further he continues:

Just as in the age of Mary, the Theotokos, death, who had reigned from Adam to her time, found when he came to her and dashed his forces against the fruit of her virginity as against a rock, *death was shattered to pieces upon her*.[23]

According to Gregory, Mary's son defeated death; and Mary herself, through her virginity, thwarted the devastating cycle of birth and death.[24] Through her virginity, Mary receives the foretaste of immortality. However, all human beings, according to Gregory, have this potential, if they practice the ascetic life.[25] What Gregory had done was give solid theological justification for acknowledging Mary's inherent power to the growing number of groups who were gathering to express their veneration and devotion to Mary. These groups now had a theological *raison d'être*, though it would be some time until they would be liturgically regularized by the Church.

Devotions to Mary

The earliest testimony to cultic activity to the Virgin comes from a fragment of a Greek manuscript that clearly invokes her divine powers of protection. This is the oldest extant prayer addressing Mary and using the term "Theotokos."[26] Giamberardini has translated the text of the fragment:

Under your mercy we take refuge, Theotokos, do not reject our supplications in necessity but deliver us from danger.

The word "deliver" in the Greek is "ῥῦσαι," the same word that occurs in the Lord's Prayer; "ῥῦσαι" is also the word used in the *Akathistos Hymn*, verse 24.

Gregory Nyssa's *Life of Gregory Thaumaturgus* (d. 270) gives evidence that personal devotion to Mary was growing in the third century. The Virgin herself commissioned the elder

Gregory to his lifelong work. The *Life* relates that Mary and John the Apostle appeared to Thaumaturgus one night in a dream. They were much larger than normal human beings. Thaumaturgus did not dare decline her wish. The dream shows that Gregory did know of the apocryphal traditions but chose not to include them in his theological treatises. Although dependent on the Gospel of John, the tradition that John the Beloved Disciple takes Mary to Ephesus and there she lives until her life on earth is finished is fully developed in the later apocryphal stories dating from the fifth century onward.

Gregory Nazianzus also gives evidence of the growing Mary devotion. In Oration 24 he writes that a certain young Thekla, a virgin, was in trouble. She prayed to the Virgin Mary to assist her, and her prayer was answered. Sozomen's account of the defeat of the Arians by Gregory Nazianzus and Theodosius I in the Church of Anastasia also includes a snippet of information about devotions to Mary during the late fourth century. Writing about the sanctity of the church itself he says:

> the power of God was there manifested by dreams, by visions, and by miraculous cures of diverse diseases; these miracles were usually attributed to the instrumentality of Mary the Holy Virgin, the Theotokos.[27]

Egeria gives the earliest testimony (350) to the feast of Hypapante, celebrated in Jerusalem forty days after Epiphany, February 14.[28] The feast commemorated the purification of Mary and the presentation of Christ in the Temple, where, according to Luke, they both met Simeon and Anna. Gregory of Nyssa also has a sermon written for the holiday.[29]

Nyssa's friend, Amphilochius of Iconium (d. 394, Gregory Nazianzus' cousin), wrote a homily specifically for the Hypapante as well. Even though this holiday is based on the New Testament account of the Presentation, it appears that it became an occasion to celebrate three things: Mary's virginity; virginity as a choice for women; and finally the three legitimate states of womanhood, virginity, marriage, and widowhood. Amphilochius' oration lauds Mary's virginity and the wondrous way it bridged the gap between the divine and the human worlds. Mary's perpetual virginity gave the incarnate God immortal flesh. And because of Mary's virginity and its pivotal role in the sacred economy, women (as well as all humanity) have the opportunity to foretaste the sublime sweetness of immortality through virginity. As Amphilochius writes, virginity is the "companion of the higher powers, and is the meeting place with incorporeal nature."[30] Women who choose to live the life of virginity no longer are under the subjugation of the command in Genesis 3: 16, which states that women must bear children in pain and be subject to their husbands. Amphilochius writes that "virginity is an unenslaved possession, a free dwelling-place, an ascetical training ornament, higher than human habits, and a release from the sufferings which occur daily from the mortal human condition."[31] Amphilochius also used the occasion of Hypapante to praise all the proper states of womanhood, extolling marriage and widowhood as well as virginity.[32]

We have already referred to another festival celebrating virginity: the Virginity Festival celebrated in Constantinople in the 420s. Proclus delivered his famous sermon as a response to Nestorius on that occasion in 428.[33] This was the first established commemoration to the Virgin in the capital. Yet from Proclus' unambiguous language, it seems there were two reasons to establish the commemoration (the μνήμη). Women were called by the Theotokos herself to celebrate their release from the sins of Eve. So first the holiday was to allow virgins – and all women – to corporately recognize and enjoy their own happy state which resulted as a consequence of the Theotokos' actions. Second, the commemoration focused on praising the Virgin Mary herself, whose gracious activities "caused all women to be honored."[34]

Although it is not explicitly stated in any source that Pulcheria instituted the Virginity Festival, it is not unlikely that she did so. When Nestorius became bishop, he was annoyed that Pulcheria organized virgins to attend vespers and wakes. Some decades later she requested that weekly vigils take place at two of her magnificent churches built in honor of the Theotokos, on Tuesdays at Hodegetria and on Wednesdays at Chalkoprateia.[35]

What is evident from this brief survey is that for three centuries most of the Fathers held Mary in a place of honor – in various degrees. Their concerns when mentioning her most often had to do with her physical state of virginity during every moment of her life – including pregnancy and birth. This focus not only helped the Fathers battle docetists and other heretics as their situations warranted, it also proved critical in developing the Christological formulations about the divine and human natures at the Councils of Ephesus and Chalcedon. Significantly, though, the Fathers' theological speculations about Mary's virginity did not enter the language of the hymns. When she was praised in liturgical settings the people only heard that she was "virgin" and "ever-virgin.'

The apocryphal stories about Mary augmented both theology and popular devotion. "Proofs" in the form of imaginative tales about Mary's sanctity, virginity, and her power entered the hymns and popular knowledge from the Apocrypha. It is clear that the popular stories about Mary were only slowly accepted by the Fathers, since only Clement of Alexandria and Gregory of Nyssa refer to them. By the fifth century evidence shows that devotions to her were conflated with celebrations of virginity in general, and celebrations of Hypapante.

Cyril of Alexandria and the Theotokos

Cyril of Alexandria's teachings on the Theotokos are among the most influential of the early fifth century. Two characteristics of Cyril's mariology bear noting: his expositions on the Virgin are firmly rooted in Biblical exegesis, and his views on the Theotokos were ultimately determined by the politics of Christology of the period. Cyril became bishop of Alexandria in 412. His uncle, Theophilus, who had preceded him in the office, had schooled him in the Alexandrian antipathy for the Constantinopolitan see. Constantinople's claim to primacy over Alexandria, issued at the Second Ecumenical Council in 381, was spurious and ludicrous to the Alexandrians. Cyril's resentments of the Church in the capital are evident in his role in the deposition of Chrysostom from the Patriarchate in 403.

Cyril saw an opportunity to refute another hierarch of the Church in Constantinople in 428, when news of Nestorius' outrageous attacks on the Theotokos reached Alexandria. "Like John Chrysostom before him, Nestorius was loquacious and tactless."[36] Cyril used the theological controversy over the Theotokos as an excuse to vehemently battle Nestorius as representative of an ecclesiastical see which had no right to dictate to Alexandria on matter of doctrine or policy. Cyril wrote letters to Nestorius in 429 and 430 to correct his theology and to discipline him. The second letter he also sent to Pope Celestine in order to enlist Rome's aid against Nestorius. Celestine was already irked at Nestorius for at least two reasons. The bishop of Constantinople had addressed a letter to the Pope as "fellow-servant," omitting the usual accolades given to the bishop of Rome. And Nestorius had foolishly welcomed Pelagians to communion. Celestine sided with Cyril and eventually appointed him as the papal representative at the upcoming proceedings against Nestorius.[37] The pope also wrote a letter to Nestorius warning him to stop teaching his heresy on pain of excommunication. He had ten days to recant.

In the meantime emperor Theodosius pre-empted Cyril's and Celestine's plans by calling for the Council of Ephesus to take place eight months hence in June 431 in order to settle the dispute. Theodosius supported his bishop, Nestorius. Cyril wrote four more letters in this period before Ephesus. The first one, again addressed to Nestorius, is a theologically sophisticated exposition of the Alexandrian view of the unity of the divine and human natures in Christ. At the end he tacked on twelve incendiary anathemas which were obviously intended to incite the bishop's anger.[38] Of Cyril's other three letters, one was addressed to emperor Theodosius and empress Eudicia and the other two were sent to Pulcheria and her sisters Marina and Arcadia.[39] These letters contain clear theological arguments for Cyril's position on the use of the term "Theotokos." It was his hope that these letters would give Pulcheria more material with which to wheedle her brother.[40] Holum points out that Pulcheria obviously did bother Theodosius, because the emperor later chastised wily Cyril for trying to sow seeds of discontent amongst the imperial family.[41]

At the Council of Ephesus Cyril's supercilious attitude towards the see of Constantinople and his overzealousness for his Christological position provoked emperor Theodosius into deposing and arresting him, although he escaped back to Alexandria a few months later. Theodosius also deposed and exiled Nestorius forever. It would take two more years before bishops and theologians of the Antiochene school would accept the term "Theotokos" and before Cyril's twelve anathemas would be dropped.[42]

Cyril is best known as an architect of Chalcedonian Christology, defending the union of the two natures of Christ against the strict dyophysite view held by Nestorius and the Antiochenes. Cyril's terminology was not so precise as it should have been – he used φύσις and ὑπόστασις interchangeably. In fact his terminology was so unclear that the Monophysites later used Cyril's work as a basis for their beliefs. Yet his thoughts and intentions were clearly discernible, so that the Orthodox position could result at Chalcedon as a consequence.

Clearly Cyril's main preoccupation throughout the battle with Nestorius was Christology. Mariology was a logical result of his Christological position. This is most clearly seen in his theological exposition to Nestorius. Editors have divided this famous letter into nineteen paragraphs.[43] The first seventeen deal with the union of the natures of Christ and with the definition of the word "hypostasis." Finally in paragraph 18 Cyril adds,

> And since the Holy Virgin brought forth as man God united to flesh according to the *hypostasis*, we say that she is the Mother of God, not because the nature of the Word had a beginning of existence from the flesh . . . [but because] he is the creator of all things.[44]

After concluding briefly in paragraph 19 that he is consistent with Church tradition, he tacks on his twelve anathemas.

This is not to say that Cyril was reticent in praising the Virgin, but rather that the central question for Cyril was the Christological definition. His hymns to the Virgin, too, while praising her highly, emphasize above all her catalytic role in the divine economy, which enables Christ to accomplish what was necessary. In Cyril's works Mary as actor is much less emphasized than she is in Proclus'. Cyril wrote two hymns to the Theotokos that are within larger orations.[45] They are both based on the acclamation "Hail" form. It will be useful to compare these hymns and his mariology with those of Proclus.

> Hail, Mary, the revered (σέμνον)
> the treasure chest of the world,
> the inextinguishable lamp,
> the crown of virginity,
> the scepter of orthodoxy
> the indissoluble temple.
> Hail the location for the uncontainable one
> the mother and virgin
> through whom the Trinity sanctifies
> through whom the honored cross is named

and revered in all the world.
through whom heaven delights
through whom the angels and archangels rejoice
through whom demons flee
through whom the devil who tempts fell from heaven . . .

In this hymn there are only two "hails," and the one in the first paragraph goes to the Trinity.

The second hymn is embedded in an elaborate greeting to the city of Ephesus. Cyril "hails" first the city of the Ephesians and then the "thrice-holy John apostle and evangelist," Mary's caretaker in Ephesus, by apocryphal tradition. Amongst his other accomplishments Cyril calls John the "cleaner of the Temple of Artemis."[46] Finally Cyril comes to the hymn to the Virgin. These are excerpted verses from the whole:

Hail to Mary, Theotokos, Virgin Mother,
Lightbearer, unstained vessel.
. . . For conceiving without seed, you gave
birth in a manner meet for a god.
Hail Mary, the temple where God rested,
more than holy, as the prophet David spoke,
crying out, "Your holy temple, marvelous in
    righteousness."[47]
Hail Mary Theotokos, through whom the prophets
cried aloud, through whom the shepherds glorified,
saying with the angels, this fearful hymn,
"glory to God in the highest, and on earth peace and
good will towards men."[48]
. . . Hail Mary, Theotokos, through whom came the true
light our Lord Jesus Christ, who said in the Gospels
"I am the light of the world."[49]
. . . Hail Mary Theotokos, through whom was announced
in the Gospels, "Blessed is he who comes in the name of
the Lord,"[50] And through whom the orthodox church
was founded in cities, villages and on islands,
. . . Hail Mary Theotokos, through whom blossomed
and shined the beauty of the resurrection.

After a cursory reading of Cyril's second hymn, one cannot help but be struck by several observations. There are numerous Biblical quotes – twelve in all. Second, in both of his hymns Cyril changes the acclamation form of "hail" in the imperative "χαῖϱε" to the present optative, second person singular, "may you be hailed" (χαίϱοις). Although grammatically the degree of difference between the imperative and optative in Greek is slight, nevertheless the optative is less direct, it "may express a command or exhortation with a force *nearly akin* to the imperative."[51] Basil of Seleucia, Proclus, Chrysippus of Jerusalem, and the author of the *Akathistos Hymn* do not use this optative form. Only Theodotus of Ancyra (d. 440), who wrote a small "hail" hymn to the Virgin, used the optative form in combination with the imperative, as did Cyril.[52] And like Cyril the majority of his verses begin with the optative. Cyril's first hymn does not even use the imperative.

Finally, Cyril emphasizes Mary's utilitarian role in the praises. He does this by repeating the phrase "through whom' (δι 'ῆς): "through whom heaven delights, through whom angels and archangels rejoice."[53] This "through whom" phrase allows Cyril to reiterate the myriad of ways that her birthgiving was a tool for God's work. Cyril's own use of the prepositional phrase effectively depersonalizes the hymn's focus on Mary and allows it to become a general hymn of praise for the salvation event. In some verses the Virgin is so absent from the text that she is merely an occasion to extol salvation history:

> through whom the only-begotten Son of God, the light, enlightened those sitting in darkness and the shadow of death, through whom the prophets foretold.[54]

In Cyril's hymns we see none of the elements of imperial panegyric that appear in Proclus' hymns or in the *Akathistos*. There are no comparisons of the Virgin with light or astral bodies, nor does the Virgin perform heroic feats through her wisdom and virtue. Most important, in Cyril's hymns the Theotokos does not redefine the Biblical events like mythology, by being assigned an active role herself in salvation history. Above all for Cyril the Virgin is an obedient servant in the Christological event. In Cyril's hymns, the Theotokos is recognizable as Mary in Luke's gospel.

In contrast to Proclus' Theotokos, Cyril's Mary continues the Alexandrian tradition beginning with Origen that Mary expressed doubts and worries about her son's fate on the cross. Her faith was imperfect. In two sermons he develops the themes of her sorrow, doubt, and her inability to believe.[55] By contrast Proclus' Annunciation dialogue between Mary and Gabriel stresses Mary's ability to believe in the angel's words, and Proclus emphasizes her wisdom and learning. She quizzes the angel about the secrets of the universe, which make her seem bold, intellectually curious, and powerful. Her questions do not stem from her stubbornness or her inability to comprehend, but from her desire to become an initiate into cosmic mysteries. She puts the archangel Gabriel on the defensive. The angel in turn has to coax her not to be so curious. Mary explains her persistence.

> Mary: I wanted to have the perfect assurance, so that I can prevail to escape all troubles.
> Gabriel: I came to announce to you the plans from the Creator of all things, not to explain to you the secrets of everything.
> Mary: Since you are a faithful angel of God, certainly you know the powers of God?[56]

Proclus' mariology was created in Pulcheria's court and around the Marian devotions she was helping to make public. It is significant that Proclus was not yet in the ecclesiastical limelight when Cyril was battling Nestorius and Theodosius. Pulcheria and Proclus were creating a local Constantinopolitan cult to the Theotokos based on Pulcheria's own imperial conceptions, perceptions, and projections of who the Theotokos was. All the while Cyril put all of his efforts into defeating Nestorius. Even though Pulcheria and Proclus had the same goal as Cyril – to defeat Nestorius – they never took their energies away from their local efforts to institute the proper veneration of the Theotokos in Constantinople. Pulcheria was fighting Nestorius on personal grounds because he had insulted her imperial dignity.

Proclus' Marian hymns betray the close ties he had with the empress Pulcheria, and the high esteem he held for her, as well as his familiarity with court rituals. The hymns show that he allowed the devices of imperial panegyric to help transform the Theotokos into a powerful imperial entity. Proclus leaves the confines of the original Biblical stories and gives Mary credit for much of the active accomplishments of salvation. When he does use Biblical references, he recontextualizes them into a radical new setting so that their entire significance has meaning only in relation to the Theotokos.

By contrast Cyril's mariology is firmly rooted in the Bible. His praise of Mary is completely within the confines of his lofty Christology. In fact his mariology is a theological exercise in testing the parameters of the *communicatio idiomatum*. His hymns bear no evidence of contact with the ritual of imperial court, or with the forms of imperial panegyric.

Cyril fought Nestorius on Christological grounds, fueled by his rivalry and indignation for the upstart Constantinopolitan see. Above all it was an ecclesiastical fight. We may imagine that if Cyril had been confronted with Pulcheria's idiosyncratic demands as Nestorius had been, he too would have refused to bow to the empress's wishes. Cyril and Nestorius actually represent the same kind of sectarian Christianity, one that remained impervious to the whims of imperial demand.

Pulcheria did not need Cyril's help to accomplish her local goals. But when she received his initial letters, she took his appeal seriously and badgered her brother, Theodosius, on Cyril's behalf. It was to her advantage to have the Alexandrian bishop fighting Nestorius. Yet she never solicited his help. Cyril's ultimate, unattainable goal – the submission of the Constantinopolitan see to Alexandria – would not have been in Pulcheria's interests. But his immediate goal – the deposition of Nestorius – was identical to hers. She needed precisely what she got: the defeat of Nestorius, the bishop who would not obey her, and finally in 434 the installation of Proclus, a bishop who would do her bidding. Pulcheria seems to have known, too, to keep the attention of bishops of other sees away from her local projects. Bishops who would not comply to her innovations – like Nestorius or Cyril – were impediments to her plans to spread the faith in her city.

Cyril realized to his dismay how powerful the imperial court was in ecclesiastical matters. It was Theodosius who called the Council of Ephesus and upstaged the papal proceedings. It was the emperor who chastized Cyril for his epistolary efforts to get Pulcheria to influence his majesty. And finally Cyril was deposed and exiled by Theodosius' command. When he escaped from his exile and went back to Alexandria, he was unsure that he was indeed victorious, even though Nestorius had been exiled.

During the period between Cyril's return to Alexandria and

437 he wrote two letters to the see in Constantinople. Although much of subsequent church history would portray Cyril as a powerful and clever hierarch, crediting him with Nestorius' utter defeat, these letters betray Cyril's weak position with regard to the court and the Church in the capital. In addition they show that in his capacity as teacher of doctrine he was neither well respected by the Constantinopolitan see, nor influential. Finally the letters amply illustrate the clash of sectarian Christianity, represented by Cyril, with the new imperial Christianity, represented by Proclus and the court. These letters prove that the theological ties that had bound Cyril, Proclus, and Pulcheria together against Nestorius were indeed quite weak after the crisis was over. Given this political climate, it becomes obvious why Cyril's mariology did not become predominant after Ephesus.

Cyril's first letter addresses Bishop Maximian, the new bishop of Constantinople who replaced Nestorius in 432. Cyril dictated the communication through the hand of his archdeacon, Epiphanius.[57] The tone of the letter presents Cyril as weak and anxious. He appears to have in fact succumbed to his worst fear – subjugation to the bishop of Constantinople.

It seems that soon after Ephesus Theodosius sent an embassy out to Antioch and Alexandria to ensure that the Antiochene bishops stop supporting Nestorian Christology, and to ensure that the Alexandrians give up Cyril's twelve anathemas, which were quite extreme. Cyril did not appreciate being pressured by imperial legates, and he begged Bishop Maximian, whom he accuses of having abandoned him, to support Cyril rather than the embassy. Then Cyril asks Maximian to "beg lady Pulcheria" to pressure the Antiochene bishops to abandon Nestorianism, to restore monies to the bereft churches in Alexandria, and finally to petition Pulcheria to install Cyril's own choice for prefect![58] The letter also states that Pulcheria was sent a missive as well.

This letter shows that the imperial court was even more firmly directing ecclesiastical policy. Cyril certainly could not have addressed any petitions to Theodosius; he had been chastised by him, then deposed and exiled. He thus pleaded for Pulcheria's help again. When Cyril's desires had coincided with Pulcheria's own, as in the case of Ephesus and events leading up to it, she had used his energies to her advantage; she had pressed Theodosius. Now it appears that she did not need him.

Cyril felt abandoned by the court and Church alike. But the letter also shows Cyril's deep sense of humiliation at having to write to Bishop Maximian. As bishop of Alexandria he was in the wretched position of being coerced by an imperial embassy and having to beg favors from the bishop of Constantinople. Indeed the last words of the letter speak volumes: "Otherwise we are about to be always afflicted."[59] Cyril's pleading secured him no advantages. The next year, 433, the Emperor's embassy obtained agreement between Cyril and the Antiochene bishops. Cyril's anathemas were dropped and the Nestorians accepted the term "Theotokos."

Cyril wrote an extremely interesting letter in 436 to Proclus, who had become the new patriarch two years before.[60] If Proclus responded, there is no extant evidence. The letter is uncharacteristic of Cyril, because he is asking that, in the name of peace and unity, the work and person of Theodore of Mopsuetia not be anthematized.[61] Theodore (d. 428) was an influential theologian in the Antiochen school. His work had greatly influenced Nestorius; but Cyril felt that since Nestorius had been duly exiled, it was unnecessary to condemn Theodore and start a new crisis in the east.

Although Proclus did not respond directly, he had occasion to agree with Cyril in principle. Around the same time an embassy from the Armenian Church came to Constantinople for clarification on certain questions of doctrine. The Church was a little over a century old, and for the past twenty-five years had been in close contact with the Antiochenes. Since the recent trouble over Nestorius and his teachings had made theology from Antioch suspect, the Armenians came to Constantinople. Proclus wrote his famous *Tome to the Armenians* in which he wrote a concise exposition of Orthodox Christology – which did not vary from Cyril's position.[62] But Proclus had always held the same Christological views as the Alexandrian bishop. Proclus did not condemn Theodore of Mopsuetia explicitly, but he corrected his views. The Armenians accepted Proclus' position, and they no longer relied upon Theodore's theology.[63]

This incident illustrates a weak connection between two bishops who had both fought so strongly against Nestorius and for the Theotokos. For those reasons alone one would have imagined much stronger bonds between them. Even though both bishops were instrumental in developing and spreading

Marian doctrine, those doctrines sprang from different sources. Proclus obviously held the same Christological views as Cyril, but they did not necessarily come from Cyril. And certainly his mariology did not derive only from this Christology. Cyril's letter points to a formal, tenuous relationship between the two hierarchs. That Proclus did not condemn Theodore in name does not mean that he obeyed Cyril, it simply indicates that he agreed with him. Cyril remained rather quiet until his death in 444. Probably fortunate for Pulcheria, he died before the Council of Chalcedon.

We see in Cyril's two letters the losing side of the conflict between sectarian and imperial Christianity. Although Cyril fought with Antiochenes theologically, and with Constantinopolitans on ecclesiastical grounds, the churches of Rome, Antioch, and Alexandria all represented basically the same ecclesiastical standpoint with regard to the see of Constantinople. And that ecclesiastical battle against the capital proved to be the tougher fight. As ancient churches preserving time-honored Christian traditions, they were now facing an imperially founded church whose institutions and rituals were marked by influences and traditions of the Roman imperial cult. And that ecclesiastical battle against the capital proved to be the tougher fight. We see the contrast between Alexandria and Constantinople more clearly in the case of Cyril's Marian hymns. For even though they extol the Theotokos in high terms, they show that Cyril is primarily concerned with Christology, and that his praise of the Theotokos is necessarily derivative of that Christology. They also demonstrate that Cyril is more conservative in his poetic models and analogies than is Proclus. Cyril's hymns do not conform to the rules of panegyric, nor do his language and metaphors stray from Biblical prototypes. Given the fact that a hymn most akin to Proclus' – the *Akathistos Hymn* – became the best known Marian hymn in the eastern liturgical cycle, it is difficult to agree that Cyril wrote the "most famous Marian hymn of Antiquity,"[64] and more importantly, that his image of Mary predominated.

Epiphanius and heretical devotions to the Virgin

Bishop Epiphanius of Salamis (d. 404) left a long chatty catalogue of the most worrisome heresies of his day. The work, called the *Panarion*, details eighty heresies in all, along with his refutation of each of them. Three of them concern the Theotokos. Epiphanius' own views on Mary are conservative, hardly saying more than the Biblical texts will allow. Nevertheless, they are for the most part representative of orthodox belief in the fourth century. He upheld her ever-virgin status; while denying her virginity *in partu*, he developed the Eve–Mary parallelism, and he called her "Theotokos."[65]

The first aberrant belief about Mary in the *Panarion* is one concerning her death. In Epiphanius' description the beliefs are presented not so much as a heresy, but as popular misconceptions that he thinks could lead to heretical devotions. He starts off by pointing to Scripture's silence about Mary's fate. His testimony shows that speculations about her death were being expressed cultically.

> They will not find Mary's death; they will not find whether she died or did not die; they will not find whether she was buried or not buried.[66]

In his typical kitchen conversation style, he continues, "I do not dare speak [on the subject] but I keep my own thoughts and I practice silence."[67] Later he sums up the speculations. People thought she died a holy virgin, or she was killed like a martyr, or "she remained alive, since nothing is impossible with God."[68] But the New Testament is silent.

But Epiphanius refuses to state his belief in any of these, and remains purposely uncommitted. What is more important than Epiphanius' opinion about Mary's death is that these speculations were becoming more widespread and were a threat to the Faith in his opinion. By refusing to commit to one of the beliefs about Mary's end, Epiphanius avoided giving episcopal sanction to any of the beliefs, and thus helped slow the process of official doctrinal definition.

The second heresy against Mary was propounded by the Antidicomarianites, the "opponents of Mary."[69] They believed that, after Christ was born, Mary lived in a sexual relationship with her husband Joseph. Epiphanius writes that they wish "to cheapen her reputation and stain people's minds." He goes on to refute the heresy not only on theological grounds, but by the recounting of cozy family lore of Joseph and Mary, as if they were his next door neighbors. He explains who was related to whom, how Joseph's sons by his previous marriage were Nazirites and so obviously revered virginity, and how Joseph, such a very old, God-fearing man, would have respected his new wife's virgin state.[70]

The third Marian heresy catalogued by Epiphanius is by far the most interesting. The group, called the Collyridians, worshipped Mary as a goddess. They were eager to put Mary in place of God.

> They say that certain women from Thrace who live there in Arabia have held this vain doctrine, so that in the name of the ever-Virgin they offer a small loaf, and meet together.[71]

But this is not the worst of their actions. They commit blasphemy beyond all bounds by consecrating a female priesthood to perform their cultic rites.[72] This cultic infraction for Epiphanius is the most heinous, having the devil as its source, and being utterly "alien" to the Holy Spirit.

In the next chapter he gives more details about the Mary worshippers. They originated in northern Scythia as well as in Thrace and spread to Arabia. They held a service which Epiphanius says only occurred once a year, but presumably could have happened more often. The women laid out loaves of bread on a cloth which covered a "square stool." The bread was offered specifically to Mary, and then the women ate it together. The breads were called "kollyris," hence the name of the sect. Epiphanius concludes his rambling refutation of the heresy with a quote from Jeremiah, who had had a very similar problem, trying to convince the women of Judah not to "sacrifice to the queen of heaven."[73] Although Epiphanius does not say the Collyridians used this phrase, one is left to wonder whether the Collyridians called Mary the "queen of heaven."

More to the point, Epiphanius expresses his grave concern that this sect had made Mary into a deity. While he acknowledges Mary's holiness, he is insistent that she is no different in nature from other saints. And, he adds, "Which of the prophets ever bade us worship a man, to say nothing of a woman?"[74] He says that Elijah, who is still alive, is not worshipped, nor is the beloved apostle John, nor Thecla, implying in a subtle way that they are somehow more venerable than Mary.[75] He finishes this line of argument with a very interesting tact; he says that "even if the account and the traditions concerning Mary's state" as it was told to her father Joachim were true, Mary still was born as a result of sexual generation. Hence she could not be divine and worthy of worship.

Epiphanius' passages on the Virgin give a brief glimpse into the burgeoning word of Marian devotion during the late fourth century. Apocryphal speculations about the end of Mary's life on earth were cause for Epiphanius' fears. Presumably the speculations were creating troubles for local priests. Even though Epiphanius would not admit which end to Mary's life he believed in, these apocryphal tales were obviously affecting this conservative bishop. When discussing the Collyridians, Epiphanius again shows influence from the *Protoevangelium of James*, even though he is explicitly leery about its trustworthiness.

The Antidicomarianites and the Collyridians both are evidence for the promient position that Marian beliefs had acquired by Epiphanius' day. They are also witness to the Church's perennial problem of having to define doctrine – in this case Marian – when faced with exuberant expressions of belief the Church deemed "heretical." The Antidicomarianite position displays the necessity to quash the reverence for Mary's ever-virgin state. By making her a human wife and mother after the birth of Christ, they removed the token of her uniqueness. When she was chosen by God, they held, Mary was a virgin and conceived Christ in her virginity. But after the birth, they contended, she joined the ranks of earthly womanhood, and her special divine favor became a past event. This allowed for three things in the Antidicomarianite communities. First, Mary was a real woman and could not be considered in any way divine; thus she was not able to be revered, praised, or worshipped. In the same vein then either the Trinity or one of the members of the Trinity would receive full attention, devotion, and worship from the community, since the danger of Marian devotion would be removed. Finally, the Antidicomarianites' insistence that Mary did not remain a virgin devalues the highly respected state of virginity in Christian society. If Christ's own mother lived as a wife with her husband Joseph and as mother to her other children after Christ's birth, the best model for the virginal/celibate life was gone. If this were the case, it was not a superior way of life to withdraw into askesis. The Antidicomarianite heresy would have been one attempt to curb the growing status and prominence of Marian devotion in the church, and to undermine the trend in society to view virginity and celibacy as a desirable, higher way of life.

The Collyridians on the surface represent the opposite extreme. Because of their women clergy, they appear to be outside the Church, whereas the Antidicomarianites could still have functioned within the ecclesiastical structure – until a bishop would excommunicate them. The Collyridian sect is evidence that in three geographical areas devotion to Mary had reached the height of organized worship.

However, when one considers some of the pertinent details about the Collyridian sect, another possibility about its origins and character comes to light. It is significant that the cult was not confined to one area only. Epiphanius says that it was prominent in Thrace, Scythia, a small area hugging the western shore of the Black Sea, and Arabia, a small slip of inland territory east of Jerusalem, southeast of Damascus, and north of Palestine. The fact that Thrace and Scythia were the locations of strong, long-lived cults to Rhea and Demeter, coupled with the fact that the Collyridians had women clergy and rituals reminiscent of Demeter's cult, lead one to the hypothesis that Mary could have been sycretized onto an original pagan goddess cult. We shall explore this possibility in the next chapter.

Chapter 6

Byzantium's bequest to the Theotokos

Mother Themis and Gaia, she has one form but many names,
not only once did she warn me how the future would come to
pass.

(Aeschylus, *Prometheus Bound*, 211–13)

From 436 onward residents of Constantinople could encounter
many potent religious symbols in the course of a day's errands.
Statues to Rhea, "the mother of the gods" according to Zosimus,[1]
and Tyche sat regally at opposite ends of the Tetrastoön. These
two goddesses, rooted firmly in the foundation legends of
Byzantium, maintained their honor and positions in the public
spaces of Christian Constantinople. Constantine's magnificent
statue atop the porphyry column wore Helios' crown and was
certainly visible from most points of the city. The residents could
pay a visit to at least two churches dedicated to the Theotokos.[2]
Depending on the occasion, according to the festal cycle, the
residents might hear these verses of the *Akathistos Hymn*:

Hail, heavenly ladder, by which God descends.
Hail, bridge, conveying those from earth to heaven.
Hail, defense against invisible foes.
Hail, firm foundation of the faith.
Hail, shelter of the world.
Hail, most excellent abode of him.
Hail, door of the august mystery.
Hail, column of virginity.
Hail, gate of salvation.
You are a wall.
Hail, unshakeable tower of the Church.
Hail impregnable wall.[3]

It is significant that these are architectural images having mostly to do with defense, protection, and shelter. The residents would also hear the following verses that evoke agricultural abundance:

He [God] made a fertile meadow for all those desiring to
    reap salvation.
Hail, O branch of the unwithering vine.
Hail, O possession of fruit untainted.
Hail, O one who cultivates the cultivator, friend of
    humanity.
Hail, O grower to the producer of our life.
Hail, O field blossoming abundant compassion.
Hail, O table, laden with abundant forgiveness.
Hail, for you make the meadow produce contentment.
Hail! the flower of incorruption.
Hail! O tree of delectable fruit, nourishing the faithful.
Hail! O well-shaded tree, under which many find shelter.[4]

These architectural and agricultural images are not specifically Biblical, nor do they coalesce with Patristic ideas of Mary. In fact the metaphors are constructed to ensure that if any images had had Biblical roots, like the "pillar of fire" (verse 11), that connection was no longer easily discernible. Where did these images come from and, more importantly, how did the Constantinopolitans hear them? What associations did the residents make when they heard the Theotokos likened to a wall or a cultivator? The answer lies in the continued presence of the foundation goddesses of Byzantium. Rhea, Tyche, Hecate, Demeter, Persephone, and Athena, all attested cults in Byzantium, provided the cultural substratum that collectively defined and expressed who the Theotokos was and what she provided – outside of ecclesiastical doctrine – for the residents of Constantinople. That the imperial court from Constantine onward supported the continued presence of Rhea and Tyche indeed helped shape the cult of the Theotokos in Constantinople. We shall explore how elements of these traditions about the goddesses survived in the *Akathistos Hymn* and in the hymns of Proclus.

Byzantium's dual goddess tradition

As we saw in the first chapter, one of the legends explaining the origins of the city of Byzantium claimed that the founder Byzas, who came from Thrace, dedicated Rhea as the Tyche of the city.[5] According to this legend Rhea and Tyche are combined into one goddess. In another foundation myth, Byzas' mother, Keroe, becomes the Tyche. Literary testimony supports the first legend, where the two deities Rhea and Tyche are combined. The *Patria* and Dionysus of Byzantium both claim that Rhea was Tyche Poliade, and queen of the city.[6] In either case, Tyche was all important to the foundation of the city.

When Constantine arrived in Byzantium, he would have found Rhea as Tyche Poliade, and another Rhea, "the mother of the gods" with a temple on the coast, along the edge of the Bosphorus.[7] The two goddesses – Tyche and the mother of the gods – are the most important foundational figures in religion for the city of Byzantium. Before Constantine, they were syncretized with Rhea, as was common in Greek religion, yet they remained distinct entities.[8] Thus Tyche was not a mother figure for Byzantium.

Constantine maintained the two-goddess tradition of Byzantium when he built Constantinople. Tyche's continued importance for the city is obvious in Constantine's elaborate dedication ceremonies and in his statuary. The new emperor reinforced the ancient city traditions of the two separate identities of Tyche Poliade and the mother of the gods most splendidly when he housed a statue of each of them – Tyche Constantinopolis and Rhea – in niches in the Tetrastoön. Zosimus relates that Constantine brought the famous statue of Rhea from Cyzicus to set up in the Tetrastoön.[9] Supposedly the Argonauts had long ago brought this statue of the goddess, flanked by two lions, to sit on Mt Didymus, overlooking Cyzicus. Zosimus complains that Constantine changed the statue of Rhea, removing the lions, and changing her hands so that she now looked "as if she were praying, and looking at the city as if she were guarding it."[10]

The mother of the gods and Tyche each were syncretized with other goddesses whose cults were active in Byzantium: Tyche with Athena, Hecate, Demeter/Kore, and finally Isis; and the mother of the gods with Rhea, Demeter/Kore, Athena, Hecate, and Isis. The Byzantines, like all Greeks, cared very little about apparent contradictions, redundancy, and unwieldy layers of successive myths when it came to their deities.[11] However, they did strive to maintain their religious rituals unchanged, because by these rituals their common beliefs and values could be perpetuated.[12] We shall now explore how certain of these beliefs about Tyche and the mother of the gods were taken up into the hymns to the Theotokos.

Tyche

Tyche and the duties of protection

Tyche was most closely connected with the welfare of the city, no matter what city in the Mediterranean honored her. Tyche, Fortuna, as a deification of the abstraction of Luck or Fortune, was neither good nor evil,[13] although from the time of Thucydides ἀγαθή Τύχῃ was in common usage and meant "in the god's name."[14] Aristophanes uses "ἀγαθή Τύχῃ" and "τυχηρῶς" interchangeably.[15] Generally speaking, in fifth-century Athens, whether one was awarded favorable Tyche or not depended on the benevolence of the gods.[16] In the Hellenistic period Tyche became more of a goddess herself. Stobaeus and Menander describe her as "all-powerful," "wise," and one who "guides" and "preserves."[17]

The growth in the popularity of Tyche is evident from the widespread practice of dedicating cities (new and old) to her in the Hellenistic and Roman period. Coins from Attaea, Tarsus, Smyrna, Ephesus, and Nicea show Tyche Poleos.[18] The precedent for this of course was in Athens, where Athena was the Tyche of the city. Yet she was never confused with ἀγαθή Τύχῃ, who received sacrifices in her own temples. The Tyche of a city and ἀγαθή Τύχῃ were not one and the same. Although the temple to Tyche in Athens is not mentioned by Pausanias, the cult to her was begun there and in Thebes in the fourth century BCE. Praxiteles made a statue of her;[19] and there is epigraphical evidence of it in Lycurgus' law on sacrifices.[20] Pausanias does mention temples to Tyche in Elis, Sicyon, Megara, and Tegea.

Tyche was honored in fact by temples, mosaics, statues, a priesthood, and sacrifices.[21] Each locale had its own customs and ways of celebrating her feast, but the holiday usually occurred right before spring planting, begun in February and March.[22] Tyche represented the city's own institutions, laws, and political uniqueness, and they became emblems of city identity in which people could take great pride.[23] Yet Tyche was a supernatural entity which blessed the town and even acted as a mediator with other gods. And not insignificantly Tyche could be a harbinger of evil. Tyche, when she appears standing on a globe, heralds evil, but it is always favorable when she appears sitting or lying down. The richer her clothes are and the prettier she is, the better the things are which one can expect from her.[24]

Tyche not only protected and guided the destinies of these cities, she personified them. Even though this personification of the polis was not new to the Greeks, the novelty lay in the consistent, widespread popularity of using Tyche – wearing a muraled crown – to protect and identify their cities in the Roman period.[25] Each city's fame, fortune, and special bond with the divine was ultimately connected with its Tyche. Libanius, a proud Antiochene, held lofty opinions of his city, which he thought was particularly beloved by the famous Tyche of the Orontes.[26]

Tyche Constantinopolis

Constantine's Tyche was crafted to *resemble* – not duplicate – Flora, the Fortuna of Rome, just as his city was the "second Rome." As any other Tyche Poleos, she had to personify the city; thus Tyche Constantinopolis had to embody the newness and uniqueness of Constantine's capital. Philostorgius, Malalas, and the author of the *Chronicon Paschale* recount that Constantine dedicated his city to Tyche Anthousa, modeled on "Flora," the Dea Roma.[27] From the time of Constantine, Tyche as Constantinopolis was represented less on coins than on commemorative silver, gold, and bronze medallions.[28] There is a confusing heaping up of symbolism in these representations: she sometimes has Victory's wings, sometimes is helmeted like Roma, is enthroned or standing, or has her typical identifying characteristics: her foot rests on a prow (or rudder), she wears a turreted crown on her head, and she holds a cornucopia and a branch in her arms.[29] Yet the bronze medallions struck in order to honor Rome and Constantinople independently show that the symbolism of Roma and Tyche was not completely conflated.[30]

In the founding legends Tyche was also connected to Athena, who as Athena Poleos was ultimately associated with the protection of the city. Athena had had a cult in Byzantium for some time. As Athena ἐκβασία she watched over the ships as they came through the Bosphorus.[31] We must remember that the *Chronicon Paschale* introduced the legend that Constantine brought the Palladium from Rome to his new captial.[32] The Palladium, whatever object it may have been, was a "highly specialized talisman," usually believed to be sent by the gods.[33] According to this legend the Palladium became Tyche Constantinopolis, effectively merging Athena and Tyche. This legend would have strengthened the separation between Rhea and Tyche, mother and protector respectively, and would have imbued Tyche with great war-like protective characteristics.

This legend about Athena seems to have provoked some jealousy amongst intellectual pagans. Zosimus' bitterness about Christianity's position in the empire comes out in the most surprising places. Even though he does not mention Constantinople's possession of the Palladium, he credits Athena's protection against Alaric as the reason Athens remained unscathed in 396. He describes the marauding Huns heading southward to Athens from Thessaly:

> But this ancient city won some divine protection for itself despite contemporary impiety, and thus escaped destruction. . . . When Alaric and his whole army came to the city, he saw the tutelary goddess Athena walking about the wall, looking like a statue, armed and ready to resist attack.[34]

Zosimus adds that he hoped that relating this story would "excite piety in all who hear it."[35] For Zosimus Athens obviously is in competition with Constantinople, which for him represents the ancient city's antithesis. Was there any goddess on the walls protecting Constantinople?

If any goddess had connection to the walls in Constantinople, it was Hecate.[36] Hecate had a cult in Byzantium from the time of its founding. Like Byzas in one legend, she had her origins in Thrace.[37] Since Hecate was guardian of "liminal places,"[38] in Byzantium small temples in her honor were placed close to the gates of the city. Hecate's importance to Byzantium was above all as deity of protection. When Philip of Macedon was about to attack the city, according to the legend she alerted the townspeople with her ever-present torches, and with her pack of dogs, which served as her constant companions. Her mythic qualities thenceforth forever entered the fabric of Byzantine history. A statue known as the "Lampadephoros" was erected on the hill above the Bosphorus to commemorate Hecate's defensive aid.[39] Her epithet "φωσφόρος" – lightbearer – named the straits of the Bosphorus, slightly corrupting her name.[40] Hecate was also worshipped in a temple in the area that would become the Hippodrome. Instead of being destroyed, the temple was absorbed into the construction of the Hippodrome, so that the memory of the cult "was perpetuated."[41]

The Theotokos and Tyche's duties

In the *Akathistos Hymn*'s section on defense, we find language evoking war and protection, walls, bulwarks, and towers. The themes are closely allied with the images and functions of Tyche. Perhaps the Greek artists took a Homeric metaphor too literally when they crafted the image of Tyche, which for over a millennium fused the connection between protection, Tyche, walls, and towers. Homer called the wall of Troy "the sacred diadems of the city."[42] Not only did walls look like a crown surrounding a city from a distance, they obviously protected inhabitants and were very important to any city's welfare. There are very few references to *specific* duties and characteristics of Tyche, but one of them is in Pausanias:[43]

> The poems of Pindar later contained references to Fortune (Tyche), and it is he who called her Supporter of the City.

Unlike Tyche, the Theotokos was not depicted wearing a turreted crown, although she was clearly identified with the walls and towers of the city. Her relationship to the walls can only be explained by a "civilization unembarrassed by its belief in the immanence of the metaphysical in the realm of the mundane."[44] She was allied with this wall imagery, however, as these hymns, prayers, and histories from the Theodosian period onward show. Since Mary was a historical person, it would not be easy to depict her in plastic imagery with Tyche's attributes. Tyche was the allegorical personification of a city. The Virgin Mary could assume the images, however, in function. Tyche's statue may have remained in the city until the ninth century, but her duties were given gradually by the populace to the Theotokos. The Theotokos assumed more of the Tyche's duties as she was increasingly – and literally – politicized.

Tyche's ancient political function of protecting and personifying the city, making it unique above all others, was assumed by the Theotokos, though it would take four centuries for the process to be complete. From the time that empress Pulcheria built the churches of the Blachernae, Hodegetria, and Chalkoprateia, to house the Virgin's shroud, icon, and cincture, respectively, her presence was in the city. She did not *personify* the city like Tyche could, she *dwelt* in the city. For the inhabitants of Constantinople, in a very literal fashion the Theotokos took on all the practical duties Tyche had provided. Yet instead of wearing the walls of the city as her crown, she became a wall and diadem. The architectural imagery of the *Akathistos Hymn* calling the Theotokos a wall, a column, a ladder, a diadem, a door, a gate, a bridge, resonates with vestiges of Tyche. These metaphors identify the Theotokos with the best a city has to offer the world as proof of its greatness and endurance: its constructions, be they temples, walls, towers, places, houses, administrative buildings, city squares, public markets, hippodromes, theatres, churches, baths, or water works. The Theotokos was identified with the physical beauty, power, and uniqueness of the polis which Tyche had only allegorized on propagandistic coins. The imagery is potent to the author and the auditor; as an "architectural support" and "refuge" she offered tangible strong protection to the faithful. And with this in mind, to be called "diadem," "tower," and "wall" in the twenty-third verse are the most powerful images of all. This language is civic and public, consistent with Pulcheria's program of integrating the Theotokos into the civic religious ceremony of Constantinople, and making her an object of public cult. This was possible because Tyche was detached from a specific myth which would have bound her to a fixed role,[45] yet the Tyche tradition was as old as Byzantium itself.

None of this means that the *Akathistos Hymn* pits Tyche and the Theotokos in direct competition, though by the seventh century they are vying for the same position. Rather the author takes some of the most potent symbols from the context of civic protection, under the aegis of Tyche, and conflates them with the identity of the Theotokos. In the *Akathistos Hymn* the

Theotokos is not yet a protector of the city, she is a powerful entity accomplishing mythic deeds on a cosmological level.

The Theotokos protects like Tyche, but the manner in which she does this is like Athena and Hecate. She is a warrior, defeating spiritual enemies of all sorts. With martial attributes the Theotokos of the *Akathistos Hymn* revises Biblical history so that there is no doubt it truly is she who is the cause of victory in every situation. The Theotokos of the hymn is a strong warrior and an invincible bulwark – for the cause of salvation. In the *Akathistos Hymn* the Theotokos is called variations on Hecate's "lightbearer" and "torchbearer" epithets. She is the "illuminator" (φωτίζουσα), "torch" (λαμπάδα), and "one shining out" (ἐκλαμπούσα).[46] Proclus' hymn is even more akin, calling her "torchbearer" (λαμπαδήφορε) and "inextinguishable light brighter than the sun" (ἄσβετον φῶς λαμπρότερον τοῦ ἡλίου).[47]

The enemies and victories attributed to the Theotokos are still spiritual, not yet physical. Although it would take several centuries before the Theotokos became the savvy general who hurls spears at barbarian enemies, Pulcheria's efforts at establishing the devotion to the Theotokos as a public cult on the model of civic religion brought the spiritual concerns of the Church outside into the public realm. Tyche's qualities for the Virgin were still, in the fifth century, new metaphors to explain Christian spiritual hopes.

Finally by the seventh century the Theotokos becomes the protector of Constantinople and the competitor of Tyche Constantinopolis.[48] It is then, in 626, that Patriarch Sergius writes a new prooimion for the *Akathistos Hymn* to rally the citizens under the protection of their general, the Theotokos, to ward off the Avar attack. All the while Tyche remains an important presence in Constantinople and will continue thus for centuries. Codinus (*c.*850) even thought that Constantine wanted to "Christianize" Tyche, so he put a cross on her (the statue's) head, which "saved" her only until Julian's reign.[49] Tyche's statue was set up on the western side of the forum.[50] Codinus also says that up until "our time" the happiness of the city depended on the honor the townspeople paid to her.[51] He explains this by giving two examples of tensions during the ninth century. Emperor Michael Rhangabe (d. 813) had to quell a popular "magic" belief by cutting off Tyche's hands, and fifty years later Bardas destroyed the statue altogether, and made her "disappear."[52] Zonaras writes that during the reign of Anastasius I (491–518) Tyche took vengeance on the City by sending a famine because the rudder she stood on had deteriorated. After her restoration, conditions returned to normal.[53] Despite Tyche's lasting physical presence, by this late date her protective duties had been assumed by the Theotokos. Indeed as J. B. Bury comments, by this time the residents of the city treated the Virgin's robe in Blachernae as a "Palladium to protect their city."[54]

Tyche as agricultural provider

Second to Tyche's protective duties was her association with agricultural abundance, and wealth. This is most obvious from her iconic representations where she holds a cornucopia and stands on a rudder.[55] In this respect she was syncretized early on in the Mediterranean with Demeter and Kore (Persephone's other name), and the ever-popular Isis. Demeter and Kore were really two inseparable goddesses honored in Byzantium with a temple on the Golden Horn, along the coast of the Bosphorus.[56] This beautiful location was also dotted with temples to other gods, including the foreign latecomers, Isis and Serapis, although their cults apparently did not include the mysteries.[57]

Demeter was above all known as the goddess of cultivation, abundance, and of good harvests. Connected to this is her epithet "thesmorphoros," "law-giving goddess of civilized life." Her most pervasive appellation is "karpophoros," "bearer of fruits." Like Tyche and Isis she was known as the "many-named" goddess, and the goddess who controlled abundance and prosperity.[58] And Kore, the intensely beloved daughter of Demeter, according to the *Orphic Hymn* appears every spring "in the growing shoots."[59]

In the Hellenistic period Tyche, Isis, and Demeter were syncretized pervasively in the Mediterranean. Evidence of this is clear in statues, prayers, and inscriptions.[60] The text in the *Oxyrynchus Papyrus* calls Isis "Tyche at Busiris."[61] The three deities shared their agrarian characteristics, depending on the customs of the specific community. In the Isis aretalogy she is the one who delivers fruits.[62] In an inscription from the Roman period Isis is called "karpophoros"; and a line from a prayer invoking Isis reads, "I find nature in full bloom of all fruits."[63]

There are more texts to Demeter and Kore than to Tyche and Isis, whose evidence is most often in inscriptions. Therefore for purposes of comparison and example, we shall refer only to Demeter and Kore. In the *Orphic Hymn* to Demeter she is called:

> giver of prosperity and wealth. You nourish the ears of corn, O giver of all, and you delight in peace and toiling labor. Present at sowing, reaping, and threshing O spirit of the unripe fruit, you dwell in the sacred valley of Eleusis. . . . Through you there is growth and blooming.[64]

Once we realize the pervasiveness of the agricultural attributions to these goddesses, some of the agrarian vocabulary used for the Theotokos in the *Akathistos Hymn* takes on a wider meaning from the context of Greco-Roman religion. Generations of people's expectations, hopes, fears, and ritual customs are embedded in the vocabulary used in the worship of the goddesses like invisible genetic codes of the culture. When the old vocabulary and images began to be used for the Theotokos, the complex spirals of meaning in the language were not suddenly erased. In fact just the opposite happened. The old language and images enriched the identity of the Theotokos, making her familiar and powerful through a flood of associations.

In verse 13 the Virgin is praised as the "tree of splendid fruit [ἀγλαόκαρπον] nourishing [τρέφονται] the faithful." In the *Orphic Hymn* to Demeter she is extolled: "Through you there is growth and blooming O illustrious companion [ἀγλαότιμος] of Bromios."[65] And in the *Homeric Hymn* to Demeter when bemoaning Kore's fate at her abduction the author writes,

> Away from her mother and of the golden sword and the splendid fruit [ἀγλαόκαρπον].[66]

And more comparisons bear examination. In verse 13 of the *Akathistos* we read of the Theotokos: "Hail, flower of incorruption." For Demeter the auditors heard this laud: "Come blessed and pure one, and laden with the fruits of summer."[67] In addition Kore is called "the one appearing in green shoots" (βλαστοῖς), and the Theotokos is the "sprouting one" (βλαστάσουσα and βλαστήσας).[68] Proclus as well uses the word βλαστάσασσα.[69]

The following verses use the same concepts, but not the same words:

> You were first to send up from below a rich and lovely
> harvest for mortals. [For Demeter][70]
> Hail, for you make the meadow produce contentment.
> [For the Theotokos][71]
> Hearken, O blessed goddess, and send forth the earth's
> fruits. [For Kore].[72]

With these examples we see that the Theotokos has been released from the confines of exclusive Biblical language and metaphors, and has entered the Olympian pantheon by cultural association through the use of language that is heavy with a long history of connection with Mediterranean goddess veneration. As part of the process of making the Theotokos an object of public cult, the author of the *Akathistos* and Proclus experimented with new language and images for the Virgin that conjured up the traditional identities of Tyche, Demeter and Kore, and Isis, goddesses who were part of the fabric of Byzantium and invested in its welfare.

Yet the hymns to the Theotokos assume these new metaphors only up to a certain point. Traditionally Tyche, Demeter and Kore, and Isis were invoked in order to bestow fertile fields, seasonable weather, plentiful harvests, and good health. By contrast, agricultural abundance becomes a metaphor for the Theotokos in salvation history. In the Theotokos hymns, the Virgin Mary is not prayed to *for* these gifts, she is praised *as* these gifts. Yet these images do not create the picture of a passive inanimate object, quite the contrary. This language, representing the arduous physical labor of an agrarian worker and fruits thereof, depicts the Theotokos as the cultivator, tiller, producer, field, and product of salvation. The author juxtaposes the cyclical, concrete, physical realities of cultivated nature with the divine gift of salvation. The Theotokos is the nexus between them. She is also likened to the cultivator of nature, and the fruit of her labors is salvation for humanity.

Paraleipomena *from the Theotokos hymns, Isis, and Athena*

Two themes appear in the Theotokos hymns that do not fit neatly into the categories of mother of the gods or Tyche.

Rather, they evoke prominent characteristics of Isis, Athena, or both. They bear mentioning.

The first one is the loom image. In his Virginity Festival panegyric, Proclus lauds the Theotokos as the "awe-inspiring loom of the *oikoumene*," on which the "robe of unity" was woven.[73] In the χαιρετισμοί he calls Mary the "weaver of the crown not braided by hands."[74] In the Isis aretalogy Isis is known as the "inventor of weaving," and one of Athena's many duties was watching over the loom.[75] Again as in the cases of similarities to other goddesses that we have reviewed, the Theotokos actually becomes the image, in this case the loom.

The second image is fleeting, only one line in verse 21 in the *Akathistos*. "Hail, that you spring forth the multi-streamed river." It is an inexplicable image without any context unless one remembers how extremely important the waterways were to Isis and the Egyptians. The Isis aretalogy claims that she is "guardian and guide, mistress of mouths of seas and rivers, watching over the Nile and regulating the flooding season of all the rivers of the earth."[76]

Isis is also "mistress of navigators," and at Heracleum "mistress of the sea."[77] Athena's temple in Byzantium, as mentioned before, looked over the Bosphorus to watch over sailors and ships. There she was called Athena "ἐκβασία," guardian of disembarkation. In other parts of the Greek world Athena had been associated with rivers and waterways.[78] In the *Orphic Hymn* to the mother of the gods she is "swayer of rivers and the sea." Verse 17 of the *Akathistos* calls Mary "a ship carrying all those who seek salvation, and a haven for all life's seafarers." Again the author's method is consistent. The Theotokos becomes the image and accomplishes the divine duty in the spiritual realm. We shall now turn to the images and identities the Theotokos assumes from the other goddess of Byzantium, Rhea, the mother of the gods.

The mother of the gods

Worship of the Great Mother, Magna Mater, whether under the name of Kotys, Cybele, or Rhea, spread to Thrace from Asia Minor.[79] From the fifth century BCE onwards the appellations "Mother of the gods," "great Mother," "Rhea," and "Cybele," were used indistinguishably in literature to denote one divine personality.[80] Traditionally Rhea had no cult, but wherever her identity merged with that of the great Mother's, as it did in Thrace, Byzantium, Cyzicus, and Pessinus, it would have been associated with the cult's famous frenzied rituals and ecstatic music.[81]

No matter which legend about the founding of Byzantium is true, that Rhea was vital to the city from its beginnings is unquestionable. Her longevity in Byzantium is remarkable.[82] Several connections with the mother of the gods and Thrace keep cropping up, in chronicles and histories, with significant ramifications. Thrace's strong devotion to Rhea was syncretized to the Mother of the gods cult from Phrygia quite early.[83] In Thrace Hecate, soon to be a significant goddess to the Byzantines, was syncretized to the mother of the gods.[84] The legend that Thracians founded Byzantium and remained tied to the city persisted well into the Christian era. It does not appear coincidental that in the fourth century CE the Collyridians, who worshipped Mary as a goddess, should have originated in Thrace. If indeed Byzantium traced its roots to Thrace, not only the cult of Rhea was brought to the new city, but also Thrace's fervor for ardent devotion to the mother of the gods. This is even further evidence that the cult of the Theotokos in Constantinople was as much Byzantine as it was Christian.

When Pulcheria turned the churches into public politicized spaces for the cause of the Theotokos, Constantinopolitans already had a long-lived cultural context – yet visible in the Tetrastoön – for venerating Rhea, the mother of the gods. They could call upon well-established verbal images to praise the Mother of God; they could invoke their inherited ways of knowing who she was and what they could expect of her. Whether the Pulcheria's new object of veneration was called "Mother of the gods" or "Mother of God," she was praised with language that for centuries and been honed, tempered, and weighted heavily with the meaning and ritual expression of a religious culture based firmly on ancestral tradition rather than on belief. There was ample room and indeed precedent in the cultural inheritance of Byzantium to accommodate a new deity – or object of veneration. But there was little or no chance to transform or revolutionize the mental categories and linguistic restrictions of the populace programmed by generations of use. And certainly a change in the meaning of language used to praise a deity could not take place in only twenty-five years (425–450). After all, it took much longer than one century to change syncretistic religious habits. We remember Theodosius II had to decree in a law that by attending church services "due reverence is paid to the Emperor when God is worshipped."[85] As we have seen, the elements of civic religion had been hardly curtailed, in contrast to pagan cult. Through Pulcheria's efforts the Theotokos was now – as it were – literally politicized, turned out into the public forum and into the consciousness of everyday Constantinopolitans. They readily accepted the Theotokos, transferring language, concepts, and expectations onto her from their rich tradition of Thracian ardor for Rhea, the mother of the gods.

What appears in the *Akathistos Hymn* and in Proclus' hymns to the Theotokos shows that a cultural transfer was taking place. Some of Byzantium's most enduring religious attitudes and traditions about the goddesses became the bequest to the Theotokos, as manifested in the language and images of these hymns. They are otherwise inexplicable by Biblical or even apocryphal hermeneutics.

We have explored the images in the hymns connected with Tyche Constantinopolis. Now we turn to the images associated with Rhea, and to those goddesses syncretized with her: Demeter and Kore, Hecate, Isis, and, in certain cases, Athena. It is important to remember that Isis was syncretized with Rhea in the Isis aretalogy, claiming "I am the eldest daughter of Kronos."[86] Demeter and Rhea were identified in Thrace; the *Orphic Hymn* mentions their mutual identity.[87] Hecate was connected with Cybele in Thrace, although in Byzantium Cybele's identification with both Rhea and Hecate did not merge the two. They remained distinct. The themes associated with these goddesses pertinent to our investigation are motherhood, nurturer, and savior.

Steps to motherhood

In the Theotokos hymns Mary's most frequent title is "virgin." There is constant play on the paradox of her virgin motherhood, her status as "bride, unwedded." Indeed, that theme is from Luke's text, and it was fully amplified in Christian apocryphal texts. Yet when we probe the traditions about the goddess most hallowed in Byzantium we find that this theme is not exclusive to Mary.

Athena is the virgin mother of Erechtheus. According to the myth Hephestos chased Athena in lust. Though he was ultimately thwarted, his semen fell on Athena's thigh. When she wiped it off onto the ground, the boy Erechtheus began to grow from it, nourished by Earth. But it was Athena who raised him in her temple and who was known as his mother.[88] Demeter bore Plouton by Iasion, but regained her virginity. Before she was abducted, Kore was a virgin. Hecate was also called "parthenos," though it was not insisted upon.[89] Neither Rhea nor Isis were known as virgins, although the latter was called "unstained" (ἀμίαντος) in Pontus.[90]

The concept of virginity in Greek religion had "nothing to do with ethics, but was a mystical power that enabled supernatural events connected with fertility to take place."[91] Verse 17 of the *Akathistos* describes Mary's childbearing in these terms of mystical power, crediting her childbearing to her power which confounded the wisest human beings, "for they are at a loss to explain how you gave birth yet abide a virgin." Proclus does not develop the theme so much, but calls Mary an "unstained bearer" (ἀμίαντε τόκε), retaining the relationship between the two concepts.[92] The necessity of having virginity and maternity together to result in fertility – a prominent concept in Greek religion – is a clear theme in the *Akathistos* and in the hymns of Proclus.[93]

Maidenhood is woven into the theme of virgin motherhood. Persephone's name is also "maiden," "Kore." Demeter is called "maiden," as are Hecate and Rhea.[94] It is in this context that Proclus' rather antiquated phrase for the Theotokos is better understood; he calls her the "virgin maiden, inexperienced in marriage, mother not born in the natural way" (παρθένε, κόρη ἀπειρόγαμε, ἀλόχευτος μήτηρ).[95] Each of these words exhibits a conscious choice on the part of Proclus to associate the Theotokos with the long tradition of powerful virgin mothers, especially the rare word "ἀλόχευτος" referring to Athena's own extraordinary birth.

Bridal images and wedding rituals are the next step in the process to motherhood. Hecate and Kore were both known as "νύμφη," "bride." Isis was the "divine bride."[96] Nuptual language features strongly in the *Akathistos* and in Proclus' hymns. In the former she is "bride unwedded" twelve times. In verse 19 she is greeted:

Hail, O bridal chamber [παόστας]) of unsown wedlock.
Hail, O bridal escort of saintly souls.

In Proclus we find this bridal imagery:

She is the bridal chamber [παόστας] in which the Logos wedded all flesh.[97]

Again we see the intense overidentification of the symbolism. The Theotokos is a "bridal chamber." She is not only an escort. Both hymns use the technical term "παόστας." It is entirely possible that residents of Constantinople had seen or knew of the "pastas," the shrine of a bridal chamber, that was used in the Mother of the gods cult to carry the goddess in procession.[98] It is likely that residents would have known about the "pastas," not only because Rhea continued to be important in the city, but because from its origins the cult of the mother of the gods was a proselytizing one.[99]

Divine motherhood

In the *Orphic Hymns* Rhea is called "mother of the gods," and "mother of Zeus"; Demeter is "divine mother of all," and Persephone the "mother of Eubouleus."[100] Isis, the many-named goddess, carried epithets of "great divine mother," "divine mother," and "mother of the gods."[101] What character-izes motherhood for these divine entities most of all is life-giving in a myriad of ways: from the mundane giving of food to the ability to make all things alive – or dead. Inextricably connected to divine motherhood are the concepts of nurturance, food, and growing physical life. The *Orphic Hymn* to the mother of the gods states it best:

Divine are your honors, O mother of the gods and nurturer of all. . . . For in the cosmos yours is the throne in the middle because the earth is yours and you give gentle nourishment to mortals.[102]

All the divine mothers have these two seemingly disparate qualities: they are due high honors in the cosmic realm because of their mighty powers; yet they take the time and care to aid lowly mortals who are stymied by their need for daily food. The divine mothers are able to see to the needs of both realms, the mortal and the immortal. It is their capacity for care for the mortal world that earned them the adage, "kourotrophos," literally "nurturer of youths," or "nursing mother." Hence these titles. The mother of the gods is the "nurturer of life," Kore, "maiden rich in fruits," she shows up in the spring "in shoots and green fruits," and she "always nourishes all – and kills them, too."[103] Demeter is hailed as "kourotrophos," and

> You nourish the ears, of corn, O giver of all, . . . Charming and lovely, you give sustenance to all mortals, . . . Through you there is growth and blooming, . . . From beneath the earth you appear and to all are gentle, O holy and youthnurturing [maid], lover of children and of fair offspring.[104]

Isis too was "affectionate and provided abundantly,"[105] "gentle," and a "giver."[106] Hecate was not a mother, but "kourotrophos" was one of her best-known names, as she took care of orphan children.[107]

The *Akathistos Hymn* has fifteen lines that praise the Theotokos as a kourotrophos. She is called "mother" three times. In the first place the hymn makes explicit that she has that divine quality of fertility, so familiar to the Greeks, that resulted from the powerful combining of virginity and motherhood.[108] "Hail to you, who has woven maidenhood into motherhood."[109] Some of the verses liken her to blossoming fields and connect her to abundance of food.[110] Some are more profound: "Hail to you, through whom creation is remade."[111] And Mary regenerates those conceived in shame.[112] We find in verse 11:

> Hail, O nourishment [τροφή], succeeding the manna,
> Hail, O servant of hallowed feasting,
> Hail to you from whom flows milk and honey.

The mother of the gods was called "τροφή" in the *Orphic Hymn* to her. Clearly there are Biblical references in these lines, yet when they are taken with the lines in verse 13, the kourotrophos image returns full force.

> Hail, O tree of spectacular fruit, nourishing the faithful.
> Hail, O well-shaded tree, under which many find shelter.
> Hail, O robe for those bare of courage,

Hail, O affection conquering all desires.
Hail, beautiful nursing-mother of virgins.
Hail, O life of mystical feasting.[113]

"Affection" (στοργή) is the same name used for Isis; "nursing-mother" is the term translating "kourotrophos," the well-known name for Hecate, Isis, and Demeter. The "kourotrophos" adage made Mary a nurturer of all people, not just her own son. Again, consistent with the author's theology, the hymn applies the maximum meaning to the adjective and Mary *becomes* the "nourishment," and the "affection," rather than only bestowing these earthly gifts. Nevertheless, it is difficult to believe that the images of "kourotrophos" and literal use of the word were unconsciously employed by the author, not intending any connections with goddesses whose presence was well attested in the life and history of Constantinople.

Soteira

The last aspect of divine motherhood is salvation and its attendant means thereto: initiation into divine knowledge. Demeter, Isis, and Hecate are the goddesses most closely allied with cults of initiation that brought them devoté(es) into the mysteries of divine knowledge. Although Hecate had no mystery cult of her own, she was credited in one of the myths with retrieving Kore from the underworld. From that point on she and her torches remained Kore's constant companions and accompanied her yearly on her journey to Hades.[114] For as the goddess who "pointed out the way" on the road, Hecate thoroughly protected her and guided her.[115] Because Hecate bridged the chasm between the divine world and the human world, her reputation as a protective guide for human beings as they proceeded in life from one transition to another was universally acknowledged. In fact, "Hecate continued to provide passage between the worlds of men and gods or between otherwise detached spheres, such as the Sensible and Intelligible Realms."[116] The *Akathistos Hymn* effectively evokes the image of the Theotokos as wise mystagogue for those seeking salvation.

Hail, O initiate of the ineffable will.
Hail, O knowledge, superseding the wise.
Hail to you, who enlightens the minds of believers.

Hail to you, who enlightens the initiates of the Trinity.
Hail, O guide of moderation for the faithful.
Hail to you, who extricates us from the depths of ignorance.
Hail to you, who illuminates many in knowledge.
Hail, for you gave guidance to the thoughtless.[117]

The Theotokos is a guide like Hecate. She is an initiate herself
into divine knowledge, as well as one who leads initiates into the
depths. She is like Isis in the aretalogy, who "pointed out the
mysteries to humanity," and who is a "guardian and guide."[118]
Where the Theotokos leads those willing to come is to the place,
or state, of salvation. She redeemed and rescued people,
uplifted humanity, and through her efforts hope for eternal
blessings is possible.[119]

Even more outstanding, however, are the Theotokos' abilities
to save. She is a "leader of spiritual remaking."[120] She is the
"healing of the body," the "salvation of the soul"; and she is
invoked to "deliver and save" those who call upon her.[121]

In the *Orphic Hymns* we note that Rhea is "redeemer" (λυτη-
ριάς); and twice she is called a "savior" just as Hecate and the
mother of the gods are named.[122] The Theotokos is not called
"savior" (σώτειρα) but she is called "salvation" (σοτηρία). Her
supplicants beseech her to "release" (λύτρωσαι) them from future
punishment.[123] As mother of the gods Rhea can send "death to
the ends of the earth"; and Kore in her hymn is "alone life and
death" to mortals.[124] Isis is the bestower of immortality, and is
the savior of all humanity.[125] The Theotokos is "hope of eternal
blessings."[126]

The *Akathistos Hymn* represents the Theotokos as a divine
entity like the mother of the gods. She has assumed – through
language common for goddess veneration – the ability to release
and save people. In the hymn she has appropriated the language of mystery cults in her cosmic recapitualation of creation
and redemption. Her experience of the annunciation, conception, and birth of the incarnate Logos became the ineffable
mystery of which she was the ultimate mystagogue.

Even after Mary's rise as the Theotokos, Rhea, the mother of
the gods, remained an undaunted presence in the capital and
elsewhere. That the customs and rituals of Rhea worship continued to be the prototype for veneration of female deities for
the people is apparent from the eighth-century testimony of

John of Damascus. He was painfully aware that some people were either syncretizing the Theotokos as the mother of the gods, or, as is more likely, were worshipping the Theotokos with the same *rituals and language* as they had employed for the worship of the mother of the gods. He explicitly warns his audience that the Virgin Mother of God is not a goddess, and most certainly she should not be worshipped with the frenzied music of the mother of the gods' rites. In fact she should not be worshipped at all – only venerated.[127]

Examining the fantastic descriptions of Mary in the most popular and influential hymns to the Theotokos as part of the cultural context of the old city of Byzantium enables the reader to understand two processes facilitating the rise of the cult of the Virgin in Constantinople. First, the authors were using language that evoked powerful associations with the age-old Byzantine goddesses, Tyche and Rhea, as well as Hecate, Athena, Demeter/ Kore, and Isis. The goddesses' duties of protection, defense, nurturance, and well-being were foisted upon the Theotokos by means of language that had been used to describe, praise, and beseech them. The Theotokos assumed a new array of powers, duties, and abilities that before had been provided to the residents by the old Byzantine deities.

Second, since the Theotokos was bequeathed these powerful attributions, she could emerge in the arena of public veneration. She became part of the fabric of city life, as she was gradually recognized as the supernatural entity who could fulfill essential public needs. Pulcheria's frequent public liturgies to the Theotokos and her magnificent churches built for the Virgin strongly reinforced this process for the residents. Yet careful auditors of the Theotokos hymns could have discerned that the power ascribed to the Theotokos was still on the spiritual level. In the hymns the Theotokos accomplished duties she had assumed from the goddesses to those seeking salvation. But most listeners of the hymn, crowded into hot, noisy churches or pushed and shoved in public squares, would not have had the luxury of extended quiet needed to listen to and ponder the full meaning of the metaphors in the hymns. At most the people would have heard the noun: "hail defense, hail destroyer, hail torch, hail kourotrophos, hail redeemer." Quiet and order were not part of Mediterranean piety; quite the opposite, correct fulfillment of ritual behavior was paramount for fulfilling one's obligation to the deities. By means of the public festivals to the Theotokos in her grand new churches, residents of Constantinople were instructed to venerate a supernatural being who could provide for the city much as the goddesses had. And in this context the object of Constantinopolitan devotion to the Theotokos could not be arguably different from the last line of the *Orphic Hymn* to the mother of the gods: "Joyously and graciously visit our deeds of piety."[128]

Conclusion

This study has attempted to explain the rise of the cult of the Theotokos in Constantinople by means of the hermeneutical presupposition that religion is fundamentally an expression of culture. The identity of the Virgin and her meaning for society has a historical context, it is culturally embedded, and most of all it is shaped by local traditions. We saw in the first three chapters that Constantine indeed did something new: he made Christianity his religion and eventually the official religion of the Roman Empire. But the only means he had of doing this was through his own modes of cultural expression which set the precedent for future generations of Christian Roman emperors. Constantine continued in his capacity as Roman emperor to act as *pontifex maximus*, dictating on matters of religious importance for the empire. He reshaped – yet retained – the rituals of the imperial cult in elaborate civic ceremonies in the Hippodrome. And he reinforced the civic religious heritage of Byzantium by ensconcing statues of the two goddesses most important to the old city of Byzantium, Tyche Constantinopolis and Rhea, in the Tetrastoön. The Theodosian dynasty acted on Constantine's precedents, elaborating laws against pagan cult, while detailing the ways their imperial personages were to be respected and venerated in the great public spaces of Constantinople. All the while residents of the city were schooled in the proper veneration of imperial images, and were accustomed to the emperor – especially Theodosius I – taking the helm in matters of religious importance during a political crisis.

Understandably, this imperial mold for Christianity in the capital was difficult for the bishops to accept. Christianity was a new faith for Byzantium, and the city's position as an important see of the empire was spurious by the traditions of the Church. It was an imperial see, not an apostolic one. But the hierarchs had little choice but to accommodate themselves to the situation. We have seen the varieties of ways they did this.

Conservative bishops like Eusebius and John Chrysostom chose the most extreme ways. Eusebius, a learned intellectual, used his pen as the weapon to fight the embarrassing errors of his hero, emperor Constantine. By means of rewriting some of the history of Constantine's acceptance of Christianity, he hoped to correct Constantine's blunders for future generations of emperors. He recontextualized Constantine's intrusions into ecclesiastical disputes. The emperor's rights to mandate on religious matters of the state had no place or precedent in Christian sectarian culture. Eusebius simply ignored Constantinople and the continuation of the imperial cult there. By recasting the peace of the Church as part of Biblical history, Eusebius perpetuated his own religious culture – sectarian Christianity – very effectively. Eusebius was able to blend his own elation about Christianity's new status in the empire with his trepidation and chagrin about the retention of the imperial *potestas* in religious matters. His writings about Constantine would continue to convince ecclesiarchs, but obviously they fell short of changing the wider religious culture of Constantinople.

The case of Chrysostom's opposition to imperial Christianity is much less subtle than Eusebius'. His virulent temper, sharp tongue, and extremely conservative vision of Christianity made him utterly unable to subordinate his episcopal dignity to the imperial court, as was expected of him. Several times he clashed with the court over civic rituals that allowed the public to venerate the imperial household.

By the time Nestorius became bishop of Constantinople, the court had had a succession of compliant bishops. Although Theodosius II supported Nestorius, his fight with the most pious member of the imperial family, Pulcheria, cost him his career and almost his life. Significantly their differences were over issues of Pulcheria's *imperial privilege* in matters religious (her receiving communion in the altar), her imperial *dictum* on the use of the title 'Theotokos,' and the manifestations of veneration for Pulcheria's imperial personage (her image above the altar). There is no doubt that the historical particularities of the Nestorian controversy brought the cult of the Theotokos to the foregound of Constantinopolitan civic religion. Pulcheria was ardently Christian, but she was equally steeped in the Roman imperial traditions of the court which had instilled in her the cultural modes of religious expression: as empress she and her image were to be venerated in panegyric and ritual behavior. She could dictate on religious matters. And finally she could turn the churches into spaces of public civic ceremonies, on the model of the Hippodrome, in order to properly venerate the Theotokos, on whom she had patterned her life.

The hierarchy of Constantinople had been watching the rituals of imperial cult in the capital for decades. They had heard the panegyrics to the emperors and empresses on anniversaries and other occasions. When the Nestorian crisis precipitated the need to settle the theological dispute at the Council of Ephesus, it also brought the Theotokos out into the public domain in Constantinople. Pulcheria demanded that the Theotokos be publicly praised in a befitting manner, on the order of an imperial panegyric, which the residents of the city were quite used to hearing. It is not surprising then that Proclus' hymns to the Theotokos are akin to his praises of Pulcheria, displaying nearly all the requirements of imperial panegyric. The most influential hymn to the Theotokos, the *Akathistos*, shows that the author experimented with the literary devices of imperial panegyric in order to properly venerate the new object of civic cult, the Theotokos. Some of the vocabulary and images are identical to Menander's panegyrics used to teach rhetors how to laud an emperor. The metaphors and devices common to panegyric made the Theotokos recognizable to the vast majority of Constantinopolitans, who were used to hearing and participating in the panegyrics as part of the elaborate ceremonies honoring the emperor.

Until the late fourth century the hierarchs and theologians of the Church had written about Mary in order to further define and clarify who Jesus Christ was, as both man and God. On the whole Patristic speculations about her revolve around her virginity during every phase of her life, her obedience as the new Eve to God, and her role in the Incarnation. These arguments effectively countered the heresies of Docetism and many varieties of Gnosticism.

Apocryphal literature, however, shows that Marian devotion was developing right alongside cautious Patristic expositions.

These popular stories, especially the *Protoevangelium of James*, made the Virgin the focus of devotion by elaborating on her life before and after the birth of Christ. What is most interesting is that very few Patristic authors allowed the apocryphal tales to influence their doctrinal writing until late in the fourth century. Marian piety, however, was spreading in spite of the Church during this period. Epiphanius was most concerned with the heretical attention and importance Mary was getting. According to him the most troublesome group was the Collyridians, who worshipped Mary with a female priesthood.

It is significant that influence from apocryphal stories about Mary does not show up in the Marian hymns of Proclus or the *Akathistos*. Their language and metaphors come from imperial panegyric and the indigenous Byzantine goddess traditions. It may sound scandalous to some that the Theotokos as depicted in these most influential hymns is represented in metaphors resounding with traditions of Tyche and Rhea. Yet without this explanation, theologians are confounded and embarrassed by the hyperbolic language which is usually saved for the Trinity. And certainly the metaphors and language are not Biblical. Thus it makes credible, *historical* sense that the city of Constantinople should produce such an identity for the Theotokos, bequeathing these divine aspects to her character for the following reasons.

First, Constantinople had no strong sectarian Christian tradition. Christianity was new to the city, and it was introduced at the behest of the emperor. Second, the civic ceremonies of the imperial cult were an integral part of life in the city, breaking up the monotony of everyday existence. The Church was witness and participator in the ceremonies, gradually experimenting with the ritual forms of public veneration and incorporating the rhetorical form of imperial panegyric into its hymns to the Theotokos. Finally, Tyche Constantinopolis and Rhea, the Mother of the gods, were deeply ingrained in the religious cultural fabric of Byzantium. Moreover, their statues were honored by Constantine himself. Hecate, Athena, Demeter and Persephone, and Isis had also had strong presences in the pre-Christian city. Consistent with syncretizing cultures, duties and functions of these goddesses were merged long before into Tyche's functions for the city, protecting and providing abundance and wealth; and into Rhea's as nurturer, mystagogue, and savior. In Constantine's statues, these syncretized goddesses and their effective presences were affirmed along with visible Tyche and Rhea. When one examines the metaphors and language of the *Akathistos* and Proclus' hymns in the context of the traditions and hymns about these goddesses, the secret cultural code embedded in the language is broken, and for a moment a world long passed away is conjured up; and the grand civic stature of the Theotokos comes to life. Like bright colored shards in the kaleidoscope, the functions of the goddesses, the imperial identity taken from the court, and the humble maiden of Luke's gospel recombined themselves into a uniquely Constantino-politan creation, the Theotokos.

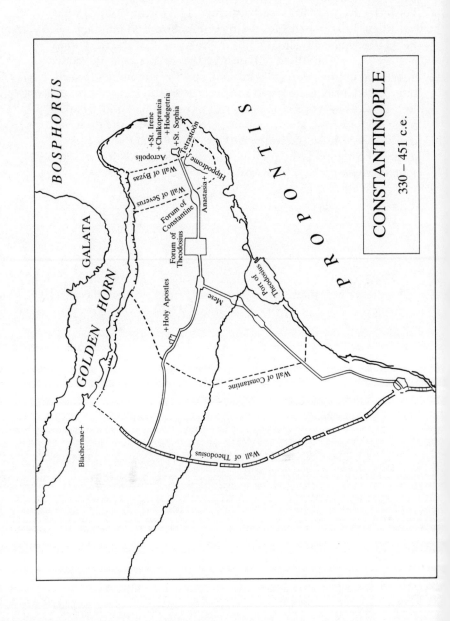

BOSPHORUS

GALATA

GOLDEN HORN

Blachernae+

+Holy Apostles

Acropolis

+St. Irene
+Chalkoprateia
+Hodegetria
+St. Sophia

Wall of Byzas

Tetrastoon

Wall of Severus

Hippodrome

Forum of
Constantine

Anastasia+

Forum of
Theodosius

Mese

Port of
Theodosius

Wall of Constantine

Wall of Theodosius

PROPONTIS

CONSTANTINOPLE

330 – 451 c.e.

Appendix

The *Akathistos Hymn*

Prooimion I

Having secretly received the command,
  the Archangel hastened unto Joseph's abode
  and spoke to the holy virgin.
He who bowed the heavens with his descending,
  is wholly contained, yet unchanged in you.
And seeing him taking the likeness of a servant in
  Your womb,
I stand in amazement and cry unto you: "Hail! O
  bride unwedded."

Prooimion II (added *circa* 626 CE)

Unto you, O Theotokos, invincible champion,
Your city, in thanksgiving ascribes the victory for the
  deliverance from sufferings.
And having your might unassailable,
  free me from all dangers, so that I may cry
  unto you: "Hail! O bride unwedded."

1

The archangel was sent from heaven to say "Hail" to the Theokotos. And with his celestial voice, envisioning you O Lord embodied, he was wonder-rapt and stood crying unto her:

Hail! to you through whom joy shall shine forth.
Hail! to you through whom the curse will vanish.

Hail! The recalling of the fallen Adam.
Hail! The redemption of Eve's tears.

Hail! O height beyond human logic.
Hail! O depth invisible even to the eyes of angels.

Hail! For you are the king's throne.
Hail! That you bear him, who bears the universe.

Hail! O star revealing the sun.
Hail! O womb of divine incarnation.

Hail! To you through whom creation is re-made.
Hail! To you through whom the creator is born a babe.

Hail! O bride unwedded.

2

Beholding herself in purity, the holy one courageously said to Gabriel: "Your strange voice seems almost unbelievable to my soul; for how do you speak of birth-giving without seed? crying:

"Alleluia."

3

Yearning to know the incomprehensible knowledge, the Virgin cried to the ministrant: "How may a son be born from a virginal womb? tell me." To her he answered in fear, yet crying thus:

Hail! O initiate of the ineffable will.
Hail! O faith of those praying in silence

Hail! To you the preface of Christ's miracles.
Hail! To you the heading of his commandments.

Hail! O heavenly ladder, by which God descended.
Hail! O bridge, conveying those from earth to heaven.

Hail! O miracle, much marveled of angels.
Hail! O trauma, much dirged of demons.

Hail! To you, who ineffably bore the Light.
Hail! To you, who revealed the Mystery to none.

Hail! O knowledge, superseding the wise.
Hail! To you, who enlightens the minds of believers.

Hail! O bride unwedded.

4

Power from the most high then overshadowed the Virgin unto
conceiving; and her fruitful womb, he made a fertile meadow
for all those desiring to reap salvation, as they sing thus:

"Alleluia."

5

Having a God-receiving womb, the Virgin hastened to Elizabeth.
Her unborn son forthwith recognizing Mary's greeting rejoiced,
and with stirrings, as though with songs, cried unto Theotokos:

Hail! O branch of the unwithering vine.
Hail! O possession of fruit untainted.

Hail! O the one who cultivates the cultivator, friend of
humanity.
Hail! O grower of the producer of our life

Hail! O field blossoming abundant compassion.
Hail! O table, laden with abundant forgiveness.

Hail! for you make the meadow produce contentment.
Hail! for you prepare a haven for souls.

Hail! O incense, acceptable for intercession.
Hail! To you who are the whole world's expiation.

Hail! O favor of God for mortals.
Hail! O boldness unto God on behalf of all mortals.

Hail! O bride unwedded.

6

The righteous Joseph having doubtful thoughts seeing you, O
pure one, and suspecting a hidden wedlock, was troubled; but
when he learned of your conception by the Holy Spirit, he
said:

"Alleluia."

7

The shepherds heard the angels extolling the presence of Christ in the flesh; and rushing as if to a shepherd, they behold Him as a spotless lamb, pastured in the womb of Mary, while praising him they said:

Hail! O mother of the lamb and shepherd.
Hail! O penfold of rational sheep.

Hail! O defense against invisible foes.
Hail! To you, who opened the gates of paradise.

Hail! for the heavenly rejoice with the earth.
Hail! for the earthly dance with the heavens.

Hail! O unsilenced mouth of the apostles.
Hail! O invincible courage of the martyrs.

Hail! O firm foundation of the faith.
Hail! O resplendent token of grace.

Hail! to you, through whom Hades was despoiled.
Hail! To you, through whom we are vested in glory.

Hail! O bride unwedded.

8

The Magi having seen the star leading to God, followed its radiance, and holding on to it as to a lantern, they found through it a mighty king; and having reached the unreachable they rejoiced and cried unto Him:

"Alleluia."

9

The sons of Chaldeans saw in the arms of the Virgin, the one whose hands had fashioned men; and sensing him as Lord, even though He had taken the form of a servant, they hastened to render homage with gifts, and exclaimed to the blessed one:

Hail! O mother of the unsetting star.
Hail! O dawn of the mystical day.

Hail! to you, who has quenched the furnace of error.
Hail! to you, who enlightens the initiates of the Trinity.

Hail! to you, who has removed the inhuman tyrant from
    his rule.
Hail! to you, who has shown Christ as the loving Lord.

Hail! to you, who has redeemed us from the pagan religion.
Hail! to you, who has rescued us from the mire of transgression.

Hail! to you, who ceased the worship of fire.
Hail! to you, who destroys the flames of passions.

Hail! O guide of moderation for the faithful.
Hail! O delight of all generations.

Hail! O bride unwedded.

10

Having become God-bearing heralds, the Magi returned to
Babylon. Executing your instructions, and having preached You
as the Christ to all, they left Herod raving, knowing not to chant:

"Alleluia."

11

Having shed the light of truth in Egypt, You expelled the
darkness of untruth; for her idols O Saviour, enduring not Your
power, toppled; and those who were freed from them cried unto
the Theotokos:

Hail! to you, who uplifted humanity.
Hail! to you, who are the downfall of demons.

Hail! to you, who treads over the error of deceit.
Hail! to you, who refuted the fraud of idols!

Hail! O sea, which drowned the symbolic Pharaoh.
Hail! O rock, refreshing those who thirst for life.

Hail! O pillar of fire, guiding those in darkness.
Hail! O shelter of the world, broader than a cloud.

Hail! O nourishment, succeeding the manna.
Hail! O servant of hallowed feasting.

Hail! to you, who are the land of promise.
Hail! to you, from whom flows milk and honey.

Hail! O bride unwedded.

12

Unto Symeon, prepared to leave this deceptive age, you were presented as an infant; but you made yourself known unto him as perfect God; wherefore he marveled at Your ineffable wisdom chanting:

"Alleluia."

13

The Creator, revealed in a new creation when He presented Himself unto us, who were made by Him; blossomed from a seedless womb, He kept her as she was, pure, so that we, seeing the miracle, may praise her saying:

Hail! the flower of incorruption.
Hail! the crown of self-restraint.

Hail! O shining token of resurrection.
Hail! to you, Who reflects the life of angels.

Hail! O tree of splendid fruit, nourishing the faithful.
Hail! O well-shaded tree, under which many find shelter.

Hail! to you who bears the guide for those who go astray.
Hail! to you, who gives birth to the redeemer of captives.
Hail! O intercessor to the righteous judge.
Hail! O forgiveness of many transgressions.
Hail! O robe for those, bare of courage.
Hail! O affection conquering all desires.

Hail! O bride unwedded.

14

Having seen the strange birth, let us estrange ourselves from the world, lifting our minds to heaven. For this reason the most-high God appeared on earth, as a humble man, wishing to draw on high, those who call out to him:

"Alleluia."

15

Wholly present on earth, yet never absent from Heaven was He, the uncircumscribed Logos. For Divine condescension, and not a mere change of location had occurred in his birth from the God-selected Virgin, who hears these praises:

Hail! O land of the infinite God.
Hail! O door of the august mystery.

Hail! O sound of doubt for the faithless.
Hail! O undoubtful pride of the faithful.

Hail! O most holy chariot of him, who is above the Cherubim.

Hail! O most excellent abode of him, who is above the Seraphim.
Hail, to you, who conducts the opposites to unity.
Hail! to you, who has woven maidenhood into motherhood.
Hail! to you, through whom transgression was loosed.
Hail! to you, through whom paradise was opened.

Hail! O key of Christ's kingdom.
Hail! O hope of eternal blessings.

Hail! O bride unwedded.

16

All the orders of angels marveled at the great work of Your incarnation; for they saw God-inaccessible, as man, to all access-ible, dwelling with us, and hearing from all:

"Alleluia."

17

O Theotokos, we see most eloquent orators mute as fish before you; for they are at a loss to explain, how you gave birth and yet abide a virgin; but we, marveling at the mystery, faithfully cry unto You:

Hail! O vessel of God's wisdom.
Hail! O treasury of his providence.
Hail! to you, who proves the wise to be unwise.
Hail! to you, who proves the sophists as foolish.

Hail! that the dreaded debaters were rendered fools.
Hail! that the inventors of myths have waned.

Hail! to you, who broke the word-webs of the Athenians.
Hail! to you, who fills the nets of the fishermen.

Hail! to you, who extricates us from the depths of ignorance.
Hail! to you who illuminates many in knowledge.

Hail! O ship carrying all who seek salvation.
Hail! O haven of all life's seafarers.

Hail! O bride unwedded.

18

When the adorner of all wished to save the world, He came unto it by himself; and being shepherd as God, he appeared for us as man; for appearing the same as we are, He called us unto himself, and as God he hears:

"Alleluia."

19

O Theotokos Virgin, you are a wall protecting all virgins, and all who hasten unto you. For the maker of heaven and earth has made you such, O pure one, having entered Your womb and taught all to call unto You:

Hail! O column of virginity.
Hail! O gate of salvation.

Hail! O leader of spiritual re-making.
Hail! O supplier of divine beneficence.

Hail! for you have regenerated those who were conceived
  in shame.
Hail! for you gave guidance to the thoughtless.

Hail! to you, who abolishes the corruptor of minds.
Hail! to you, who gave birth to the sower of purity.

Hail! O bridal chamber of unsown wedlock.
Hail! to you, who brings the faithful to the Lord.

Hail! O beautiful nursing-mother of virgins.
Hail! O bridal-escort of saintly souls.

Hail! O bride unwedded.

20

Every hymn falls short in describing the multitude of your
manifold mercies; for if we were to praise you with hymns, equal
in number to the sands of the sea, we would do nothing compar-
able to what you, O holy king, have done for us, who cry unto
You:

"Alleluia."

21

As a light-bearing torch, shining upon those in darkness we
behold the holy virgin; for enkindling the celestial light, she
guides everyone to divine knowledge, and by her radiance
illuminating the mind, may she be honoured loudly as follows:

Hail! O ray of the mystical sun.
Hail! O flash of the unsetting light.

Hail! O lightning, illuminating the souls.
Hail! that you astound as thunder your foes.

Hail! that you shed the light of great brilliancy.
Hail! that you spring forth the multi-streamed river.

Hail! to you, who depicts the sign of the font of Siloam.
Hail! to you, who did remove the stain of sin.

Hail! O shower, cleansing the conscience.
Hail! O vessel, brimming with rejoicing.

Hail! O fragrance of Christ's sweetness.

Hail! O life of mystical feasting.

Hail! O bride unwedded.

22

Wanting to grant grace for all ancient debts, the redeemer of mankind came of his own, to those, alien to the realm of his grace; and tearing up the writ of indebtedness, he hears from all:

"Alleluia."

23

Praising your Son, we all praise you, O Theotokos, as a living temple; for dwelling in your womb, the Lord, who holds the universe in his hand, sanctified and glorified you and taught all to cry unto you:

Hail! O tabernacle of God the Logos.

Hail! O saint, greater than all saints.

Hail! O ark, gilded by the Holy Spirit.

Hail! O inexhaustible treasure of life.

Hail! O precious diadem of devout kings.

Hail! O venerable boast of pious priests.

Hail! O unshakable tower of the Church.

Hail! O impregnable wall of the kingdom.

Hail! to you, through whom trophies of victory are assured.

Hail! to you, through whom enemies are vanquished.

Hail! to you, who are the healing of my body.

Hail! to you, who are the salvation of my soul.

Hail! O bride unwedded.

24

O Holy Mother, worthy of all praise, who brought forth the Logos, the holiest of all saints, accept this present offering, and deliver all from every distress, and release from the future punishment those, who cry with you:

"Alleluia."

Notes

Preface

1 Walter Burkert, *Greek Religion*, John Raffan (trans.), Cambridge, MA, Harvard University Press, 1985, p. 322.
2 G. E. M. de Ste Croix, "Why Were the Early Christians Persecuted?" *Studies in Ancient Society*, M. I. Finley (ed.), London, Routledge & Kegan Paul, 1974, p. 238.
3 Helmut Koester, *Introduction to the New Testament*, 2 vols, *History, Culture, and Religion of the Hellenistic Age*, vol. 1, Philadelphia, Fortress Press, 1983, p. 364. When the cult of Dionysus came to Rome in 186 BCE, the government severely curtailed its activities. It took a century for the government to allow the Isis cult in the city limits. Caligula (*c.*40 CE) lifted the prohibitions.
4 Koester, op. cit., pp. 365, 396; Ste Croix, op. cit., p. 217; Josephus, *Wars*, H. St J. Thackeray (trans.), *LCL*, 3 vols, London, William Heinemann, 1925, vol. 2, 10.4.
5 Robert L. Wilken, *The Christians as the Romans Saw Them*, New Haven, Yale University Press, 1984, p. 67.
6 Ste Croix, op. cit., p. 228.

1 Greco-Roman civic religion versus "The Kingdom of God on Earth"

1 Eusebius, *Life of Constantine* 27–31; Socrates, *Eccl. Hist.* 1.2; Sozomen, *Eccl. Hist.* 1.3–5.
2 H. W. G. Liebeschuetz, *Continuity and Change in Roman Religion*, Oxford, Clarendon Press, 1989, p. 278.
3 Eusebius, *Life of Constantine* 28.
4 Liebeschuetz, op. cit., p. 279; and Timothy D. Barnes, *Constantine and Eusebius*, Cambridge, MA, Harvard University Press, 1981, p. 43.
5 J. Rufus Fears, "Ruler Worship," in Michael Grant and Rachel Kitzinger (eds), *Civilization of the Ancient Mediterranean*, 3 vols, New York, Charles Scribner's Sons, 1988, vol. 2, p. 1018.
6 See Ramsay Macmullen, *Paganism in the Roman Empire*, New Haven,

Yale University Press, 1981, pp. 90–4; and Philostratus, *Life of Apollonius of Tyana*, F. C. Conybeare (trans.), *LCL*, London, William Heinemann, 1912. In this *vita*, Philostratus (*c.*215) evokes the religious atmosphere of the third century. Apollonius was a religious reformer who encouraged a life dedicated to morality and discipline. He abhorred animal sacrifice, superstitious rites, and all forms of religious emotionalism. For descriptions of use of augury by the Tetrarchs see Lactantius, *On the Death of the Persecutors*, *ANF*, vol. 7, 12.14.

7   Liebeschuetz, op. cit., p. 281.
8   ibid., pp. 285–6; Macmullen, op. cit., p. 93; W. H. C. Frend, *The Rise of Christianity*, Philadelphia, Fortress Press, 1984, pp. 274–5.
9   Eusebius, *Eccl. Hist.* 10.6.1; 10.7.20: "For when they render supreme service to the Deity, it seems they confer incalculable benefit on the affairs of the state."
10 Theodoret, *Eccl. Hist.* 1.11.
11 Johannes A. Straub, "Constantine as ΚΟΙΝΟΣ ΕΠΙΣΚΟΠΟΣ," *DOP*, 1967, vol. 21, p. 147; and Barnes, op. cit., p. 245.
12 Barnes, ibid., p. 208.
13 Judith Herrin, *The Formation of Christendom*, Princeton, Princeton University Press, 1987, p. 24. After 312 Constantine dissolved the praetorian guard.
14 Zosimus, *New History*, Ronald T. Ridley (trans.), Canberra, Australian Association for Byzantine Studies, 1982, 2.29; and Gilbert Dagron, *Naissance d'une capitale*, Paris, Presses universitaires de France, 1974, p. 21. Dagron believes that the personal religious scruples of Constantine are not the reason he chose to leave Rome.
15 Sozomen, *Eccl. Hist.* 2.3.
16 ibid.
17 For Thrace, Dio Cassius, *Roman History*, Earnest Cary (trans.), *LCL*, 9 vols, London, William Heinemann, 1927, vol. 9, 74.6–8; John Malalas, *Chronographia*, Elizabeth Jeffreys, Michael Jeffreys, and Roger Scott (trans.), Melbourne, Australian Association for Byzantine Studies, 1986, 13.7; Pliny, *Natural History*, H. Rackham (trans.), *LCL*, 10 vols, London, William Heinemann, 1942, vol. 2, 4.46; Ausonius, *Order of Famous Cities*, Hugh G. Evelyn White (trans.), *LCL*, 2 vols, London, William Heinemann, 1919, vol. 1, 13; see also Gibert Dagron"s discussion of the later (eighth–tenth centuries CE) patriographer"s obsession with the foundation legend in *Constantinople imaginaire*, Paris, Presses universitaires de France, 1984, p. 78. These authors, he says, write stilted accounts, since they are unable to deal with let alone "propose a concrete representation of a transfer from Rome to the east." Nevertheless, they preserve the founding legend.
18 Lydus, *De magistriibus populi Romani*, Richard Wünsch (ed.), Stuttgart, Teubner, 1967, 30.70.
19 "Byzantium," *Dictionary of Greek and Roman Geography*, London, John Murray, 1872, p. 657.
20 John Malalas, *Chronographia* 13.7.

21 Polybius, *Histories*, W. R. Paton (trans.), *LCL*, 6 vols, London, William Heinemann, 1922, vol. 2, 4.45–53.
22 ibid., 4.38.
23 ibid.
24 ibid., 4.38.3–6.
25 ibid., 4.38.10.
26 Dio Cassius, *Roman History* 75.13.
27 ibid., 75.14.
28 J. B. Bury, *History of the Later Roman Empire From the Death of Theodosius I to the Death of Justinian*, 2 vols, New York, Dover Publications, 1958, vol. 1, p. 75.
29 Dagron, *Naissance*, p. 17.
30 ibid., as he cites *Hist. aug.*, "Caracalla," 1.7.
31 ibid., p. 372.
32 Frend, op. cit., p. 212.
33 Dagron, *Naissance*, p. 372.
34 ibid.
35 ibid.
36 Frend, op. cit., p. 212.
37 See the *Acts of the Scillitan Martyrs*, the *Martydom of Perpetua and Felicitas*, in H. Mursurillo (ed.), *The Acts of the Christian Martyrs*, Oxford, Clarendon Press, 1972, pp. 86–9, 106–31, and Origen"s account of his father's execution in Eusebius, *Eccl. Hist.* 6.2.
38 Polybius, *Histories* 4.38.
39 Pliny, *Letter to Trajan*, in Agnes Cunningham (ed.), *The Early Church and State*, Philadelphia, Fortress Press, 1982, pp. 27–9.
40 Frend, op. cit., p. 284.
41 Eusebius, *Eccl. Hist.*, for Jerusalem, 3.35, 5.12; Rome, 3.2, 4.1, 4, 10, 19; Antioch, 3.22, 4.20; Alexandria, 3.21, 4.1, 10, 19.
42 Socrates, *Eccl. Hist.* 1.37.
43 Theodoret, *Eccl. Hist.* 3.
44 Sozomen, *Eccl. Hist.* 29.
45 *Chronicon Paschale* 10, Michael Whitby and Mary Whitby (trans.), Liverpool, Liverpool University Press, 1989. The translators state that "Metrophanes is unlikely to have been the first bishop," and give the references to Francis Dvornik"s book, *The Idea of Apostolicity in Constantinople and the Legend of the Apostle Andrew*, Cambridge, Harvard University Press, 1958, pp. 156–8. Yet in these pages Dvornik gives irrefutable evidence against there having been a bishop before Metrophanes. He shows in painstaking detail that the legend of the Apostle Andrew was unknown in Constantinople until the seventh century, and in fact would have been counter-productive to Constantine"s plans for the church. See also Straub"s article, "Constantine as ΚΟΙΝΟΣ ΕΠΙΣΚΟΠΟΣ," pp. 38–55; and also Dvornik, pp. 20–98.
46 Zosimus, *New History* 2.29–30.
47 "λυσιτελεῖν" is a purely political word, "to gain or profit by."
48 Libanius, *Pro templis*, in *Orationes*, R. Foerster (ed.), 12 vols, Hildesheim, Georg Olm Verlag, 1963, vol. 3, 30.6.

49 Zosimus, *New History* 2.31.
50 Hesychios, *Patria* 15, Theodore Preger (ed.), New York, Arno Press, 1975, p. 6.
51 Dagron, *Naissance*, p. 369.
52 ibid., as he cites Hesychios, *Patria* 11.
53 ibid., p. 30, as he quotes Dionysus of Byzantium, *Anaplus Bospori*, Rudolf Güngerich (ed.), Berlin, Weidmann, 1958, pp. 8, 13, 14; and the *Patria* 7.
54 ibid., see p. 370, ff. 9, Inscriptions, *R E* 3, coll. 1147.
55 John Malalas, *Chronographia* 13.13.
56 Richard Krautheimer, *Three Christian Capitals*, Berkeley, University of California Press, 1983, p. 55.
57 ibid.
58 ibid.
59 John Malalas, *Chronographia* 13.7.
60 See the ekphristic poem on the statues in the baths of Zeuxippos by Christodorus (491–518 CE), in *Anthologia Graeca*, Hermann Beckby (ed.), 4 vols, Munich, Ernst Heimeran Verlag, 1965, vol. 2.
61 Zosimus, *New History* 2.31.
62 Philostorgius, *Historia ecclesiastica*, *Die Griechischen Christlichen Schriftsteller*, 39 vols, Leipzig, Hinrich''s Buchhandlung, 1913, vol, 2, 1.2.17. "οὗτος ὁ θεομάχος καὶ τὴν Κωνσταντίνου εἰκόνα, τὴν ἐπὶ τοῦ πορφυροῦ κιόνος ἱσταμένην, θυσίαις τε ἱλάσκεσθαι καὶ λυχνοκαίαις θυμιάμασι τιμᾶν, καὶ εὐχὰς προσάγει ὡς θεῷ καὶ ἀποτροπαίους ἱκετηρίας τῶν δεινῶν ἐπιτελεῖν τοὺς Χριστιανοὺς κατηγορεῖ."
63 A. Frowlow, "La dédicace de Constantinople dans la tradition byzantine," *Revue de Science Religieuse*, 1944, vol. 127, pp. 75–8.
64 John Malalas, *Chronographia* 3.20–21; *Chronicon Paschale* 528; Zonaras, *Annales*, in *Epitome Historiarum*, 5 vols, L. Dindorf (ed.) Leipzig, Teubner, 1868–74, vol. 3, 13.3, 25–31.
65 Socrates, *Eccl. Hist.* 1.16.
66 The Palladium is Pallas Athena, sent by Zeus to Troy. Roman tradition claimed that the Palladium was rescued from the fires of Troy by Aeneus and taken to Italy. It was then ceremoniously placed in the *penus Vestae* as a pledge for the safety of Rome. See Dionysius Halicarnassus, *Roman Antiquities*, Earnest Cary (trans.), *LCL*, 7 vols, London, William Heinemann, 1927, vol. 1, 69; Cicero, *Philippics*, Walter Ker (trans.), *LCL*, London, William Heinemann, 1919, 11.24.
67 See Frowlow, op. cit., p. 75.
68 *Chronicon Paschale* 330.
69 John Malalas, *Chronographia* 13.8.
70 Dagron, *Naissance*, p. 307.
71 ibid., pp. 37–42, 312, 315.
72 Hesychios, *Patria* 15.
73 Dagron, *Naissance*, pp. 367–9.
74 *Chronicon Paschale* 328.
75 ibid., p. 373.
76 Krautheimer, op. cit., pp. 62–3.

77 ibid., p. 63.
78 ibid., p. 61.
79 Straub, op. cit., p. 40.
80 Liebeschuetz, op. cit., pp. 198–9.
81 Ramsay Macmullen, *Christianizing the Roman Empire*, New Haven, Yale University Press, 1984, p. 15.
82 Frend, op. cit., p. 275. He discusses Philostratus and Lactantius with regard to blood sacrifice.
83 *Cod. Theo.* 15.12.1.
84 Eusebius, *Life of Constantine* 2.48.
85 H. Dessau (ed.), *Inscriptiones latinae selectae*, 3 vols, Berlin, Weidmann, 1892, vol. 1, 705; and L. Brehier and P. Batiffiol, *Les survivances du culte imperial romain*, Paris, A Picard, 1920, p. 14.
86 Dessau, ibid.; Brehier and Batiffiol, ibid.
87 Sozomen, *Eccl. Hist.* 2.5.
88 ibid., 2.4.
89 ibid., 2.5.
90 ibid., 2.5.
91 Alan Cameron, "The Latin Revival of the Fourth Century," in Warren Treadgold (ed.), *Renaissances before the Renaissance*, Stanford, Stanford University Press, 1984, p. 53.
92 Macmullen, *Christianizing*, p. 49. He built churches in Rome, Aquileia, Trier, Antioch, Nicomedia, Jerusalem, Cirta, Savaria, and Constantinople.
93 ibid., p. 140, as he quotes Henry Chadwick (1978).
94 Straub, op. cit., pp. 48–9. For a thorough analysis arriving at the opposite viewpoint see Timothy D. Barnes, "Emperor and Bishops, A.D. 324–344: Some Problems," in *AJAH*, 1978, vol. 3, pp. 53–75. Professor Barnes writes on p. 53 that scholars "must accordingly discard the narrative of the ecclesiastical historians" (among them Socrates, Philostorgius, Sozomen, Theodoret) in order to reconstruct a realistic account of Constantine's ecclesiastical policies. Scholars must rely on Eusebius' *Life of Constantine* and Athanasius' letters and apologia. Although Professor Barnes's careful reconstructions from the writings of these two bishops present a strong case, I believe that Eusebius and Athanasius do not give us a more "truthful" story. Rather they present accounts of the Council of Nicea and events surrounding it from their own viewpoints. They are two conservative sectarian Christian bishops who had a real stake in omitting – or overlooking – the fact that Constantine presided over the Council. Athanasius may simply have not recognized Constantine's presiding position or his theological suggestions because the emperor was not clergy and was not baptized. That Constantine continued to view himself as the one responsible for theological truth for the empire is evident from his bullying correspondence to Arius, in which he threatened Arius with exile. Constantine calls himself the "man of God." (See Norman H. Baynes, *Constantine the Great and the Christian Church*, London, Oxford University Press, 1976, p. 21.) Neither Eusebius

nor Athanasius necessarily would have been more objective just because they were contemporaries of Constantine. When one considers how much physical evidence remained through the centuries of Constantine"s version of the imperial cult in Constantinople and how many written testimonies there were describing it, it is difficult to be convinced that the accounts of Eusebius and Athanasius about Constantine's ecclesiastical activities are balanced, objective, or more truthful than those of the historians two generations later. These later church historians, whether truthful or not, represent versions that were widely *accepted* as truth, and more or less corroborate the physical evidence of Constantine's Constantinople.

95 Straub, ibid.
96 ibid., p. 51.
97 Eusebius, *Life of Constantine* 4.24; see Barnes, "Emperor and Bishops," p. 57, for an opposing view. If Constantine had taken such a diminutive role at the Council of Nicea and had been so accommodating to the bishops, it seems unlikely that Eusebius would have had to be so adamant in this section explaining why there are bishops "outside" and bishops "inside" the Church.
98 See Baynes, op. cit., pp. 22–3. Constantine's letter to Athanasius, *c.*327, betrays an "Emperor turned theologian."
99 "pontifex, pontifices," *ODCC*, 1970, p. 860. It is significant here to note that Sozomen, 1.9, says that Constantine changed the laws toward celibates and virgins, allowing them to make wills before puberty, as Romans had allowed Vestal Virgins to do at age 6, "and the Emperor was even *more influenced* by this example than by his reverence for religion."
100 Eusebius, *Life of Constantine* 3.7.
101 Timothy D. Barnes, "Panegyric, history, and hagiography," in Rowan Williams, *The Making of Orthodoxy. Essays in Honor of Henry Chadwick*, Cambridge, Cambridge University Press, 1989, p. 114.
102 ibid.
103 Barnes, *Constantine and Eusebius*, p. 249.
104 Straub, op. cit., p. 52.
105 Eusebius, *Life of Constantine* 2.38.
106 Cyril Mango, "Antique Statuary and the Byzantine Beholder," *DOP*, 1963, vol. 17, pp. 56–7.
107 Barnes, *Constantine and Eusebius*, p. 248. See the discussion especially of churches in Nicomedia, Jerusalem, and Antioch.
108 Krautheimer, op. cit., p. 58.
109 Eusebius, *Life of Constantine* 4.71.
110 Krautheimer, op. cit., p. 60.
111 Frend, op. cit., p. 287.
112 ibid.
113 Krautheimer, op. cit., p. 67.
114 ibid.
115 ibid.

116 Dagron, *Naissance*, p. 378; and Macmullen, *Christianizing*, p. 15.
117 Liebeschuetz, op. cit., p. 299.
118 *Cod. Theo.* 16.10.3.
119 ibid., 5.20.1.

2 The Theodosians and paganism

1 Gregory Nyssa''s famous remark about the bakery, *PG* 46.557.
2 H. W. G. Liebeschuetz, *Continuity and Change in Roman Religion*, Oxford, Clarendon Press, 1989, p. 296.
3 Gilbert Dagron, *Naissance d'une capitale*, Paris, Presses universitaires de France, 1974, p. 379.
4 Gregory Nazianzus, Oration 33, *NPNF*, vol. 7, 1–3.
5 Gregory Nazianzus, *PG* 37.1253.
6 ibid., 377.
7 Socrates, *Eccl. Hist.* 4.32.
8 ibid.
9 ibid.
10 ibid. John Malalas adds that Valens "thoroughly mistreats Christians," *Chronographia*, Elizabeth Jeffreys, Michael Jeffreys, and Roger Scott (trans.), Melbourne, Australian Association for Byzantine Studies, 1986, 13.34.
11 Zosimus, *New History*, Ronald T. Ridley (trans.), Canberra, Australian Association for Byzantine Studies, 1982, 4.37.
12 Liebeschuetz, op. cit., pp. 301–3. Liebeschuetz sees Gratian and Theodosius as the first truly Christian emperors, breaking with what he terms the "Constantinian compromise." This in my view is correct for the city of Rome and the west. In the east, while it is true that Theodosius' policies are more effective at eradicating paganism, there is no rupture with Constantinian traditions and ceremonies. In fact, as will be seen, the Church in the east begins to experiment in greater participation in the civic rituals of Constantinople, as it gradually acclimatizes to the wider culture and to Christian emperors. Through this experimentation the Church begins to invent its rituals and symbols as the new state religion.
13 John Malalas, *Chronographia* 13.34.
14 Socrates, *Eccl. Hist.* 5.
15 ibid.
16 ibid.
17 ibid.
18 John Malalas, *Chronographia* 13.34.
19 Ausonius, *Thanksgiving for his Consulship*, Hugh G. E. White (ed. and trans.), *LCL*, 2 vols, London, William Heinemann, 1921, vol. 2, 9, 14.
20 Sozomen, *Eccl. Hist.* 7.4.
21 Theodoret, *Eccl. Hist.* 5.6.
22 ibid. 5.11.
23 John Malalas, *Chronographia* 13.39.

24 ibid.
25 ibid.
26 Sozomen, *Eccl. Hist.* 7.15.
27 ibid.; Socrates, *Eccl. Hist.* 5.16.
28 Sozomen, *Eccl. Hist.* 7.15.
29 Zosimus, *New History* 4.37.
30 *Cod. Theo.* 16.10.10–12.
31 Zosimus, *New History* 4.33.
32 Sozomen, *Eccl. Hist.* 7.15.
33 ibid., 7.13.
34 ibid., 7.20.
35 *Chronicon Paschale* 289 (year 391), Michael Whitby and Mary Whitby (trans.), Liverpool, Liverpool University Press, 1989.
36 *Cod. Theo.* 16.7.1–5.
37 ibid., 16.7.1.
38 ibid., 16.7.5.
39 Zosimus, *New History* 4.59.
40 ibid.
41 ibid., 4.33. A law of 384 also hints at his lavish tastes. It declares that "no private person" should be able to distribute "silk garments as gifts at any public exhibition of games." *Cod.Theo.* 15.9.1.
42 Sozomen, *Eccl. Hist.* 7.23; Zosimus, *New History* 4.4.1; Theodoret, *Eccl. Hist.* 5.20; Socrates omits the entire incident.
43 Zosimus, *New History* 4.41.
44 Sozomen, *Eccl. Hist.* 7.23; John Chrysostom, *Concerning the Statues*, *NPNF*, vol. 9, 21.4, 7, 13. Chrysostom uses the occasion to illustrate his position that the ecclesiastical hierarchy is above the secular powers. "Heavens, how great is the power of Christianity, that it restrains and bridles a man who has no equal upon earth; a sovereign powerful enough to destroy and devastate all things; and teaches him to practice such philosophy as one in a private station has not been likely to display" (21.13). He does not deal with the subject of the statues *per se* until the end of the chapter. There he tells the emperor that he can set up new images; and if his behavior is virtuous, his grateful subjects will set up spiritual "statues" of him in their hearts. Chrysostom quotes an anecdote supposedly from Constantine, which shows how lightly Chrysostom and allegedly the emperor took the subject of statues. He does acknowledge that the hooligans who caused the trouble in the first place by knocking down the statues should not have treated them with contempt. But the overall theme of the sermon is not images or statues, but rather one of Chrysostom"s favorite themes, how to withstand tribulation. He gives as models to his flock examples of great people from the Bible who overcame adversity.
45 W. H. C. Frend, *The Rise of Christianity*, Philadelphia, Fortress Press, 1984, p. 275. "The imperial statues were becoming the imperial icons of Byzantine times."
46 Sabina MacCormack, *Art and Ceremony in Late Antiquity*, Berkeley, University of California Press, 1981, p. 67.

47 ibid.
48 ibid.
49 Zosimus, *New History* 4.37.
50 Zosimus, *New History* 4.33, 50.
51 Socrates, *Eccl. Hist.* 6.
52 *Cod Theo.* 15.5.2.
53 Sozomen, *Eccl. Hist.* 7.24; Theodoret, *Eccl. Hist.* 5.17–18. The latter relates none of this preliminary story, and calls the violence in Thessaloniki "a sedition."
54 Sozomen, *Eccl. Hist.* 7.25.
55 Theodoret, *Eccl. Hist.* 5.28.
56 ibid.
57 Sozomen, *Eccl. Hist.* 7.25.
58 Theodoret, *Eccl. Hist.* 5.28.
59 As we shall see, Pulcheria tangled with Nestorius over this very issue.
60 Sozomen, *Eccl. Hist.* 8.20.
61 ibid.
62 ibid., and H. W. G. Liebeschuetz, *Barbarians and Bishops*, Oxford, Clarendon Press, 1990, pp. 196–7. Professor Liebeschuetz, discussing the biases and limitations of the Church historians in their versions of the deposition of Chrysostom, says they convey little about secular politics, only the details of personality conflicts. He shows that the deposition of Chrysostom was related to his political strength. "The East was not used to having a bishop of Constantinople who could be an independent power in its politics" (p. 195). The views in this chapter concur with Liebeschuetz"s observations.
63 *Cod Theo.* 16.10.17.
64 ibid., 178.
65 John Chrysostom, *Commentary on the Acts of the Apostles*, 39.3, *NPNF*, vol. 11, p. 240; see Liebeschuetz, *Barbarians*, p. 186.
66 Liebeschuetz, ibid.
67 ibid., pp. 182–3.
68 Frend, op. cit., p. 752.
69 *Cod Theo.* 16.10.15.
70 ibid., 16.10.18.
71 Liebeschuetz, *Barbarians*, p. 188.
72 John Chrysostom, *Discourse on Blessed Babylas*, in Margaret A. Schatkin and Paul W. Harkins (trans.), *Saint John Chrysostom, Apologist*, Washington, Catholic University of America Press, 1985, p. 104.
73 Liebeschuetz, *Barbarians*, p. 188.
74 ibid.
75 Please see the discussion of "sectarian" in the Preface, p. viii.
76 *Cod Theo.* 16.10.14.
77 ibid., Constantine, 2.8.1; Theodosius, 2.8.18, 2.8.21.
78 Theodosius, 2.8.20.
79 ibid., 2.8.24.

80　ibid., 2.8.25.
81　ibid., 15.9.2.
82　ibid., 15.1.44.
83　Kenneth Holum, *Theodosian Empresses*, Berkeley, University of California Press, 1982, p. 77.
84　Theophanes, *Chronographia*, C. de Boor (ed.), Hildesheim, Georg Olms, 1963, 80; and Holum, op. cit., p. 88.
85　Holum, ibid.
86　Sozomen, *Eccl. Hist.* 9.1.
87　ibid.; see also Theophanes, *Chronographia* 81.
88　Sozomen, *Eccl. Hist.* 9.1.
89　ibid.; see also Theophanes, *Chronographia* 81; Theodoret, *Eccl. Hist.* 36. Gannadius of Marseilles (*c.*480) wrote in the *Hieronymus de viris inlustribus*,William Herding (ed.), Leipzig, Teubner, 1879, p. 93, that Atticus, bishop of Constantinople, was quite influential on young Pulcheria''s ideas of faith and virginity.
90　Socrates, *Eccl. Hist.* 7.22.
91　ibid.
92　John Malalas, *Chronographia* 14.3–6; *Chronicon Paschale* 420.
93　Theodoret, *Eccl. Hist.* 5.37.
94　*Cod. Theo.* 16.10.19.
95　ibid.
96　ibid., 16.10.20.
97　ibid., note 47, p. 475, "They are officials in pagan cult and ritual."
98　Averil Cameron and Judith Herrin (eds and trans.) *Constantinople in the Early Eighth Century: the Parastaseis Syntomoi Chronikai*, Leiden, Brill, 1984, p. 268. Apparently this order to remove the statues was not carried out. Statues in the baths of Severus were casualties of the fire during the Nika Revolt of 532. The Constantinianai baths, established in 345, were also decorated with statues. The *Parastaseis*, ch. 73, remarks that they "fell down and caused great wonder."
99　*Cod. Theo.* 16.10.21. Two other laws, issued in 423 and 435, reiterated the prohibitions against pagan cult.
100　Dagron, op. cit., pp. 292–3.
101　*Chronicon Paschale* 450; John Malalas, *Chronographia* 14.16.
102　Dagron, op. cit., pp. 269–71. He discusses at some length the conflicting versions of the building projects.
103　*Cod. Theo.* 3.8.
104　Alan Cameron, *Circus Factions*, Oxford, Clarendon, 1976, p. 230.
105　ibid., p. 231.
106　ibid.
107　Andreas Alföldi, "Die Ausgestaltung des Monarchischen Zeremoniells am Romischen Kaiserhofe," *Mitteilungen des Deutschen Archaeologischen Instituts*, Romische Abteilung, 1934, vol. 49, pp. 45–93; Cameron, op. cit., p. 232. MacCormack, op. cit., pp. 18–22; J. B. Bury, *History of the Later Roman Empire From the Death of Theodosius I to the Death of Justinian*, 2 vols, New York, Dover Publications, 1958, p. 15.

108 See note 107.
109 ibid.
110 Cameron, op. cit., p. 77.
111 Dagron, op. cit., p. 282.
112 ibid.
113 ibid.
114 *Chronicon Paschale* 416. Bury states that the usual place for acces-
     sion was the Hippodrome. See op. cit., p. 86. He also states that
     after 450 the city prefect no longer crowned the emperor (p. 11).
     After 450 the Patriarch crowned the emperors. Bury makes it clear
     that the Patriarchal crowning of each sovereign never became
     constitutionally necessary, it only became custom. The Patriarch,
     Bury says, was not representing the Church in doing so. "The
     Patriarch acted as representative of the State. . . . The consent of
     the Church *was not formally necessary* to the inauguration of a
     sovran."
115 Dagron, op. cit., p. 317.
116 Cameron, op. cit., p. 231.
117 MacCormack, op. cit., p. 9.
118 Dagron, op. cit., pp. 279–80

3   Theodosius, Pulcheria, and the civic ceremonies

1 Sabina MacCormack, *Art and Ceremony in Late Antiquity*, Berkeley,
   University of California Press, 1981, pp. 22–32.
2 ibid., 35.
3 ibid., 36.
4 ibid., 38.
5 Arcadius and Theodosius II were chastised by historians for not
   demonstrating any military abilities. They hardly ever left the
   palace complex, let alone the city. See Theodoret, *Eccl. Hist.* 5.36;
   Sozomen, *Eccl. Hist.* 9; Socrates, *Eccl. Hist.* 6.23; and W. H. C.
   Frend, *The Rise of Christianity*, Philadelphia, Fortress Press, 1984,
   p. 746.
6 H. W. G. Liebeschuetz, *Barbarians and Bishops*, Oxford, Clarendon
   Press, 1990, p. 277; Alan Cameron, *Circus Factions*, Oxford,
   Clarendon Press, 1976, p. 177; and MacCormack, op. cit., pp.
   56–68.
7 MacCormack, ibid.
8 Andreas Alföldi, "Die Ausgestaltung des Monarchischen
   Zeremoniells am Romischen Kaiserhofe," *Mitteilungen des Deutschen
   Archaeologischen Instituts*, Romische Abteilung, vol. 49, 1934, pp.
   76–9.
9 See Chapter 2, pp. 00–00.
10 *Cod. Theo.* 15.4.1.
11 ibid.
12 ibid.
13 ibid.
14 ibid., 15.5.5.

15 *Chronicon Paschale* 415, Michael Whitby and Mary Whitby (trans.), Liverpool, Liverpool University Press, 1989.
16 John Malalas, *Chronographia*, Elizabeth Jeffreys, Michael Jeffreys, and Roger Scott (trans.), Melbourne, Australian Association for Byzantine Studies, 1986, 14.20. Socrates, *Eccl. Hist.* 7.1, states that Anthemius the praetorian prefect, under whose charge Theodosius was as a minor, built the walls.
17 Elizabeth Clark, "Ascetic Renunciation and Feminine Advancement," *Anglican Theological Review*, 1981, vol. 63, p. 257.
18 Kenneth Holum, *Theodosian Empresses*, Berkeley, University of California Press, 1982, p. 137.
19 Sozomen, *Eccl. Hist.* 9.1, 9.3.
20 Barhadbeshabba, *PO* 9, François Nau (trans.), Paris, Firmin-Didot, 1913, p. 565.
21 ibid.
22 *Chronicon Paschale* 416.
23 ibid., 415.
24 John Malalas, *Chronographia* 14.2; this is earliest mention of the blues and greens. See Alan Cameron, op. cit., pp. 230–46, for discussion of the ceremonial role of claque acclamation of blues and greens.
25 Socrates, *Eccl. Hist.* 22 (year 423).
26 ibid., 7.23.
27 John Malalas, *Chronographia* 14.22.
28 See MacCormack, op. cit., pp. 1–45. Panegyric will be discussed much more fully in Chapter 4.
29 ibid., p. 8.
30 ibid., p. 4.
31 The form of panegyric and the form of hymn will be discussed in Chapter 4.
32 Proclus, *PG* 65.788–789, translated in Holum, op. cit., p. 138.
33 Barhadbeshabba, op. cit., p. 565.
34 Francis Dvornik, *The Idea of Apostolicity in Constantinople and the Legend of the Apostle Andrew*, Cambridge, MA, Harvard University Press, 1958, p. 139.
35 Sozomen, *Eccl. Hist.* 7.21.
36 Samuel, *Chronicon Paschale* 406; Joseph and Zechariah, 415; Anthemius, John Malalas, *Chronographia* 14.20.
37 *Chronicon Paschale* 396.
38 Holum, op. cit., p. 137.
39 Theophanes, *Chronographia*, C. de Boor (ed.), Hildesheim, Georg Olms, 1963, 86–7.
40 Holum, op. cit., p. 104.
41 ibid., pp. 107–9.
42 ibid., p. 109.
43 Sozomen, *Eccl. Hist.* 9.2.
44 ibid.
45 Holum, op. cit., pp. 136–7.
46 Socrates, *Eccl. Hist.* 45; Theodoret, *Eccl. Hist.* 5.36.

47 Theodoret, *Eccl. Hist.* 5.36.
48 Nestorius, *Corpus Marianum Patristicum*, A. Campos (ed.), Burgos, Ediciones Aldecoa, 1976, vol. 4/1, 2956, 2980.
49 See Martin Jugie, *Nestorius et la controverse nestorienne*, Paris, Beauchesne, 1912, and Friedrich Loofs, *Nestorius and His Place in the History of Christian Doctrine*, Cambridge, Cambridge University Press, 1914, pp. 49–69.
50 Socrates, *Eccl. Hist.* 7.32.
51 ibid.
52 ibid., 7.29.
53 *Lettre à Cosme*, PO 13, François Nau (trans.), Paris, Firmin-Didot, 1916, p. 278.
54 Nestorius, *Bazaar of Heracleides*, G. Drivers and L. Hodgson (eds and trans.), Oxford, Clarendon, 1925, p. 103.
55 Barhadbeshabba, op. cit., p. 528.
56 ibid., p. 565.
57 Nestorius, *Baz. Her.* 148.
58 Barhadbeshabba, op. cit., pp. 565–6.
59 *Lettre à Cosme*, op. cit., p. 279.
60 ibid., " 'Laisse-moi entrer selon ma coutume.' Mais il lui dit, 'Ce lieu ne doit être foulé que par les prêtres.' Elle lui dit, 'Pourquoi n'ai-je pas enfanté Dieu!' Il lui dit, 'Toi, tu a enfanté Satan,' et il la chassa de la porte du Saint des saints. Elle partit irritée, elle trouva l'empereur et lui rencontra la chose. 'Par ta vie, ma soeur, et par la couronne qui est sur ta tête, je ne cesserai pas avant d'avoir tiré vengeance de lui.' "
61 Nestorius, *Baz. Her.* 96–7.
62 J. N. D. Kelly, *Early Christian Doctrines*, San Francisco, Harper & Row, 1978, p. 311.
63 Richard A. Norris Jr. (trans. and ed.), *The Christological Controversy*, Philadelphia, Fortress Press, 1980, p. 131. Loofs, op. cit., pp. 31, 32. He quotes Nestorius as preaching before the year 430, "I have already repeatedly declared that if anyone of you or anyone else be simple and has a preference for the term 'Theotokos', then I have nothing to say against it – only do not make a goddess of the Virgin."
64 Holum, op. cit., pp. 154–5.
65 ibid.
66 ibid.
67 Proclus, *PG* 65.680–681.
68 Giovanni Mansi, *Sacrorum Conciliorum* 47 vols, Florence and Paris, 1760–1901, vol. 4, 671a, 681b.
69 Nestorius, *Baz. Her.* 265–9.
70 Mansi, op. cit., vol. 3, 543–4.
71 Nestorius, *Baz. Her.* p. xxii.
72 Frend, op. cit., p. 769.
73 Holum, op. cit., pp. 209, 211.
74 Frend, op. cit., p. 770.
75 Holum, op. cit., p. 215; Holum relates that there was an earlier

church built for Mary in Constantinople. He is convinced that Pulcheria built this one also, but before the Council of Ephesus.
76 Theophanes, *Chronographia* 105; Theodore the Reader, *PG* 86.200, 86.168.
77 Norman H. Baynes, "The Supernatural Defenders of Constantinople," in *Byzantine Studies and Other Essays*, London, University of London, 1955, pp. 257–60.
78 Theodore the Reader, *PG* 86.165A.
79 Raymond Janin, *La géographie écclésiastique de l'empire byzantine*, Paris, Centre national de la recherche scientifique, 1953, p. 169.
80 Holum, op. cit., pp. 142–3.
81 *Oratio de sancta Maria*, *PG* 115.560–566, and from *Codex Paris. gr.* 1447, fol. 257–8, as translated by Cyril Mango, *The Art of the Byzantine Empire 312–1453, Sources and Documents*, Englewood Cliffs, Prentice-Hall, 1972, p. 35. "We shall mention also the following . . . namely that in those days the aforesaid illustrious men Galbius and Candidus dedicated with all glory and honor an enormous image of our Lady the Mother of God. To the right and left of her upon this image are two angels and, on either side, St. John the Baptist and St. Conon."
82 Theodore Synkellos, *De obsidione constantinopolitana* in A. Mai (ed.), *Nova Bibliotheca Patrum* 6.431. "ἐν ϐλαχέρναι· ἅγιον οἶκον τῆς θεομήτορος."
83 Janin, op. cit., p. 169.
84 John of Damascus, *PG* 96.748–752, as translated by Walter J. Burghardt, SJ, *The Testimony of the Patristic Age Concerning Mary's Death*, Westminster, MD, Newman Press, 1961, p. 35. The John of Damascus legend is also testimony for Jerusalem as the location of Mary's death. The tangled arguments over whether Mary passed away in Ephesus or in Jerusalem are beyond the scope of this study. The "transitus Mariae" speculations began in earnest with Epiphanius' gossipy *Panarion* (*The Panarion of St. Epiphanius, Selected Passages*, Philip R. Amidon, SJ (trans.), Oxford, Oxford University Press, 1990), 78.10–11. He reports the ambiguous views current about her "falling asleep" and "passing away," and he is careful not to commit himself one way or the other. The Dormition Assumption of Mary entered into liturgical devotions officially at the end of the fifth century. In 600 emperor Maurice instituted August 15 as the commemoration of the "κοίμησις τῆς Θεοτόκου." See also Martin Jugie, *La Mort et l'Assomption de la Sainte Vièrge: Etude historico-doctrinale*, Vatican, 1944, and Jugie, "La mort et l'assomption de la sainte Vièrge dans la tradition des cinq premiers siècles," *Echoes d'orient*, 1926, vol. 2, pp. 129–43.
85 Janin, op. cit., p. 246.
86 Nicephorus Callistus excerpting Theodore the Reader, *PG* 86.200.
87 The fourth-century devotions to the Virgin will be discussed in Chapter 4.
88 *Lettre à Cosme*, op. cit., p. 279.

4 Imperial cult, panegyric, and the Theotokos

1 Chris A. Faraone, *Talismans and Trojan Horses*, Oxford, Oxford University Press, 1992, p. 12.

2 H. W. G. Leibescheutz, *Continuity and Change in Roman Religion*, Oxford, Clarendon Press, 1989, p. 51.

3 See Duncan Fishwick's book, *The Imperial Cult in the Latin West*, 2 vols, Leiden, Brill, 1991, vol. 2.1, and S. R. F. Price, *Rituals and Power*, Cambridge, Cambridge University Press, 1984, for excellent surveys and discussions of the emperor cult. The title of the former book is misleading; much of this volume deals with evidence from the eastern part of the empire too.

4 F. E. Hadcock, "The Achievement of Augustus," in J. B. Bury, S. A. Cook, and F. E. Adcock (eds), *The Cambridge Ancient History*, 12 vols, Cambridge, Cambridge University Press, 1923–39, vol. 10, p. 586.

5 Price, op. cit., p. 231.

6 Fishwick, op. cit., ch. 8.

7 ibid., p. 522.

8 Price, op. cit., p. 203, where he quotes several other scholars.

9 Nicolaus Sophistae, *Progymnasmata*, Joseph Felten (ed.), Leipzig, Teubner, 1913, pp. 47–71.

10 Toivo Viljamaa, *Studies in Greek Encomiastic Poetry of the Early Byzantine Period*, Helsinki, Helsingfors, 1968, p. 20.

11 George Kennedy, *Greek Rhetoric Under the Christian Emperors*, Princeton, Princeton University Press, 1983, p. 26.

12 Viljamaa, op. cit., p. 20.

13 Kennedy, op. cit., p. 63.

14 ibid.

15 Viljamaa, op. cit., p. 22; and Sabina MacCormack, *Art and Ceremony in Late Antiquity*, Berkeley, University of California Press, 1981, pp. 5–6.

16 MacCormack, op. cit., pp. 6–8.

17 ibid.

18 Viljamaa ventures a political reason: "the growing threat from the barbarians as well as pursuit of official favor" (p. 9).

19 Alan Cameron, "The Latin Revival of the Fourth Century," in Warren Treadgold (ed.), *Renaissances before the Renaissance*, Stanford, Stanford University Press, 1984, p. 53.

20 Viljamaa, op. cit., p. 12.

21 Cameron, op. cit., p. 287.

22 Viljamaa, op. cit., p. 22.

23 ibid., pp. 27–8.

24 ibid., p. 29.

25 ibid., p. 132.

26 ibid., pp. 71–83, asyndeton, omitting the conjunction; antithesis, opposites and contrasts; pleonasm, an excess of words; paranomasia, plays on words.

27 ibid., p. 15; and *Anthologia Graeca*, Hermann Beckby (ed.), 4 vols,

Munich, Ernst Heimeran Verlag, 1965, vol. 15.9: "ἔχεις δ' ἐρικυδέα μορφὴν τὴν Ἀγαμεμνονέην, ἀλλ' οὐ φρένας οἶνος ὀρίνει. ἐς πινυτὴν δ' Ὀδυσῆι δᾶφρονι παν σε εἴσκω, ἀλλὰ κακῶν ἀπάνευθε δόλων."

28 Viljamaa, op. cit., p. 116.
29 *Anth. Gr.* 16.65.
30 ibid., "Ἔκθορες ἀντολίηθε, φαεσφόρος ἥλιος ἄλλος, Θευδόσιε, θνητοῖσι, πόλου μέσον, ἠπιόθυμε, ὠκεανὸν παρὰ ποσσὶν ἔχων μετ' ἀπείρονα γαῖαν, πάντοθεν αἰγλήεις, κεκορυθμένος, ἀγλαὸν ἵππον, ῥηιδίως, μεγάθυμε, καὶ ἐσσύμενον κατερύκων." Interestingly the line is quoted in Liddell, Scott, Jones, *Greek–English Lexicon*, Oxford, Clarendon Press, 1978, p. 1436, as coming from *Anth. Gr.* 14.139, by Metrodorus, fourth century CE. In the German edition referring to poem 14. 139, Hermann Beckby says the line "ἀπ' ανατολλίης πόλον ἤλατο χρύσεα κύκλα ἠελίου" is a quote, and the poet asks a certain Diodorus to tell him what it means. Beckby says the poem is anonymous, not by Metrodorus.
31 *Anth. Gr.* 16.65; Homer *Illiad*, A. T. Murray (trans.), *LCL*, 2 vols, Cambridge, MA, Harvard University Press, 1924–5, 20.498; Homer *Odyssey*, A. T. Murray (trans.), *LCL*, 2 vols, Cambridge, MA, Harvard University Press, 1976–80, 8.520, 13.121.
32 *Anth. Gr.* 9. 400; "Ὅταν βλέπω σε, προσκυνῶ, καὶ τοὺς λόγους, τῆς παρθένου τὸν οἶκον ἀστροφον βλέπων, εἰς οὐρανὸν γάρ ἐστι σου τὰ πράγματα, Ὑπατία σέμνη, τῶν λόγων εὐμορφία, ἄχραντον ἄστρον τῆς σοφῆς παιδεύσεως."
33 The first three lines replicate Gregory Nazianzus' poem, *PG* 37.507.
34 *Anth. Gr.* 1.102; "Ὦ πάντων ἐπέκεινα – τί γὰρ πλέον ἄλλο σε μέλψω; Πῶς σε ἐν πάντεσσιν ὑπείροχον ἐξονομήνω; πῶς δὲ λόγῳ μέλψω σὲ, τὸν οὐδὲ λόγῳ περιληπτόν;"
35 ibid., 1.105. Ἡ μὲν σοφὴ δέσποινα τῆς οἰκουμένης, ὑπ' εὐσεβοῦς ἔρωτος ἠρεθισμένη, πάρεστι δούλη, προσκυνεῖ δ' ἑνὸς τάψον, ἡ πᾶσιν ἀνθρώποισι προσκυνουμένη. Ὀ γὰρ δεδωκὼς τὸν θρόνον καὶ τὸν γάμον τέθνηκεν ὡς ἄνθρωπος, ἀλλὰ ζῇ θεός. κάτω μὲν ἠνθρώπιζεν, ἦν δ' ὡς ἦν ἄνω."
36 MacCormack, op. cit., p. 18.
37 ibid., p. 23.
38 Menander, 378.10, as quoted by MacCormack, op. cit., p. 20.
39 MacCormack, op. cit., p. 20.
40 ibid., p. 21, and MacCormack"s translation of Menander, p. 282. These words are particularly important: savior, σωτῆρα; wall, τεῖχος; most radiant star, ἀστέρα φανώτατον; nourisher, τροφέα; sweetness on the day, ἡδίστης δὲ ἡμέρας; light more radiant than the sun, ἡλίου φῶς φαιδρότερον.
41 See Chapter 3, p. 59.
42 ibid., p. 42.
43 ibid., p. 45.
44 ibid., pp. 56–8.
45 See Chapter 3, pp. 66–7, for the references to Holum and MacCormack who have full discussions of the phenomenon, and see MacCormack, op. cit., pp. 64–5.

46 *Panégyriques latines*, Edouard Galletier (ed. and trans.), 3 vols, Paris, Société d'éditions "les belles lettres," 1952, vol. 2, pp. 165–98.
47 ibid., 32.2.
48 ibid., 34.2–4.
49 ibid., 34.2, 35.3.
50 ibid., 36–7.
51 ibid., 38.
52 ibid., 32.1.
53 ibid., 32.8.
54 ibid., 38.4.
55 ibid., 33.
56 ibid., 34.
57 ibid., 38.
58 Julian, *The Works of Emperor Julian*, Wilmer Cave Wright (ed. and trans.), *LCL*, 3 vols, London, William Heinemann, 1913, vol. 1, *Panegyric to Constantius* p. 105.
59 ibid., p. 117.
60 Julian, *The Works of Emperor Julian*, Wilmer Cave Wright (ed. and trans.), *LCL*, 3 vols, London, William Heinemann, 1913, vol. 1, *Oration to Eusebeia*, p. 281.
61 ibid., p. 327.
62 ibid., p. 320.
63 ibid., p. 345.
64 Ausonius, *Thanksgiving for the Consulship*, Hugh G. E. White (ed. and trans.), *LCL*, 2 vols, London, William Heinemann, 1921, vol. 2, p. 221.
65 ibid.
66 ibid., p. 225.
67 ibid., p. 231.
68 ibid., p. 223.
69 ibid., p. 245.
70 ibid., pp. 231, 239.
71 ibid., p. 241.
72 ibid., p. 231.
73 ibid., p. 221.
74 ibid., p. 239.
75 Pacatus, *Panegyrius Theodosio*, in Edouard Galletier (ed. and trans.), *Panégyriques latines*, 3 vols, Paris, Société d'éditions "Les belles lettres," 1952, vol. 3, pp. 68–114.
76 ibid., 3.6.
77 ibid., 4.5.
78 ibid., 18.3.
79 ibid., 6.3.
80 ibid., 6.4. Galletier, in astonishment, writes this note in ff. 1, p. 74: "Véritable acte d''adoration pour la personne impériale et sa puissance divine."
81 ibid., 21.2; human qualities, 7.1.
82 ibid., 16.2.
83 ibid., 17.3.

84 ibid., 22.1.
85 ibid., 22.5.
86 ibid., 27.5.
87 ibid., 8.4.
88 ibid., 44.5.
89 ibid., 27.5.
90 ibid., 28.3.
91 ibid., 21.4.
92 ibid., see Galletier"s ff. 3, p. 88.
93 ibid., 21.1.
94 Viljamaa, op. cit., p. 25.
95 Kennedy, op. cit., p. 70.
96 Fishwick, op. cit., pp. 571–2.
97 MacCormack, op. cit., p. 50.
98 Athanasius, *Against the Heathen*, *NPNF*, vol. 4, p. 9. Constantine was the last emperor to be officially deified by the senate.
99 ibid.
100 Price, op. cit., p. 203.
101 ibid.
102 T. D. Barnes has convincingly shown that Chapters 1–10 of the *Praise of Constantine* were written for the Tricennalia. Chapters 11–18 constitute a separate second oration delivered a few months later in Jerusalem to praise the emperor"s building of the Church of the Holy Sepulchre. The two works were not intended to form a whole. See "Two speeches by Eusebius," in *Early Christianity and the Roman Empire*, London, Variorum Reprints, 1984, xvi, pp. 341–5.
103 ibid., p. 342.
104 Eusebius, *In Praise of Constantine*, *NPNF*, vol. 2, pp. 581–610, ch. 5.
105 ibid.
106 ibid.
107 ibid.
108 Ramsay Macmullen, *Paganism in the Roman Empire*, New Haven, Yale University Press, 1981, p. 77.
109 Socrates, *Eccl. Hist.* 5.
110 José Grosdidier de Matons, *Romanos le Mélode et les origines de la poésie religieuse à Byzance*, Paris, Beauchesne, 1977, p. 15.
111 ibid., p. 8.
112 ibid.
113 ibid.
114 ibid., p. 6.
115 St. Gregory Nazianzus, *Three Poems*, in Denis Molaise Meehan, OSB (trans.), *The Fathers of the Church*, Washington, Catholic University Press, 1987, vol. 75, pp. 114–15.
116 ibid. Gregory by his own admission was an unwilling patriarch and not up to the degree of vigor and strength needed to accommodate the court and lead the people.
117 Socrates, *Eccl. Hist.* 5.6; Sozomen, *Eccl. Hist.* 7.3–7.6.
118 Sozomen, *Eccl. Hist.* 8.8.
119 Socrates, *Eccl. Hist.* 6.3.

120 ibid.
121 ibid.
122 *The Oxford Dictionary of the Christian Church*, p. 799, dates the council some twenty years after 345.
123 Giovanni Mansi, *Sacrorum Conciliorum*, 47 vols, Florence and Paris, 1760–1901, vol. 2, 563–74.
124 ibid., canon 39.
125 ibid., canon 53.
126 ibid.
127 ibid.
128 ibid., canon 55.
129 See Robert L. Wilken, *The Land Called Holy*, New Haven, Yale University Press, 1992, pp. 11–115.
130 Egeria, *Egeria's Travels*, John Wilkinson (ed. and trans.), London, SPCK, 1971, 24.1–12.
131 Gregory Nyssa, *On Pilgrimages*, *NPNF*, vol. 5, pp. 382–3.
132 Grosdidier de Matons, op. cit., pp. 12–13.
133 ibid., p. 15.
134 ibid.
135 ibid., p. 13. Grosdidier de Matons cites the *Life of St. Auxentius* (*c.*440), *PG* 114.1480.
136 ibid.
137 Grosdidier de Matons, op. cit., p. 13.
138 ibid.
139 MacCormack's work has shown that the Church's welcoming of relics to the capital during the fifth century took on salient aspects of the *adventus* ceremony of the Roman emperor cult. See pp. 64–6.
140 Proclus, *PG* 61.737–738; Cyril of Alexandria, *PG* 77.1033–1036; Chrysippus of Jerusalem, *PO* 19.218–219; Basil of Seleucia, *PG* 85.444, 448; Theodotus, *PG* 77.1389–1412.
141 The scholarship of F. J. Leroy and R. Caro has convincingly shown that these sermons are genuine works of Proclus. See F. J. Leroy, *L'homiletique de Proclus de Constantinople*, Citta del Vaticano, Biblioteca Apostolica Vaticana, 1967, pp. 267–70; Robert Caro, *La homiletica mariana griega en el siglo V*, Dayton, University of Dayton, 1972, pp. 308–24.
142 The first half of this oration leading up to these verses is quoted in Chapter 3.
143 Proclus, *PG* 65.681.
144 Proclus, *PG* 65.788.
145 ibid., 720.
146 ibid., 710–12.
147 ibid., 711, "ὁ παρθένε, κόρη ἀπειρόγαμε, ἀλόχευτος μήτηρ." This will be dealt with more fully in Chapter 6.
148 ibid., 753.
149 *PG* 61.737–738; in Migne this hymn is listed as part of the "spuria" under Chrysostom. S. A. Campos has attributed it to Proclus, as have Leroy and Caro. See Sergios Alvarez Campos, O F M (ed.),

Corpus Marianum Patristicum, 4 vols, Burgos, Ediciones Aldecoa, 1976, vol. 1, pp. 35, 61–3.

150 Campos, ibid.

151 *Anth. Gr.*, Prokne, 9.452; Aphrodite, 13.1; Hermes, 9.91; Mithras Firmicus, *de err. prof. rel.* 19.1; *Homeric Hymns*, Demeter, 13.1.

152 *Akathistos Hymn*, *PG* 92.1335–1348; see the Appendix of this book for the full English text. Grosdidier de Matons, op. cit., and Constantine Trypanis, *Fourteen Early Byzantine Cantica*, *Wiener byzantinistische Studien* 5, Wien, Hermann Bohlaus, 1968. Trypanis includes a critical edition; although the differences are slight, I have chosen to work with the version in Migne because it is the one used liturgically in the Greek Orthodox Church, and hence the one heard by the people. For the most influential studies on the *Akathistos Hymn* itself, see P. F. Krypiakiewicz, "De hymni acathisti auctore," *Byzantinische Zeitschrift*, 1909, vol. 18, pp. 356–82; R. A. Fletcher, "Three Early Byzantine Hymns," *Byzantinische Zeitschrift*, 1958, vol. 52, pp. 53–65; Casimir Emereau, "Hymnographi Byzantini-Acathisti auctore," *Echoes d'Orient*, 1922, vol. 21, pp. 59–83; Thomas Maria Wehofer, *Untersuchungen zum Lied d. Romanos auf die Wiederkunft des Herrn*, Wien, Keiserlice Akademie der Wissenschaften, 1907, vol. 154.5; Egon Wellesz, "The Akathistos," *DOP*, 1955, vol. 9/10, pp. 131–72.

153 Hilda Graef, *Mary, A History of Doctrine and Devotion*, London, Sheed & Ward, 1965, p. 129.

154 Michael O'Carroll, CSSp, *Theotokos*, Wilmington, DE, Michael Glazier, 1986, pp. 8–9.

155 The liturgical formula "sing, bridegroom, rejoice, bridgroom, rejoice at the new light" (Αἶδε νύμφε, χαῖρε νύμφε, χαῖρε νέον φῶς) is attested to by Firmicus as part of the Mithas liturgy; in Firmicus, *de err. prof. relig.*, 19.1, as quoted in Franz Cumont, "The Dura Mithraeum," in John R. Hinnells (ed.), *Mithraic Studies*, 2 vols, Manchester, Manchester University Press, 1971, vol. 1, p. 200.

156 ibid.

157 Krypiakiewicz, op. cit., pp. 356–82. This was the holiday that Proclus named the "Virginity Festival."

158 Fletcher, op. cit., p. 63.

159 Paul Maas and Constantine Trypanis, *Sancti Romani Melodi Cantica*, Oxford, Clarendon, 1963, p. xiv.

160 Grosdidier de Matons, op. cit., p. 16.

161 For translations of Ephraim's hymns to the Virgin from Syriac into Latin, see *Sancti Ephraem Syri Hymni et Sermones*, Thomas Josephus Lamy (ed. and trans.), 4 vols, Mechliniae, H. Dessain, 1886, vol. 2, pp. 585–602, 630–42; for study of influence see Casimir Emereau, *Saint Ephraem le Syrien*, Paris, Etudes critiques de littérature et de philologie byzantine, 1918.

162 *Anth. Gr.* 16.39, Aphrodite and the Muses; 9.108, Zeus and Eros; 9.134, Tyche and a mortal; 9.294, Leonidas and Xerxes; 9.627, Eros and the Nymphs.

163 See these examples of Greek acrostic poetry and inscriptions: *Anth.*

Gr. 9.524, 525; *CIG* 4310. These range over a long period of time illustrating popularity.

164 Grosdidier de Matons, op. cit., pp. 20–4.

165 Antithesis, opposites and contrasts; assonance, noticeable recurrence of sound in successive words; anaphora, repetition of a word or phrase at the beginning of successive clauses; isocolon, a line of equal members or clauses; and Kennedy, op. cit., p. 183.

166 Grosdidier de Matons, op. cit., p. 24.

167 Maas and Trypanis, op. cit., p. xiv.

168 ibid., and Grosdidier de Matons, op. cit., p. 37.

169 See Viljamaa's categories, p. 132. The genre of kontakion was just emerging; it was not yet a set form.

170 *PG* 65.742–758.

171 Wellesz, op. cit., p. 154.

172 Kennedy, op. cit., p. 70.

173 Viljamaa, op. cit., p. 98.

174 ibid., p. 99.

175 Trypanis has shown on the basis of meter that Prooimion I (τὸ πρόσταχθεν μυστικῶς) is the original. See op. cit., p. 21.

176 Romanos Melodos (*c.*560) is the most famous hymnographer of the Orthodox Church. Church tradition credits him with authorship of the *Akathistos*. Grosdidier de Matons's book successfully refutes the tradition.

177 Verses 9, 11, 23.

178 They will be dealt with in Chapter 6.

179 Ausonius likened Gratian words to "sustaining milk from the sincerest breast"; see note 70.

180 Kennedy, op. cit., p. 168, quoting the fourth-century rhetor, Lachares, who commented on rhetors" ignorance of Greek meter; he himself wrote in accentual rhythm!

181 See verses 1, 3, 9, 11, 13, 17, 19, 21, 23.

182 Averil Cameron, *Christianity and the Rhetoric of Empire*, Berkeley, University of California Press, 1991. For the best discussion about the use of paradox in Christian literature, see pp. 165–9.

183 ibid., p. 7.

5 The hierarchs' Mary

1 H. W. G. Liebescheutz, *Barbarians and Bishops*, Oxford, Clarendon Press, 1990, p. 179.

2 Ignatius of Antioch, Epistle to the Ephesians 7: 2, *ANF*, vol. 1.

3 Justin Martyr, *Dialogue With Trypho* 66; *Apology* 1.33, *ANF*, vol. 1.

4 Irenaeus of Lyons, *Against Heresies* 5.19, 3.16, *ANF*, vol. 1.

5 Tertullian, *On the Flesh of Christ* 23, *ANF*, vol. 1; apocryphal literature will be discussed below.

6 Clement of Alexandria, *Stromata* 7.16, *ANF*, vol. 2.

7 Origen, *Commentary on John* 1.34, 37; *Commentary on Matthew* 10.17; *ANF*, vol. 10; "Theotokos" is in two fragments of his *Commentary on Luke*, 41, 80.

8 ibid.
9 Averil Cameron, *Christianity and the Rhetoric of Empire*, Berkeley, University of California Press, 1991, p. 100.
10 *Ascension of Isaiah*, in Willis Barnstone (ed.), *The Other Bible*, San Francisco, Harper & Row, 1980, p. 530.
11 *Odes of Solomon*, in Willis Barnstone (ed.), *The Other Bible*, San Francisco, Harper & Row, 1980, Ode 19, pp. 279–80.
12 *Protoevangelium of James*, in Willis Barnstone (ed.), *The Other Bible*, San Francisco, Harper & Row, 1980, pp. 385–403.
13 Athanasius, *PG* 18.568.
14 Athanasius, *PG* 26.349, 161, 296.
15 "Saint Athanase: Sur la Virginité," in L.-Th. Lefort (trans.), *Le Muséon*, 1929, vol. 42, pp. 197–274. On the attribution see Peter Brown, *Body and Society*, New York, Columbia University Press, 1988, pp. 254–5.
16 Eusebius, *PG* 24.1033.
17 Ephraem Syrus *Hymnen*, in Edmund Beck (ed. and trans.), *CSCO*, Louvain, 1903; "Bride of Christ," *Hymen de nativitate*, *CSCO* 187,61, 11,2; "ear conception," *Hymen de nativitate*, *CSCO* 187,3,1,16; "purification by Holy Spirit," *Hymnen de ecclesiae*, *CSCO* 199,88,36,2; "immortal flesh," *Hymnen de virginitate*, *CSCO* 224,3,3.
18 See Brown, op. cit.
19 Basil, *PG* 29.180; 31.1465.
20 Gregory Nazianzus, *PG* 37.1565; 26.80; 36.633.
21 Gregory Nazianzus, Epistle 101.4–6; *PG* 37.177.
22 Gregory of Nyssa, *On Virginity*, *NPNF*, vol. 5, p. 359.
23 ibid.
24 Brown discusses Mary's virginity in this context of overcoming death in op. cit., pp. 445–6.
25 Gerhart B. Ladner, "Anthropology of Gregory of Nyssa," *DOP*, 1958, vol. 12, p. 93. See especially pages 88–95.
26 Gabriele Giamberardini, *Il culto mariano in Egitto nei primi sei secoli: Origine-Sviluppo-Cause*, Jerusalem, Franciscan Printing, 1967, ch. 6. It is housed in the John Rylands Library in Manchester. After twenty-one years, the library published the manuscript in 1938. The opening line, "Under your mercy . . ." was until then thought to be a western medieval prayer to the Virgin, the famous "sub tuum presidium." But scholars have dated the papyrus to the third century.
27 Sozomen, *Eccl. Hist.* 7.5.
28 Egeria, *Egeria's Travels*, John Wilkinson (ed. and trans.), London, SPCK, 1971, 26.
29 Gregory of Nyssa, *PG* 46.1151–1182.
30 Amphilochius of Iconium, *PG* 39.37, "ὡς ἄνω δυνάμεων συνόμιλος, ὡς τῶν ἀσωμάτων φύσεων σύνδρομος."
31 ibid., "ἡ παρθενία ὡς ἀδούλωτον κτῆμα, ὡς ἐλεύθερον ἐδιάτημα, ὡς ἀσκητικὸν ἐγκαλώπισμα, ὡς τῆς ἀνθρωπινῆς ἔξεως ἀνωτέρα, ὡς τῶν ἐπ' ἀνάγκαις παθῶν ἀπολυθεῖσα."
32 ibid., "καλὸν γὰρ τῶν τριῶν ταγμάτων ἀπομνημονεῦσαι."

33 Martin Jugie, *La Mort et l'Assomption de la Sainte Vièrge, Studi e testi*, no. 114, Vatican, 1944, p. 175.
34 See Chapter 3, pp. 67–8.
35 See Chapter 3, pp. 70–1.
36 W. H. C. Frend, *The Rise of Christianity*, Philadelphia, Fortress Press, 1984, p. 754.
37 ibid., p. 756.
38 ibid., p. 757.
39 Kenneth Holum, *Theodosian Empresses*, Berkeley, Unversity of California Press, 1982, pp. 158–61.
40 ibid., p. 161.
41 ibid.
42 Frend, op. cit., p. 761.
43 Cyril of Alexandria, *St. Cyril of Alexandria, Letters 1–50*, John I. McEnerney (trans.), Washington, Catholic University Press, 1985, Letter 17, pp. 80–92.
44 ibid., p. 89.
45 Cyril of Alexandria, *PG* 77.992; 77.1032–1036.
46 ibid., 77.1032.
47 Psalm 64: 6.
48 Luke 2: 4.
49 John 8: 12.
50 Matthew 21: 9.
51 Herbert Weir Smyth, *Greek Grammar*, Cambridge, MA, Harvard University Press, 1976, no. 1820, p. 406.
52 Cyril of Alexandria, *PG* 77.1392–1393.
53 Cyril of Alexandria, *PG* 77.992.
54 ibid.; the *Akathistos* uses this form, too, yet without the effect of mitigating the Virgin's active role.
55 Cyril of Alexandria, *PG* 73.228; 74.661–664.
56 Proclus, *PG* 65.740. This dialogue too is in contrast to one of the famous ones by Ephraim the Syrian. Gabriel must repeat over and over to Mary how she is to conceive by the Holy Spirit. Mary is in turn terrorized by the news, then incredulous, and even stupid. She finds the message "exceedingly difficult." See *Sancti Ephraem Syri Hymni et Sermones*, Thomas Josephus Lamy (ed. and trans.), 4 vols, Mechliniae, H. Dessain, 1886, vol. 2, 594–6.
57 Cyril of Alexandria, *St. Cyril of Alexandria, Letters 51–110*, John I. McEnerney (trans.), Washington, Catholic University Press, 1985, pp. 188–92.
58 ibid., paragraphs 5, 7, 9, 10.
59 ibid., p. 192.
60 One of the outcomes of the Council of Ephesus was that the bishops of Constantinople, Rome, Antioch, Alexandria, and Jerusalem were now to be called "patriarchs."
61 Cyril of Alexandria, op. cit., Letter 72, pp. 72–4.
62 Frend, op. cit., p. 763.
63 ibid.

64 Johannes Quasten, *Patrology*, 3 vols, Westminster, MD, Newman Press, 1963, vol. 3, p. 131. This line is often quoted about Cyril.
65 Epiphanius, *Panarion* 30.20; 77.8; 78.7–14, 18; 79.3. Epiphanius, *Opera*, G. Dindorf (ed.), Leipzig, 1859, vols 1–3, and *The Panarion of St. Epiphanius, Selected Passages*, Philip R. Amidon, SJ (trans.), Oxford, Oxford University Press, 1990.
66 ibid., 78.10, translated by Walter J. Burghardt, SJ, *The Testimony of the Patristic Age Concerning Mary's Death*, Westminster, MD, Newman Press, 1961, p. 5.
67 ibid.
68 ibid., 78.28, Burghardt, p. 6.
69 *Panarion*, Amidon, p. 348.
70 *Panarion* 78.13–17, Amidon, pp. 350–1.
71 ibid., 78.23, p. 351.
72 ibid.
73 Jeremiah 44: 15–26.
74 *Panarion* 79.5, Amidon, p. 353.
75 ibid., p. 354.

6   Byzantium's bequest to the Theotokos

1 See Zosimus, *New History*, Ronald T. Ridley (trans.), Canberra, Australian Association for Byzantine Studies, 1982, 2.31, and Chapter 1, ff. 66, p. 17.
2 In 438 there were at least two churches dedicated to the Virgin: the prefect Cyrus built one in 437, and the "first-founded" church to Mary, built before Ephesus, was perhaps built by Pulcheria. Kenneth Holum, *Theodosian Empresses*, Berkeley, University of California Press, 1982, p. 143.
3 *Akathistos Hymn*, verses 3, 7, 11, 15, 19, 23.
4 ibid., verses 4, 5, 13.
5 ibid., Chapter 1, ff. 22, ff. 55, pp. 11, 16.
6 Gilbert Dagron, *Naissance d'une capitale*, Paris, Presses universitaires de France, 1974, p. 368; Dionysus of Byzantium, *Anaplus Bospori*, Rudolf Güngerich (ed.), Berlin, Weidmann, 1958, 52, 74, 75; Hesychios, *Patria* 6, Theodore Preger (ed.), New York, Arno Press, 1975, pp. 22–3.
7 See note 6.
8 *The Orphic Hymns*, Apostolos Athanassakis (ed. and trans.), Missoula, Scholar's Press, 1977, 27. Rhea is identified with Demeter, Cybele, and the mother of the gods.
9 Zosimus, *New History* 2.33.
10 ibid.
11 Theodora Hadzisteliou Price, *Kourotrophos*, Leiden, Brill, 1978, p. 12.
12 ibid.
13 Liddell, Scott, Jones, *Greek–English Lexicon*, Oxford, Clarendon Press, 1978, p. 825.

14 ibid.
15 Aristophanes, *Birds*, Benjamin Rogers (trans.), *LCL*, Cambridge, MA, Harvard University Press, 1965, 435, 675, 1720.
16 Euripides, *Electra*, Arthur S. Way (trans.), *LCL*, London, William Heinemann, 1912, 890.
17 Stobaeus, *Eklogai*, Augustus Meineke (ed.), Leipzig, Teubner, 1860, 1.6.1; *Anthologion*, Augustus Meineke (ed.), Leipzig, Teubner, 1855, 13.
18 Theodore Mionnet, *Des medailles romaines*, Paris, A. Aubry, 1858, Phrygia 273; Cilicia 416, 458; Ionia 1132, 408, 434; Bythinia 237.
19 Pausanias, *Descriptions of Greece*, W. H. S. Jones (trans.), *LCL*, Cambridge, MA, Harvard University Press, 1935–64, 9.39.5.
20 *CIG* 162, fragment C.
21 *CIG* 4555, 2024, 3171.
22 ibid., 4303.
23 Fernand Allègre, *Etude sur la déesse grècque Tyche*, Paris, Leroux, 1889, pp. 184–5.
24 Artemiodorus, *Oneirocriticon*, Roger Pack (ed.), Leipzig, Teubner, 1963, 2.42.12.
25 Mionnet, op. cit., Phrygia 273; Cilicia 416, 458; Ionia 1132.
26 Libanius, *Orationes*, Richard Foerster (ed.), 12 vols, Hildesheim, Georg Olms Verlag, 1963, vol. 1, II.180.
27 Philostorgius, *Eccl. Hist.* 2.1.2.17; John Malalas, *Chronographia*, Elizabeth Jeffreys, Michael Jeffreys, and Roger Scott (trans.), Melbourne, Australian Association for Byzantine Studies, 1986, 13.7; *Chronicon Paschale*, Michael Whitby and Mary Whitby (trans.), Liverpool, Liverpool University Press, 1989, 528. There are significant differences between Dea Roma in Rome, Dea Roma in the Greek cities of the eastern provinces during the Roman period, and the Greek goddess or personification, Tyche. Constantine's Tyche is only externally modeled on Dea, Roma, just as his city was. Tyche Constantinopolis never became Dea Roma. This is obvious from coins and medals minted during the fourth century. Given the long tradition of Tyche in Byzantium, it can be assumed that her identity was separate and well known before Constantine. For Dea Roma see Ronald Mellor, *Thea Rome*, Göttingen, Van Den Hoek & Ruprecht, 1975, pp. 20–6; for coins and medals see Francesco Gnecchi, *I medaglioni romani*, 4 vols, Bologna, Forni Editore, 1912, vol. 2, pp. 136–8; and Justin Sabatier, *Descriptions générales des monnaies byzantines*, 2 vols, Paris, Rollin et Fenardent, 1862, vol. 1, p. 4,29.
28 Gnecchi, op. cit.
29 Andreas Alföldi, *The Conversion of Constantine and Pagan Rome*, H. Mattingly (trans.), Oxford, Clarendon Press, 1948, p. 3; and Andreas Alföldi, "On the Foundation of Constantinople," *JRS*, 1947, vol. 37, p. 16.
30 Gnecchi, op. cit., vol. 2, pp. 132.2, 4.
31 Dagron, op. cit., p. 370.
32 Chapter 1, ff. 71, p. 19.

33 Chris A. Faraone, *Talismans and Trojan Horses*, Oxford, Oxford University Press, 1992, p. 7.
34 Zosimus, *New History* 5.6.
35 ibid.
36 Dagron, op. cit., p. 369.
37 Lewis R. Farnell, *The Cults of the Greek States*, 5 vols, New Rochelle, NY, Caratzas Brothers, 1977, vol. 2, pp. 505, 508, 509.
38 Sarah Iles Johnston, *Hekate Soteira*, Atlanta, Scholar's Press, 1990, p. 24.
39 Hesychios, *Patria* 27, p. 11, and Farnell, ibid., vol. 2, p. 508.
40 Dionysus of Byzantium, *Anaplus Bospori* 36.
41 Dagron, op. cit., p. 372.
42 Homer, *Iliad*, A. T. Murray (trans.), *LCL*, 2 vols, Cambridge, MA, Harvard University Press, 1924–5, 16.100; Homer, *Odyssey*, A. T. Murray (trans.), *LCL*, 2 vols, Cambridge, MA, Harvard University Press, 1976–80, 13.388.
43 Pausanias, op. cit., 4.30.6.
44 Anthony Cutler, *Transfigurations, Studies in the Dynamics of Byzantine Iconography*, University Park, PA, Pennsylvania State University Press, 1975, p. 119.
45 Allègre, op. cit., p. 136.
46 Verses 9, 17, 21; 21; 13.
47 Proclus, *PG* 61.737.
48 Averil Cameron, "The Theotokos in Sixth-century Constantinople," *Journal of Theological Studies*, 1978, vol. 29, p. 89; see Theodore Synkellos' account of the Avar siege in *De obsidione constantinopolitana*, A. Mai (ed.), *Nova Bibliotheca Patrum*, 6.425. The Theotokos is the protector of the city and strategic genius behind the military victory. In the Canon of Andrew of Crete (d. 720), *PG* 97.1385, military victory is assured in the Theotokos.
49 Codinus, *De officialibus palatii Constantinopolitani et de officiis magnae ecclesiae liber*, *CSHB*, Bonn, Dindorf, 1839, 25.40–48; Friedrich Wilhelm Unger, *Quellen des Byzantinische Kunstgeschichte*, Vienna, W. Braumuller, 1878, p. 50.
50 Codinus, *De officialibus* 47.
51 ibid., 48.
52 ibid., 48.
53 Zonaras, *Epitome Historiarum*, 5 vols, L. Dindorf (ed.), Leipzig, Teubner, 1868–74, vol. 3, 14.4.
54 J. B. Bury, *History of the Later Roman Empire, From the Death of Theodosius I to the Death of Justinian*, 2 vols, New York, Dover Publications, 1958, vol. 1, p. 239; and Averil Cameron and Judith Herrin (eds and trans.), *Constantinople in the Early Eighth Century: the Parastaseis Syntomoi Chronikai*, Leiden, Brill, 1984, chs. 34, 38, 56. There is also competition in this later period about whom the city was dedicated to, Tyche or the Theotokos. See Cameron and Herrin, pp. 240, 242–3, and A. Frowlow, "La dédicace de Constantinople dans la tradition byzantine," *Revue de Science Religieuse*, 1944, vol. 127, pp. 61–127.

55 Pausanius, op. cit., 2.7.5; 6.25.4.
56 Dionysus of Byzantium, op. cit., 14.
57 Dagron, op. cit., p. 370.
58 *Orphic Hymns*, 72.3, 40; Athanassakis posits that the *Orphic Hymns* were collected and written down in the late third century; and the Isis aretalogy in W. L. Knox, "The Divine Wisdom," *Journal of Theological Studies*, 1937, vol. 38, p. 230.
59 *Orphic Hymns*, 29.
60 Apuleius, *The Golden Ass*, W. Addlington (trans.), *LCL*, 2 vols, Cambridge, MA, Harvard University Press, 1965, vol. 2; Isis is called "Ceres." For Isis borrowing Tyche's cornucopia, see Françoise Dunand, *Le culte d'Isis dans le bassin oriental de la méditerranée*, 3 vols, Leiden, Brill, 1973, vol. 3, p. 104; vol. 2, p. 56.
61 Bernard P. Grenfell and Arthur S. Hunt (eds), *Oxyrhynchus Papyri*, 59 vols, London, Oxford University Press, 1915, vol. 11, 1380.185. In the Isis aretalogy she is called by Demeter's name, "lawgiver" (thesmophoros); Knox, op. cit., p. 231.
62 Knox, op. cit., p. 230.
63 Dunand, op. cit., vol. 3, p. 104.
64 *Orphic Hymns*, 40.
65 ibid.
66 *The Homeric Hymns*, Apostolos Athanassakis (ed. and trans.), Baltimore, Johns Hopkins University Press, 1984, 2,4, and 23.
67 *Orphic Hymns*, 40.
68 ibid., 29.
69 Proclus, *PG* 61.737.
70 *Orphic Hymns*, 40.
71 *Akathistos Hymn*, verse 5.
72 *Orphic Hymns*, 29.
73 Proclus, *PG* 65.681.
74 Proclus, *PG* 61.737–738.
75 Grenfell and Hunt, *Ox. Pap.* vii.145–6, and Walter Burkert, *Greek Religion*, John Raffan (trans.), Cambridge, MA, Harvard University Press, 1985, p. 139.
76 Grenfell and Hunt, *Ox. Pap.* vi.120–3; Knox, op. cit., p. 213.
77 Grenfell and Hunt, *Ox. Pap.* iii.60, Knox, ibid.
78 Farnell, op. cit., vol. 1, pp. 268–9.
79 Jane Harrison, *Prolegomena to Greek Religion*, Cambridge, Cambridge University Press, 1903, p. 560.
80 Farnell, op. cit., vol. 2, pp. 292, 302, 304.
81 Burkert, op. cit., p. 178, not in Arcadia or Athens.
82 Farnell, op. cit., vol. 2, p. 293.
83 ibid., p. 298.
84 ibid., vol. 3, p. 507. Athanassakis surmises with justification that the *Orphic Hymns* were written down in Thrace. Hymn 27 identifies Rhea and Demeter. Johnston, op. cit., pp. 66, 68.
85 See Chapter 3, ff. 254.
86 Knox, op. cit., p. 230.
87 *Orphic Hymns*, 27; p. 117.

88 Burkert, op. cit., p. 143.
89 Farnell, op. cit., vol. 2, p. 518.
90 Grenfell and Hunt, *Ox. Pap.* v.108.
91 Price, op. cit., p. 203.
92 Proclus, *PG* 61.737.
93 ibid.; see also *Akathistos Hymn*, verses 4, 17.
94 *Orphic Hymns*, 1, 14, 29, 40.
95 Proclus, *PG* 65.753; see Chapter 4, ff. 147, p. 88.
96 Günther Roeder, *Urkunden zur Religion des alten Aegypten*, Jena, E. Diedrichs, 1915, 63.3.
97 Proclus, *PG* 65.681.
98 Farnell, op. cit., vol. 3, p. 302.
99 ibid.
100 *Orphic Hymns*, 14, 40, 29.
101 Roeder, op. cit., 63.3, and H. Junder, *Der grosse Pylon des Tempels der Isis zu Philae*, Vienna, R. M. Rohrer, 1958, pp. 21, 24, 29, 232, 267–76.
102 *Orphic Hymns*, 27.
103 ibid., 27, 29.
104 ibid., 40.
105 Grenfell and Hunt, *Ox. Pap.* vi.130, 132.
106 ibid., i, ii, 12, 13.
107 Hesiod, *Theogony*, Hugh G. Evelyn White (trans.), *LCL*, London, William Heinemann, 1926, 450.
108 This is a prominent theme in Proclus also.
109 Verse 15.
110 Verse 5.
111 Verse 1.
112 Verse 19.
113 Verses 19, 21.
114 Burkert, op. cit., pp. 171, 222.
115 ibid., p. 23.
116 ibid.
117 Verses 3, 9, 17, 19.
118 Knox, op. cit., p. 231, and Grenfell and Hunt, *Ox. Pap.* p. 202.
119 Verses 9, 11, 15.
120 Verse 19.
121 Verses 23, 24.
122 *Orphic Hymns*, 1, 14, 27.
123 Verses 23, 24.
124 *Orphic Hymns*, 14, 29.
125 Grenfell and Hunt, *Ox. Pap.* p. 202.
126 Verse 15.
127 John of Damascus, *PG* 96.741–744.
128 *Orphic Hymns*, 27.

References

Primary sources

Acts of the Scillitan Martyrs, in H. Mursurillo (ed.), *The Acts of the Christian Martyrs*, Oxford, Clarendon Press, 1972.

Anthologia Graeca, Hermann Beckby (ed.), 4 vols, Munich, Ernst Heimeran Verlag, 1965.

Apuleius, *The Golden Ass*, W. Addlington (trans.), *LCL*, 2 vols, Cambridge, MA, Harvard University Press, 1965.

Aristophanes, *Birds*, Benjamin Rogers (trans.), *LCL*, Cambridge, MA, Harvard University Press, 1965.

Artemiodorus, *Oneirocriticon*, Roger Pack (ed.), Leipzig, Teubner, 1963.

Ascension of Isaiah, in Willis Barnstone (ed.), *The Other Bible*, San Francisco, Harper & Row, 1980.

Ausonius, *Order of Famous Cities*, Hugh G. Evelyn White (trans.), *LCL*, 2 vols, London, William Heinemann, 1919.

——, *Thanksgiving for the Consulship*, Hugh G. E. White (ed. and trans.), *LCL*, 2 vols, London, William Heinemann, 1921.

Barhadbeshabba, *Patrologia Orientalis*, François Nau (trans.), vol. 9, Paris, Firmin-Didot et Cie, 1913.

Campos, Sergios Alvarez, OFM (ed.), *Corpus Marianum Patristicum*, 4 vols, Burgos, Ediciones Aldecoa, 1976.

Chronicon Paschale, Michael Whitby and Mary Whitby (trans.), Liverpool, Liverpool University Press, 1989.

Cicero, *Philippics*, Walter Ker (trans.), *LCL*, London, William Heinemann, 1919.

Codinus, *De officialibus palatii Constantinopolitani et de officiis magnae ecclesiae liber*, *CSHB*, Bonn, Dindorf, 1839.

Cyril of Alexandria, *St. Cyril of Alexandria, Letters 1–50*, John I. McEnerney (trans.), Washington, Catholic University Press, 1985.

——, *St. Cyril of Alexandria, Letters 51–110*, John I. McEnerney (trans.), Washington, Catholic University Press, 1985.

Dessau, H. (ed.), *Inscriptiones latinae selectae*, Berlin, Weidmann, 1892.

Dio Cassius, *Roman History*, Earnest Cary (trans.), *LCL*, 9 vols, London, William Heinemann, 1927.

Dionysius Halicarnassus, *Roman Antiquities*, Earnest Cary (trans.), *LCL*, 7 vols, London, William Heinemann, 1927.

Dionysus of Byzantium, *Anaplus Bospori*, Rudolf Güngerich (ed.), Berlin, Weidmann, 1958.

Egeria, *Egeria's Travels*, John Wilkinson, (ed, and trans.), London, SPCK, 1971.

Sancti Ephraem Syri Hymni et Sermones, Thomas Josephus Lamy (ed. and trans.), 4 vols, Mechliniae, H. Dessain, 1886, vol. 2.

Ephraem Syrus, *Hymnen*, in Edmund Beck (ed. and trans.), *Corpus Scriptorum Christianorum Orientalium*, 59 vols, Louvain, Secretariat du Corpus SCO, 1959–74.

Epiphanius, *The Panarion of St. Epiphanius, Selected Passages*, Philip R. Amidon, SJ (trans.), Oxford, Oxford University Press, 1990.

Euripides, *Electra*, Arthur S. Way (trans.), *LCL*, London, William Heinemann, 1912.

Gannadius of Marseilles, *Hieronymus de viris inlustribus*, William Herding (ed.), Leipzig, Teubner, 1879.

Giovanni Mansi, *Sacrorum Conciliorum*, Florence and Paris, 47 vols, 1760–1901.

St Gregory Nazianzus, *Three Poems*, in Denis Molaise Meehan, OSB (trans.), *The Fathers of the Church*, Washington, Catholic University Press, 1987.

Grenfell, Bernard P. and Arthur S. Hunt (eds), *Oxyrhynchus Papyri*, 59 vols, London, Oxford University Press, 1915.

Hesiod, *Theogony*, Hugh G. Evelyn White (trans.), *LCL*, London, William Heinemann, 1926.

Hesychios, *Patria*, Theodore Preger (ed.), New York, Arno Press, 1975.

Homer, *Iliad*, A. T. Murray (trans.), *LCL*, 2 vols, Cambridge, MA, Harvard University Press, 1924–5.

——, *Odyssey*, A. T. Murray (trans.), *LCL*, 2 vols, Cambridge, MA, Harvard University Press, 1976–80.

The Homeric Hymns, Apostolos Athanassakis (ed. and trans.), Baltimore, Johns Hopkins University Press, 1984.

John Chrysostom, *Discourse on Blessed Babylas*, in Margaret A. Schatkin and Paul W. Harkins (trans.), *Saint John Chrysostom, Apologist*, Washington, Catholic University of America Press, 1985.

John Malalas, *Chronographia*, Elizabeth Jeffreys, Michael Jeffreys, and Roger Scott (trans.), Melbourne, Australian Association for Byzantine Studies, 1986.

Josephus, *Wars*, H. St. J. Thackeray (trans.), *LCL*, 3 vols, London, William Heinemann, 1925.

Julian, *The Works of Emperor Julian*, Wilmer Cave Wright, (ed. and trans.), *LCL*, 3 vols, London, William Heinemann, 1913, vol. 1, *Panegyric to Constantius*, 133–269; *Oration to Eusebeia*, 275–345.

Lettre à Cosme, François Nau (trans.), *Patrologia Orientalis*, vol. 13, Paris, Firmin-Didot, 1916.

Libanius, *Orationes*, Richard Foerster (ed.), 12 vols, Hildesheim, Georg Olms Verlag, 1963.

Lydus, *De magistriiibus populi Romani*, Richard Wünsch (ed.), Stuttgart, Teubner, 1967.

Martydom of Perpetua and Felicitas, in H. Mursurillo (ed.), *The Acts of the Christian Martyrs*, Oxford, Clarendon Press, 1972.

Nestorius, *Bazaar of Heracleides*, G. Drivers and L. Hodgson (eds and trans.), Oxford, Clarendon Press, 1925.

——, *Corpus Marianum Patristicum*, A. Campos (ed.), Burgos, Ediciones Aldecoa, 1976.

Nicolaus Sophistae, *Progymnasmata*, Joseph Felten (ed.), Leipzig, Teubner, 1913.

Odes of Solomon, in Willis Barnstone (ed.), *The Other Bible*, San Francisco, Harper & Row, 1980.

The Orphic Hymns, Apostolos Athanassakis (ed. and trans.), Missoula, Scholar's Press, 1977.

Pacatus, *Panegyrius Theodosio*, in Edouard Galletier (ed. and trans.), *Panegyriques latines*, 3 vols, Paris, Société d'éditions "les belles lettres," 1952.

Panégyriques latines, Edouard Galletier (ed. and trans.), 3 vols, Paris, Société d'éditions "les belles lettres," 1952.

Pausanias, *Descriptions of Greece*, W. H. S. Jones (trans.), *LCL*, Cambridge, Harvard University Press, 1935–64.

Philostorgius, *Historia ecclesiastica*, *Die Griechischen Christlichen Schriftsteller*, 39 vols, Leipzig, Hinrich's Buchhandlung, 1913.

Philostratus, *Life of Apollonius of Tyana*, F. C. Conybeare (trans.), *LCL*, London, William Heinemann, 1912.

Pliny, *Letter to Trajan*, in Agnes Cunningham (ed.), *The Early Church and State*, Philadelphia, Fortress Press, 1982.

——, *Natural History*, H. Rackham (trans.), *LCL*, 10 vols, London, William Heinemann, 1942.

Polybius, *Histories*, W. R. Paton (trans.), *LCL*, 6 vols, London, William Heinemann, 1922.

Protoevangelium of James, in Willis Barnstone (ed.), *The Other Bible*, San Francisco, Harper & Row, 1980.

Stobaeus, Anthologion, Augustus Meineke (ed.), Leipzig, Teubner, 1855.

——, *Eklogai*, Augustus Meineke (ed.), Leipzig, Teubner, 1860.

Theodore Synkellos, *De obsidione constantinopolitana*, in A. Mai (ed.), *Nova Bibliotheca Patrum*, vol. 6.

The Theodosian Code, Clyde Pharr (trans.), Princeton, Princeton University Press, 1952.

Theophanes, *Chronographia*, C. de Boor (ed.), Hildesheim, Georg Olms, 1963.

Zonaras, *Epitome Historiatum*, 5 vols, L. Dindorf (ed.), Leipzig, Teubner, 1868–74.

Zosimus, *New History*, Ronald T. Ridley (trans.), Canberra, Australian Association for Byzantine Studies, 1982.

Secondary sources

"Saint Athanase: Sur la Virginité," in L.-Th. Lefort (trans.), *Le Muséon*, vol. 42, 1929.

Alföldi, Andreas, "Die Ausgestaltung des Monarchischen Zeremoniells am Romischen Kaiserhofe," *Mitteilungen des Deutschen Archaeologischen Instituts*, Romische Abteilung, vol. 49, 1934, 45–93.

——, "On the Foundation of Constantinople," *JRS*, vol. 37, 1947, 10–16.

——, *The Conversion of Constantine and Pagan Rome*, H. Mattingly (trans.), Oxford, Clarendon Press, 1948.

Allègre, Fernand, *Etude sur la déesse grècque Tyche*, Paris, Leroux, 1889.

Barnes, Timothy D., "Emperor and Bishops, A.D. 324–344: Some Problems," in *AJAH*, vol. 3, 1978, 53–75.

——, *Constantine and Eusebius*, Cambridge, MA, Harvard University Press, 1981.

——, "Two speeches by Eusebius," in *Early Christianity and the Roman Empire*, London, Variorum Reprints, 1984.

——, "Panegyric, history, and hagiography," in Rowan Williams, *The Making of Orthodoxy: Essays in Honor of Henry Chadwick*, Cambridge, Cambridge University Press, 1989, 94–103.

Baynes, Norman H., "The Supernatural Defenders of Constantinople," in *Byzantine Studies and Other Essays*, London, University of London, 1955.

——, *Constantine the Great and the Christian Church*, London, Oxford University Press, 1976.

Brehier, H. and P. Batiffiol, *Les survivances du culte impérial romain*, Paris, A. Picard, 1920.

Brown, Peter, *Body and Society*, New York, Columbia University Press, 1988.

Burghardt, Walter J., SJ, *The Testimony of the Patristic Age Concerning Mary's Death*, Westminster, MD, Newman Press, 1961.

Burkert, Walter, *Greek Religion*, John Raffan (trans.), Cambridge, MA, Harvard University Press, 1985.

Bury, J. B., *History of the Later Roman Empire From the Death of Theodosius I to the Death of Justinian*, 2 vols, New York, Dover Publications, 1958.

Cameron, Alan, *Circus Factions*, Oxford, Clarendon Press, 1976.

——, "The Latin Revival of the Fourth Century," in Warren Treadgold (ed.), *Renaissances before the Renaissance*, Stanford, Stanford University Press, 1984, 42–58.

Cameron, Averil, "The Theotokos in Sixth-century Constantinople," *Journal of Theological Studies*, vol. 29, 1978, 79–108.

——, *Christianity and the Rhetoric of Empire*, Berkeley, University of California Press, 1991.

Cameron, Averil and Judith Herrin (eds and trans.), *Constantinople in the Early Eighth Century: the Parastaseis Syntomoi Chronikai*, Leiden, Brill, 1984.

Caro, Robert, *La homiletica mariana griega en el siglo V*, Dayton, University of Dayton Press, 1972.

Clark, Elizabeth, "Ascetic Renunciation and Feminine Advancement,"

Anglican Theological Review, vol. 63, 1981, 240–57.

Cumont, Franz, "The Dura Mithraeum," in John R. Hinnells (ed.), *Mithraic Studies*, 2 vols, Manchester, Manchester University Press, 1971.

Cutler, Anthony, *Transfigurations, Studies in the Dynamics of Byzantine Iconography*, University Park, PA, Pennsylvania State University Press, 1975.

Dagron, Gilbert, *Naissance d'une capitale*, Paris, Presses universitaires de France, 1974.

——, *Constantinople imaginaire*, Paris, Presses universitaires de France, 1984.

Dictionary of Greek and Roman Geography, London, John Murray, 1872.

Dunand, Françoise, *Le culte d'Isis dans le bassin oriental de la méditerranée*, 3 vols, Leiden, Brill, 1973.

Dvornik, Francis, *The Idea of Apostolicity in Constantinople and the Legend of the Apostle Andrew*, Cambridge, MA, Harvard University Press, 1958.

Emereau, Casimir, *Saint Ephraem le Syrien*, Paris, Etudes critiques de littérature et de philologie byzantine, 1918.

——, "Hymnographi Byzantini-Acathisti auctore," *Echoes d'Orient*, 1922, vol. 21, 59–83.

Faraone, Chris A., *Talismans and Trojan Horses*, Oxford, Oxford University Press, 1992.

Farnell, Lewis R., *The Cults of the Greek States*, 5 vols, New Rochelle, NY, Caratzas Brothers, 1977.

Fears, Rufus J., "Ruler Worship," in Michael Grant and Rachel Kitzinger (eds), *Civilization of the Ancient Mediterranean*, 3 vols, New York, Charles Scribner's Sons, 1988, vol. 2, 1009–25.

Fishwick, Duncan, *The Imperial Cult in the Latin West*, 2 vols, Leiden, Brill, 1991.

Fletcher, R. A., "Three Early Byzantine Hymns," *Byzantinische Zeitschrift*, 1958, vol. 52, 53–65.

Frend, W. H. C., *The Rise of Christianity*, Philadelphia, Fortress Press, 1984.

Frowlow, A., "La dédicace de Constantinople dans la tradition byzantine," *Revue de Science Religieuse*, vol. 127, 1944, 61–127.

Giamberardini, Gabriele, *Il culto mariano in Egitto nei primi sei secoli: Origine-Sviluppo-Cause*, Jerusalem, Franciscan Printing, 1967.

Gnecchi, Francesco, *I medaglioni romani*, 4 vols, Bologna, Forni Editore, 1912.

Graef, Hilda, *Mary, A History of Doctrine and Devotion*, London, Sheed & Ward, 1965.

Grosdidier de Matons, José, *Romanos le Mélode et les origines de la poésie religieuse à Byzance*, Paris, Beauchesne, 1977.

Hadcock, F. E., "The Achievement of Augustus," in J. B. Bury, S. A. Cook, and F. E. Adcock (eds), *The Cambridge Ancient History*, 12 vols, Cambridge, Cambridge University Press, 1923–39, vol. 10.

Harrison, Jane, *Prolegomena to Greek Religion*, Cambridge, Cambridge University Press, 1903.

Herrin, Judith, *The Formation of Christendom*, Princeton, Princeton University Press, 1987.

Holum, Kenneth, *Theodosian Empresses*, Berkeley, University of California Press, 1982.

Janin, Raymond, *La géographie écclésiastique de l'empire byzantine*, Paris, Centre national de la recherche scientifique, 1953.

Johnston, Sarah Iles, *Hekate Soteira*, Atlanta, Scholar's Press, 1990.

Jugie, Martin, *Nestorius et la controverse nestorienne*, Paris, Beauchesne, 1912.

——, "La mort et l'assomption de la sainte Vièrge dans la tradition des cinq premiers siècles," *Echoes d'orient*, vol. 2, 1926, 129–43.

——, *La Mort et l'Assomption de la Sainte Vièrge: Etude historico-doctrinale*, Vatican, 1944.

——, *La Mort et l'Assomption de la Sainte Vièrge*, Studi e testi, no. 114, Vatican, 1944.

Junder, H., *Der grosse Pylon des Tempels der Isis zu Philae*, Vienna, R. M. Rohrer, 1958.

Kelly, J. N. D., *Early Christian Doctrines*, San Francisco, Harper & Row, 1978.

Kennedy, George, *Greek Rhetoric Under the Christian Emperors*, Princeton, Princeton University Press, 1983.

Knox, W. L., "The Divine Wisdom," *Journal of Theological Studies*, vol. 38, 1937, 230–7.

Koester, Helmut, *Introduction to the New Testament*, 2 vols, *History, Culture, and Religion of the Hellenistic Age*, vol. 1, Philadelphia, Fortress Press, 1983.

Krautheimer, Richard, *Three Christian Capitals*, Berkeley, University of California Press, 1983.

Krypiakiewicz, P. F., "De hymni acathisti auctore," *Byzantinische Zeitschrift*, 1909, vol. 18, 356–82.

Ladner, Gerhart, B., "Anthropology of Gregory of Nyssa," *DOP*, 1958, vol. 12, pp. 59–94.

Leroy, F. J., *L'homiletique de Proclus de Constantinople*, Citta del Vaticano, Biblioteca Apostolica Vaticana, 1967.

Liddell, Scott, Jones, *Greek–English Lexicon*, Oxford, Clarendon Press, 1978.

Liebeschuetz, H. W. G., *Continuity and Change in Roman Religion*, Oxford, Clarendon Press, 1989.

——, *Barbarians and Bishops*, Oxford, Clarendon Press, 1990.

Loofs, Friedrich, *Nestorius and His Place in the History of Christian Doctrine*, Cambridge, Cambridge University Press, 1914.

Maas, Paul and Constantine Trypanis, *Sancti Romani Melodi Cantica*, Oxford, Clarendon Press, 1963.

MacCormack, Sabina, *Art and Ceremony in Late Antiquity*, Berkeley, University of California Press, 1981.

Macmullen, Ramsay, *Paganism in the Roman Empire*, New Haven, Yale University Press, 1981.

——, *Christianizing the Roman Empire*, New Haven, Yale University Press, 1984.

Mango, Cyril, "Antique Statuary and the Byzantine Beholder," *DOP*, 1963, vol. 17, 53–75.

——, *The Art of the Byzantine Empire 312–1453, Sources and Documents*, Englewood Cliffs, Prentice-Hall, 1972.

Mellor, Ronald, *Thea Rome*, Göttingen, Van Den Hoek and Ruprecht, 1975.

Mionnet, Theodore, *Des medailles romaines*, Paris, A. Aubry, 1858.

Norris Jr., Richard A. (ed. and trans.), *The Christological Controversy*, Philadelphia, Fortress Press, 1980.

O"Carroll, Michael, CSSp, *Theotokos*, Wilmington, DE, Michael Glazier Inc., 1986.

Price, S. R. F., *Rituals and Power*, Cambridge, Cambridge University Press, 1984.

Price, Theodora Hadzisteliou, *Kourotrophos*, Leiden, Brill, 1978.

Quasten, Johannes, *Patrology*, 3 vols, Westminster, MD, Newman Press, 1963.

Roeder, Günther, *Urkunden zur Religion des alten Aegypten*, Jena, E. Diedrichs, 1915.

Sabatier, Justin, *Descriptions générales des monnaies byzantines*, 2 vols, Paris, Rollin et Fenardent, 1862.

Ste Croix, G.E.M. de, "Why were the Early Christians Persecuted?" *Studies in Ancient Society*, M. I. Finley (ed.), London, Routledge & Kegan Paul, 1974.

Smyth, Herbert Weir, *Greek Grammar*, Cambridge, MA, Harvard University Press, 1976.

Straub, Johannes A. "Constantine as ΚΟΙΝΟΣ ΕΠΙΣΚΟΠΟΣ," *DOP*, 1967, vol. 21, 139–55.

Trypanis, Constantine, *Fourteen Early Byzantine Cantica, Wiener byzantinistische Studien* 5, Wien, Hermann Bohlaus, 1968.

Unger, Friedrich Wilhelm, *Quellen des Byzantinische Kunstgeschichte*, Vienna, W. Braumuller, 1878.

Viljamaa, Toivo, *Studies in Greek Encomiastic Poetry of the Early Byzantine Period*, Helsinki, Helsingfors, 1968.

Wehofer, Thomas Maria, *Untersuchungen zum Lied d. Romanos auf die Wiederkunft des Herrn*, Wien, Keiserlice Akademie der Wissenschaften, 154.5, 1907.

Wellesz, Egon, "The Akathistos," *DOP*, 1955, vol. 9/10, 131–72.

Wilken, Robert L., *The Land Called Holy*, New Haven, Yale University Press, 1992.

——, *The Christains as the Romans Saw Them*, New Haven, Yale University Press, 1984.

Index

Agia Sophia, church of 26, 31,
33, 37, 49–51, 55–6
Akathistos Hymn 62; composition
89–92; English translation
149–58; form 90–2; as imperial
panegyric 145–6; rhetorical
devices 92–7, 111, 121–2,
127–9, 131–3, 135–40, 147
Alexander, Bishop of
Constantinople 14
Ambrose of Milan 36, 38–9, 63
Amphilochius of Iconium 105–6
Anastasia, church of the 81, 105
Anastasius, Emperor 30
Anastasius, presbyter 54
Anthemius, hymnographer 84
Anthousa (Dea Roma/Flora)
17–19, 21, 27, 125
Antidicomarianites 117–20
Antiochus, imperial eunuch 41–2
Aphrodite 12, 16, 33, 89
Apollo 12, 15–16, 47
Arcadius, Emperor: against
Arians 82; death 41; family 37;
imperial cult ritual 47–8;
legislation 37–40, 43, 48
Arians: in Constantinople 54,
79–82; hymnography 80–2;
opposition to 24, 30–2
Artemis 12, 15, 33, 110
Athanasius 77, 103
Athena: in Athens 124; in
Byzantium 16, 122–3; in
Constantinople 18–19, 126,

141, 146; in panegyric 67, 72,
88, 96; as protectress 129,
132–3; as virgin 136
Atticus, Bishop of Constantinople
49–50
Augustus 8–9, 63
Ausonius, panegyrist 32, 73–4
Auxentius of Syria,
hymnographer 84

Bacchus 33, 76
Bardas, Emperor 129–30
Basil, Bishop of Caesarea 31,
103
Basil of Seleucia, hymnographer
85, 111
Blachernae, church of 57–8, 128,
130
Borborians 54
Byzantium, city of: choice as
capital 9; Christianity 13–14;
paganism 12, 16, 19, 21,
121–4, 134–5; pre-
Constantinian history and
legends 10–14 (*see also* Byzas);
public construction 11–12;
statues 12, 15; Tetrastoön
12, 15; *see also* Septimius
Severus
Byzas 10, 12, 15, 19, 123, 129

Caracalla, Antoninus, Emperor
11, 16
Celestine, Pope 56, 108

Chalcedon, Council of (451) 57–8, 107, 109, 116
Chalkoprateia, church of 57–8, 106, 128
Christianity: holidays 40–1, 48, 90–1, 105–7 (*see also* Hypapante, feast of; Virginity Festival); orthodox doctrine of 32–3, 57, 106–9, 115–17, 119; as sectarian stance 3, 40, 113, 116, 144; *see also* civic religion, Greco-Roman
Chronicon Pascale: on Byzantium 14; on Constantine 125–6; on Constantinople 17–19; on Theodosius II 50
Chrysippus of Jerusalem, hymnographer 86, 111
civic religion, Greco-Roman: ceremonies in Constantinople 20, 30, 45–6; and Christianity 1–4, 9, 27–8, 33–4, 37, 40–1, 46, 50, 59–62, 76–9, 85, 114, 116, 128–9, 135, 141, 146; definition 2; distinguished from paganism 1–2, 21–3, 34–5, 38–9, 41, 45, 63; panegyric in 68; practices (*c.* 420) 47–8; *see also* individual emperors/esses; emperor cult; imperial imagery
Clement of Alexandria 12, 102, 107
Codinus, historian 129
coinage; *see* imperial imagery
Collyridians 118–20, 134, 146
Constans, Emperor 29
Constantine, Emperor: and Arianism 24; Christianization of empire 1, 3, 21–3, 26–8, 143; civil religious practice 40; conversion 7–9; distaste for pagan sacrifice 21–3, 63; foundation of Constantinople 9–10, 14, 16–18; imperial cult ritual 7, 17, 19, 20–1, 27–8, 35–6, 45, 47, 61, 69, 70–1, 78, 143; pagan religious practice 3, 15–16, 19–21, 27–8, 45, 123,

125, 129, 143; understanding of Christianity 8–9, 23–8, 37; *see also* individual historians
Constantinople: Augusteon in 19; Christianity 30, 39–40, 146; city prefect in 44–46; civic religion 38, 146; dedication ceremonies 17; Forum 16–17; Great Palace 16; imperial cult 36–9; liturgy 79; map of 148; paganism 3, 16–20, 30, 39, 122–30, 134–5, 137, 143; public construction 17; senate basilica 17; Tetrastoön 3, 17, 19–20, 121, 123, 134, 143; Theotokos cult 1, 57–60, 96–7, 106, 112, 121–2, 127–30, 134, 141–7; Zeuxippon baths 18; *see also* individual churches and historians; Constantine; Hippodrome, in Constantinople
Constantinople I, Council of (381) 32, 82, 107
Constantius II, Emperor 29, 52, 65, 71–2
Cybele 2, 19, 133, 135
Cyril of Alexandria: against Nestorius 54, 56, 107–9, 112–14; Christology 109, 113, 115; deposition of 113–16; at Ephesus, Council of 56, 108; hymns to Theotokos 85, 109–11, 116; mariology 107–14
Cyrus of Panopolis: as City Prefect of Constantinople 44, 49; and encomiastic poetry 65–6; and imperial panegyric 96

Damasus, Pope 4, 32–3
Dea Roma: *see* Anthousa
Decian persecutions 3
Demeter: as agricultural provider 130–2; in Byzantium 16, 122–3; in Constantinople 141, 146; in literature 89; as mother 123–9; as Rhea 135; in Thrace 120, 135; as virgin 136

Dio, historian 11
Dionysus cult 2
Dionysus of Byzantium, historian
123
Dioscourii 12
Docetists 106
Donatists 30

Egeria, pilgrim 84, 105
emperor cult: bishops against
77–8, 116; dynamics of 21,
62–4, 74, 76; *see also* individual
emperors/esses; civic religion,
Greco-Roman; encomiastic
poetry; panegyric
encomiastic poetry: and
Christianity 63; examples of
66–8; forms of 65–6; *topoi* of
92–3; *see also* individual
authors; hymns; panegyric
Ephesus, Council of (431) 56–7,
89, 107–8, 113–14, 145
Ephraim the Syrian 91, 93, 103
Epiphanius of Salamis: on
Marian heresies (*Panarion*)
116–20, 146; mariology 117
Eudokia, Empress 43, 57, 65,
67–8, 96
Eudoxia, Empress: children of
37; and Chrysostom 37, 82;
death of 41
Eusebeia, Empress 72–3, 96
Eusebius of Caesarea: on
Constantine 15, 23–7; on
Constantinople 9, 13–14, 26;
on Nicaea 24–5; panegyric to
Constantine 78; religio-political
philosophy 25–7, 63, 144
Eusebius of Dorylaeum 55
Eusebius Scholasticus 65

Flavian, Bishop of Antioch 35
Flora: *see* Anthousa

genius, emperor's 8, 17, 21, 33
Gratian, Emperor: imperial cult
ritual 40, 73–4; and paganism
31–3
Great Church: *see* Agia Sophia

Gregory of Nazianzus: and
Constantinople 30, 81–2;
on Mary 103–5, 107; poetry 79
Gregory of Nyssa: on Arianism
30; on Mary 103–5, 107; on
pilgrimage 84

Hagia Sophia: *see* Agia Sophia
Hecate: in Byzantium 12, 15–16,
122–3, 126–7; in
Constantinople 141, 146; as
kourotrophos 138–9; as mother
134, 138–9; as protectress 129;
as Rhea 135; as *soteria* 139–40;
as virgin 136
Helena, mother of Constantine
19
Helios: in Byzantium 12; in
Constantinople 17, 19–20, 27,
33, 121
Hera 10, 16
heresies: *see* individual names
Hermes Trimegistos 16, 32, 89
Hesychios, *Patria* compiler 123
Hesychius of Miletus 10
Hippodrome, in Constantinople:
under Arcadius 38; under
Constantine 3, 16–21, 27, 30,
45, 143; *kathisma* in 16, 20, 50,
85; and Pulcheria 43, 49,
59–60, 88; under Severus
11–12, 127; under Theodosius
I 35; under Theodosius II 44,
46–7, 49–51
Hodegetria, church of 57–8, 106,
128
Holy Apostles, church of 26–7,
52
Honorius, Emperor 34, 37–9
hymns: Christian 4, 79–80, 83–5
(*see also* Laodicea, Council of);
in civic ceremonies 77;
heretical 80; pagan 77, 85, 89;
to Theotokos (*chairetismoi*) 69,
85–97, 109–12, 116, 132, 141,
146; *see also* individual
hymnographers; *Akathistos
Hymn*
Hypapante, feast of 105–7

Ignatius of Antioch 101
imperial imagery: of Arcadius 41, 47–8; of Constantine 17–20, 26–7, 35, 47, 121; in emperor cult 63; of Eudoxia 37; of Helena 19; of Pulcheria 49–50, 54, 60, 144; of Severus 12, 35; of Tetrarchs 47; of Theodosius I 35, 40, 47, 143; of Theodosius II 45–9
Irenaeus of Lyons, on Mary 102
Isaiah, Ascension of 102
Isis: as agricultural provider 130–2; as bride 136; in Byzantium 123–4; in Constantinople 141, 146; in Greco-Roman religion 2, 16; as mother 137–9; as Rhea 135; as *soteira* 139–41; as weaver 132–3

James, Protoevangelium of 102–3, 119, 146
John Chrysostom: deposition of 107; Eudoxia, invectives against 37; as liturgist 82; on Mary 101; relics of 53; on Theodosius I 35; understanding of Christianity 38–40, 63, 144
John Malalas, historian: on Constantine 125; on Constantinople 16–18; on Theodosius II 44, 50–1
John of Damascus 58, 141
Judaism 2–3
Julian, Emperor: imperial cult ritual 78; as panegyrist 71–3, 96; and Theotokos 129
Justinian, Emperor 90
Justin Martyr 101–2
Juvenal, Patriarch of Jerusalem 58

kathisma: see Hippodrome, in Constantinople
kontakion 91–2
Kore: *see* Persephone
Kotys: *see* Rhea

Laodicea, Council (*c.* 360) 83–4
legislation, imperial: *see* individual emperors
Leo I, Emperor 58
Leo I, Pope 57
Libanius of Antioch 15–16, 27, 35, 125
Luke, Gospel of 88–9, 93, 101–2, 105, 111, 135, 147

Magna Mater: *see* Rhea
Manicheans 54
Marcion, Emperor 57–8
Mary, mother of Jesus: as agricultural provider 131–2; apotheosis of 1, 3, 59–61, 97, 104, 118–20, 127–42, 146–7; as bride 103, 136–7; cincture of 57–8, 128; early Christian devotion to 104–7, 117–20, 146; early Christian literature on 101–7, 145–6 (*see also* individual authors and works); as ever-virgin 102–7, 117–19, 135–6; heresies concerning 117–20; icon of 57, 128; as *kourotrophos* 138–9; as *panagia* 103; as protectress 127–30; relics of 58; as second Eve 101–3, 117; shroud of 57–8, 128; as *soteira* 139–40; as Theotokos 3–4, 55–7, 60, 90, 102–5, 107–10, 117, 145; *see also Akathistos Hymn*; Constantinople; hymns, to Theotokos; Hypapante, feast of; Virginity Festival
Maximian, Bishop of Constantinople 57, 114–15
Menander, rhetorician 68, 71, 92, 96, 124, 145
Metrophanes, Bishop of Byzantium 14
Michael Rhangabe, Emperor 129
Mithras 2, 89
Monophysites 109
mother of the gods: *see* Rhea
mystery religions: *see* individual deities

Nazarius, panegyrist 70–1
Nestorians 3, 56, 62, 85, 114–15,
    144–5
Nestorius, Bishop of Constantin-
    ople: background of 53, 115; at
    Ephesus, Council of 56, 1058;
    mariology 53–5; and Pelagians
    108; against Pulcheria 54–5,
    106, 113, 144; religious
    reforms 54; Theotokos,
    opposition to 46, 86, 107
Nicaea, Council of (325) 24
Nicephorus Callistus, historian
    57, 59
Nicolaus Sophistae, rhetorician
    64
Novatians 54

Origen 12, 102, 111
Orpheus 32
Orphic Hymns 130–1, 133, 135,
    137–40, 142

Pacatus, panegyrist 74–6, 96
paganism: see individual deities
    and emperors; Byzantium;
    Constantinople
Palladas, poet 67
panegyric: Adventus 47, 51–3, 59,
    68–9; categories of 64;
    examples of 70–6; form of
    64–5; imperial 3, 47, 60–5,
    68–9, 78, 86–8, 95–7, 111–13,
    144; see also Akathistos Hymn;
    encomiastic poetry
Patria: see Hesychios
Pausanias, historian 124, 127
Pelagianism 108
Persephone (Kore): as
    agricultural provider 122,
    130–2; in Byzantium 16,
    122–3, 130, 132; in
    Constantinople 141, 146; in
    literature 88, 137; as maiden
    135–6, 138; as Rhea 135; as
    soteria 139–41
Peter of Alexandria 103
Philostorgius: on Constantine
    125; on Constantinople 17

Pliny the Younger 13
poetry: see encomiastic poetry
Polybius, historian 10–11, 13
pontifex maximus: Constantine 8,
    24, 26, 40, 143; Gratian 31–2,
    73; Pulcheria 59; Theodosius
    II 49
Proclus of Constantinople:
    against Nestorius 88, 112; as
    bishop 53, 113, 115–16;
    hymnographic style 91–2;
    Pulcheria, panegyric to 51, 60,
    86–8; Theotokos, hymns to 51,
    62, 85–9, 96, 111–12, 122, 129,
    131–2, 135–7, 145–7;
    Theotokos, orations on 51,
    55–6, 62, 86–7, 106, 133
Procopius, historian 17
Pulcheria: against Nestorius 46,
    53–5, 56, 60, 108, 113; and
    Chalcedon, Council of 57–8;
    Christianity, support to 49–50,
    52, 57–9; civic religious
    practice 50, 55, 59–61, 128–9,
    134–5, 141; as co-regent 42–3;
    and Cyril of Alexandria
    113–14; imperial cult ritual
    60–1, 86–8, 145; Marian
    devotion 51, 54–5, 57–61, 106,
    112, 129, 145; paganism,
    opposition to 43; and relics
    52–3, 59; supernatural claim
    54–5, 60–1, 86–8; as virgin 42,
    49, 59–60, 86–8

Quartodecimani 54

relics of saints 46, 50, 52–3, 58–9,
    63, 69; see also individual
    imperial sponsors; Mary,
    mother of Jesus
Rhea: in Byzantium 15–16, 19,
    122–3, 134; in Constantinople
    3, 17, 20–1, 27, 121, 124, 126,
    137, 141, 146–7; as divine
    mother 137; goddesses
    associated with 135; history of
    cult 133–4; as maiden 136; as
    soteira 140; in Thrace 120

Romanos Melodos 89, 93
Rome: Christianity in 28;
   paganism in 9–10, 21, 27, 31,
   34, 63, 125

St Anastasia, church of: *see*
   Anastasia, church of the
St Irene, church of 26
Septimius Severus, Emperor: and
   Byzantium 11–16; Christian
   persecutions 12–14; imperial
   cult ritual 8, 12–13, 17, 21, 35
Serapis 2, 16, 33, 130
Sergius, Patriarch of
   Constantinople 129
Sissinius, Bishop of
   Constantinople 50
Socrates, historian: on
   Constantine 7, 15; on
   Constantinople 14, 17; on
   emperor's role in Church 31;
   on liturgy 79; on Pulcheria 43;
   on Theodosius I 35, 81; on
   Theodosius II 50
Sol Invictus 8, 20, 47
Solomon, Odes of 102
Sozomen, historian: on Ambrose
   of Milan 36; on Chrysostom
   37; on Constantine 15, 22–3;
   on Constantinople 9, 14; on
   Pulcheria 42, 49, 53; on
   Theodosius I 33–5, 81–2,
   105

Tertullian 12, 102
Tetrarchy 26, 36, 47, 61, 68–9
Themistius, philosopher 31
Theodore of Mopsuestia 53,
   115–16
Theodoret of Cyrus: on
   Constantinople 14; on
   Constantinople I, Council of
   32; on Theodosius I 36; on
   Theodosius II 43, 53
Theodosius I, Emperor: against
   paganism 33–5; and
   Christianity 32, 143; civic
   religious practice 34–7, 47, 82;
   Constantinople, entrance into

81–2; imperial cult ritual 35–7,
   40, 65, 74–6, 96; legislation
   34–5, 40; and relics 52
Theodosius II, Emperor: against
   paganism 43–5; and
   Chalkoprateia church 58;
   Christianity, support of 52;
   civic religious practice 46,
   49–51; death 57; and Ephesus,
   Council of 56, 108, 113–14;
   imperial cult ritual 46–7, 96;
   legislation 43–4, 46, 48–9, 135;
   and Nestorius 54, 56, 108;
   Pulcheria's influence on 42;
   and relics 52
Theodotus of Ancyra,
   hymnographer 86, 111
Theon, philosopher 32
Theophilus, Bishop of
   Alexandria 107
Theotokos: *see* Mary, mother of
   Jesus
Trajan, Emperor 13, 75
Tyche: as agricultural provider
   130–2; in Byzantium 10,
   15–16, 122–3, 132; in
   Constantinople 3, 17–21, 27,
   45, 121, 124–30, 141, 146–7;
   Eusebius on 26; history of cult
   124–5; as protectress 127–30;
   see also Anthousa

Valens, Emperor 31, 65, 137
Vespasian, Emperor 11
Via Egnatia 11, 16
Virginity Festival (memorial to
   Theotokos) 51, 55–6, 86, 106

Zeus 10, 16, 88
Zeuxippos: *see* Apollo;
   Byzantium, pre-Constantinian
   history and legends; Helios
Zonaras, historian 17, 130
Zosimus, historian: on Athena
   126; on Byzantium 9, 15–16;
   on Constantine 20, 27, 123; on
   Constantinople 17, 19, 121; on
   Gratian 31; on Theodosius I
   33–5